Veiled in Goodness

A Catholic Guide For Young Women

Seeking Marriage & Motherhood

Kira G. King

Originally published in Savannah, Georgia by Wymberly Communications, llc
www.kiragking.com

Printed with ecclesiastical permission
✠ Stephen D. Parkes
Bishop of Savannah
September 11, 2025

ISBN: 979-8-218-43234-8

To the Holy Family.
I consecrated my life to you, and it has never been the
same since.

To the young women who sat through these talks and all
those who read this little book. Please remember you are in
this world but not of this world.

To my girls. May you always keep your gaze on Him who
loves you.

To my husband, Arthur. Thank you for marrying me.

Salve, Regina, mater misericordiae;
vita, dulcedo et spes nostra, salve.
Ad te clamamus exsules filii Hevae.
Ad te suspiramus gementes et flentes
in hac lacrimarum valle.
Eia ergo, advocata nostra,
illos tuos misericordes oculos ad nos converte.
Et Iesum, benedictum fructum ventris tui,
nobis post hoc exsilium ostende.
O clemens, o pia, o dulcis Virgo Maria.

Table of Contents

Prologue

"Lord, keep Your grace in my heart. Live in me so that Your grace be mine. Make it that I may bear every day some flowers and new fruit."
- St. Gianna Beretta Molla

In the early Summer of 2023, I was still in many ways confined to the denim-colored couch in my sunroom. Learning how to juggle two beautiful daughters, both with their own needs, had been my vocation for the past year, ever since I discovered we were (finally) pregnant with our second child. It felt like I'd lived on that blue couch that year, and here I was again, but this time, snuggling and soothing a four-month-old baby while trying to allow my 4-year-old daughter to get her afternoon nap.

Funny things happen to your self-esteem when you feel confined. You start to look for more purpose where you are, a purpose that is within your limitations. My second pregnancy was a cakewalk compared to many women's pregnancies, but compared to my first pregnancy, the second time around was an incredibly humbling experience. I was not given the orders to be bedridden, but since our baby bundle was situated so low in my uterus, I was given the orders to accept my fate of being couch-ridden. So, there I sat most of my day for nearly ten months.

Then one Friday, after I was sure I had just slept wrong and wasn't actually in labor and after I made sure to fulfill our curbside fresh egg orders, I waddled ever-so-gracefully... into the doctor's office, to make sure all was right before the weekend. A quick whisk away to the operating room for a c-section, and our baby was here. A beautiful little eternal soul now rested in our arms. Peyton Lillis came two and a half weeks early, and she was perfect. Her big sister, Piper, was thrilled. Truly. And so began trimester four (the one people rarely talk about), and I found myself spending most of my days back on the blue couch.

It was there that I discovered, and I mean *really* discovered, my Catholic faith. There, I learned for the first time in my life how to begin to trust God, offer my day up to His Son, and weep with the Virgin Mary in unison. It took us nearly eight months to get pregnant with little Peyton. It went from a, "We'll just put it in God's hands, and we'll get pregnant when He decides" to, "God, *why*? Why haven't you given us another child? What is your will for us? Are we meant to adopt?" Eight months is not a long time in the grand scheme of things, and countless women go through much more extended periods of waiting in agony or never get that positive pregnancy test, but as every month goes by, your heart breaks that much more. You begin to feel sorrow, a feeling much more than sadness.

We slowly strengthened our faith when our first daughter entered the world. We knew it was up to us to pass Catholicism and a love of God to her, but we also said... "There's time. We'll wait until she's a little older." One of the best things that could have ever happened to us regarding our faith was when churches went online during the COVID-19 pandemic. We could watch Mass right from our home, from our bed even! It was wonderful. Now, if they would just send communion through Amazon, our little millennial life would be perfect. Well, they never did that (thankfully!), and as weeks and months went by and churches opened back up, we started gracing their doors once or twice a month but never every Sunday. We stuck true to our generation's fear of commitment.

I don't remember when it strictly landed in our minds that our actions offended God. We knew sin went against God, but for so long, we didn't care. We knew not attending Mass was a sin, but we never cared enough to learn why. And then, one day, it all made sense. How could we willingly, *willingly*, not only offend God but choose not to receive the Body of Christ!? We're idiots! That is Jesus Christ's body and blood on that altar, and He willingly died to give it to *us*. Here we were, looking at the gift of His very self, and saying, "No thank you. We're good without it." I started frantically learning about all of the Eucharistic miracles. I binged Catholic podcasts, lectures, and videos like I was preparing for the biggest test of my life. I became a devoted patron of thriftbooks.com and Catholic publishing companies. I told Arthur, my husband, to budget a hundred or so dollars a month for books about Catholicism.

Purpose began to unfold, even while I sat stagnant on our sunroom's blue couch looking out over the gardens I was neglecting and the animals I longed to tend to on our little homestead. Arthur and I knew something was missing in our lives, but we didn't know where to get it. Here was the answer! We would find other 'idiots' from our generation and younger ones who are growing up in this warped culture and get together to talk about Jesus. And because I can't just focus on the small, my mind went straight to the big picture. Together in Christ, all of us would save this world from the wickedness and snares of the devil, and it would be great! The Holy Spirit was hard at work. Real hard.

We invited older couples we knew over for dinner to pick their brains on how to start an outreach ministry. I created a website and came up with a cheesy but catchy name, Farm to Jesus. You know, like farm to table. And, we came up with a plan. We'd host a bi-monthly dinner party for millennials, Gen Zers, and anyone else who wanted to come. Arthur would get to use his desire for a restaurant to feed the masses. I would organize topics for discussion on what scripture, Church teachings, saint stories, and prayers meant for us *right now* in this moment, in this life, for us and our children.

All of that binge-watching lectures now made sense! It wasn't just for me and my knowledge. It wasn't just for my husband and our children. It was for those of us who, despite living in a world more connected than ever, still experience loneliness, those of us who have forgotten why

God put us here on this earth and what we should do about it.

Mother Teresa once said that out of all the countries she had ever visited, America was the poorest country in the world. How can that be? The United States is far wealthier than the streets of Calcutta. She went on, "America suffers most from the poverty of loneliness." Gut-punch.

Would we have labeled our indifference as loneliness? Admittedly, no, but as I look back on that time and don't forget to add the effects of the isolation of the pandemic, that's what it was. Well, what's the remedy for loneliness? Community. What is the foundation for all community? Love of God. What does a love of God call us to do? Serve and love others. Why? Because they matter! We all matter and mean everything to the God who knows every hair on our head. (Matthew 10:26–31). We live in a world that has forgotten God, but we will not forget. We will remember because He is the reason we are here. He is the reason we are more than just dust. He is our everything.

And that, dear friends, is how I ended up giving talks on the vocation of wifehood and motherhood to young women at St. Vincent's Academy and began writing them down here for you. You may be saying, "No, no. You skipped some parts." To which I graciously respond, I did not. When I began to say, "Yes, God. I am your vessel. Use me for Your divine will," my life started changing. Things started happening that I did not control. I assure you. There were a few times I responded to His push, "Are you sure, Lord? That's a lot. I'm not sure I want to." He gently pushed again, and in true Southern fashion, I said, "Yes, sir."

I decided to put these talks to paper because they might be helpful to you as you mature from girlhood to womanhood. My hope is that these talks and discussions are relatable to your chapter in life and that they help you prepare for your future marriage and, God willing, motherhood. I've tried to answer all of the questions I received from the students after each talk. During these months, I've also interlaced my interior thoughts to show how saying yes to God isn't always convenient or comfortable. I hope this little book helps you begin to say yes to God. I pray that you become the wife and mother He intended you to be if that is your vocation. I implore you to look to Our Lady as your example. Her one yes to God changed not only the entire world but all of eternity.

Living this vocation as God designed it may be the road less traveled in our current world, but what a road! I can promise you that it will make all the difference. One student asked me what my future looks like. I thought it was kind of a silly question, but then I smiled. I don't know, but He does. I'm sure it will be a daring tale and a marvelous adventure, full of many peaks and valleys. What I do know is that at the end of it, I want to be with Him in paradise. I'd like for you to be there too.

Dear sister, you were made for heaven, and the vocation of being a wife and mother is a glorious road to help get you there. Together, we will go along this scenic yet sometimes steep terrain, beginning with prayer and how your relationship with God is the foundation for your entire life. What does it mean to be Catholic woman? We will venture through how to find a community that will help you grow in holiness, where and how to find the 'one,' and discernment on whether or not he is the one God has placed before you for marriage. From there, we will climb to the heights of what a Catholic marriage looks like, the beauty of intimacy and the sexual embrace within marriage, and then to what it means to be a Catholic mother. What does it look like to be a Catholic wife and mother? Lastly, there will be a summary to help us gather our thoughts.

Through the ups and downs you may face, I hope this little book helps you to remember that you may be *in* this world, but you are not *of* this world.

Chapter 1

Prayer

"Let your door stand open to receive [God], unlock your soul to Him, offer Him a welcome in your mind, and then you will see the riches of simplicity, the treasures of peace, the joy of grace. Throw wide the gate of your heart, stand before the sun of the everlasting light."
- St. Ambrose

Come, Holy Spirit. Please give me the words these girls need to hear. God, I'm yours. Use me to tell them what You want them to know. Aly Aleigha, thank you thank you for making beautiful, Catholic music that is helping to calm my nerves. Parallel parked the bright red mom bus on the first try. Still got it. Found my old computer classroom. That teacher hated me. I am terrified of public speaking. I have to sit down. Maybe they won't see my hands shake if I sit the whole time. Then it's more like a conversation. That'll work. Here we go.

Hey, y'all. My name is Kira King, and I don't know you, and you don't know me. The only thing I know we have in common is that 15 years ago, I tripped down the same stairs as you do now and became an expert on parallel parking in these downtown streets. This old school has a lot of stairs. I don't really know how I got here. It started with a few friends and I talking, separately, about how we found it strange that we went to an all-girls Catholic high school and somehow weren't taught how to be a Catholic wife or mother. They tried to prep us for college but didn't have much to say about the vocation that 90% of us would choose as God's will for our lives. "Yeah, someone should do something about that! You should go talk to them," I said.

"No, Kira. You should," said three separate women I grew up with. That's how it started, and here I am. I will be giving you six talks ranging from our topic today, which is prayer, to when you're off on your own and looking for a community and your future spouse, discerning whether or not he's the one to marry, the beauty of a God-centered marriage and understanding Biblical wifely submission (not slavery or servitude) to intimacy and the sexual embrace in marriage and finally, to motherhood. I have left my 8-month-old baby and my four-year-old to be here. My husband took time off work to watch them so I could come here. I only tell you that to show you that saying yes to God isn't always the most convenient thing to do, but this is important. You're important, so here I am.

Today, we're going to talk about prayer. What does your prayer life look like? Do you talk to God? But before we get into prayer, I need you to know something. I don't know any of you, but you matter to me. I care about you so much that I left my babies and came down here to talk to you about the vocation God is calling most of you to, being a wife and God-willing, a mother. You're growing up in a world that is so different from mine. Yes, there are many similarities, but you have already been subjected to things by our culture that weren't even on our radar at your age. You've been exposed to a culture I can't even fathom, and I think you all need to hear that YOU MATTER. I think maybe some of you may have forgotten that.

Why do you matter? You know, when they handed my husband and me our daughter for the first time at the hospital, they handed us a human being that needed to be fed and changed, clothed and taken care of, which is all fine and well. I babysat a lot and had younger siblings. I know how to take care of a baby. But, then we realized the gravity of the situation. We weren't just handed a baby with natural needs to take care of. We were handed a human soul, a human soul that lives **FOREVER**. Do you see how I emphasized that word- forever? Because it means foreverrr, all eternity. It's kind of a big deal. When we realized that, we realized God had entrusted us with a *human soul*. I'm a human soul that will live forever. Each one of you is a human soul that will live forever. Understanding the length of time our soul will last, can you now understand why you matter? Can you see how what you do, even right now in this moment, matters?

My parents are divorced. My mom remarried and had children, so I have siblings in Savannah. My dad remarried and had children, so I have siblings in Florida. I have a sister in Florida who is your age. I asked her to write you a letter, not for you to compare yourself to, but to see what type of prayer life is attainable even at your age. What she didn't mention is that our father has narcissistic personality disorder. This illness has affected her life every single day since the day she was born. She also fell head over heels for a boy last year. Have any of y'all done that? She was planning their future when he broke up with her because she wouldn't have sex with him. Her life isn't perfect. Some of you may have bad experiences in your past, even traumatic. Some of you may not be able to relate to that at all. Praise God. Either way, her name is Ysabel, but she goes by Yzzy. She wrote this for you. Here it is.

Hey y'all! I'm Kira's sister, Yzzy, from Florida, and I'm 17 almost 18 (as of December). I've had a pretty interesting journey with my faith. Even though I was born and raised Catholic, I've really only embraced my faith recently within these last three years. I've been through many challenges and hardships, especially involving difficult relationships with difficult people. In short, there was only so much that I could do and that the world could do before I had to turn to God to ask Him to help me. I started to lean into the idea of trusting Him completely and putting my life in His hands— which is not an easy task by any stretch. This idea became the central point of my life, and it gives me such a peace to know that I don't have to have my life entirely figured out. I put my trust in God and I know that He will take care of me. Like Jesus in the Garden of Gethsemane, I constantly find myself saying, "Not by my will, but yours be done."

I usually find myself talking to God each day and setting my intentions before Him consistently. Again, I give it to Him in accordance with His will because I know He knows much better than I do. I trust that He will lead me down a path much better than I could ever imagine. For instance, I've been praying about which college I would go to because I've never felt pulled towards any specific college when I visited them. Well, that was before I visited Franciscan University. When I visited that campus, I had an internal feeling that this college was where God intended for me to be, even though it is literally in the middle of Ohio. Why on earth would I ever choose a college that far away from my home and family? Even more, why would I go out of my way to go there when I can go to an in-state college for in-state tuition?! I have no clue, but I can honestly say I believe that's where God wants me to go. And I'm happy to say that I did get accepted in about early-mid October! There was no way that He wasn't involved with that decision and call, and I'm definitely going to listen to it.

Segueing beautifully into my next idea is that God truly does speak to us, just not in the way that we expect. We want it to be loud and grand, but God doesn't work like that. As I told a friend of mine one day, "God can truly be everywhere. We just have to stop for a moment to listen to His voice and see His beauty all around us." There are some thoughts that I really can't explain and can only contribute to God, such as Franciscan. I just stopped to pay attention and listen to Him. Building this relationship with Him has taken time, but I find it so easy now to see Him in everything. I want to be able to live my life to its fullest in accordance with His will and be a living witness to

Him. I go about my daily life and am able to recognize the little blessings He has given me, like the Latin prayer Anima Christi being connected with my Youth Group or swing dancing with my parish friends after Mass, knowing I have always wanted to swing dance. He truly does speak, and it doesn't have to be in words.

It did take a while for me to actually start this relationship with God, though. It helped to start a simple night prayer "routine" where I prayed 3 simple prayers before I go to bed. I've gotten to the point now, though, where I've added 3 more prayers to it. Another piece of the puzzle was joining my parish's youth group. It helped me to see I wasn't alone in my faith journey and that there are others in the same boat as me. It has been a tremendous influence on me to surround myself with like-minded people when it comes to the faith. I have people praying for me, and I for them. I feel like I truly belong to such an incredible community. I can't explain the joy that I have when I meet my friends after Mass in the Social Hall. That moment alone gives me something to truly look forward to in the weekends, which fosters feelings of hope and excitement. This part has only really occurred within the last 3 months, but it has helped bolster my involvement in my faith. A recent friend of mine and I talk about this quite frequently how these people have changed our lives simply by living and being at this parish. It's amazing what a community can do.

Another aspect that truly changed my life was going to Portugal, especially Fátima, during WYD this year. I felt so grace-filled during the entire trip, and I really grew closer to Our Lady. It's hard to explain, but I had such peace (again) and true inner joy when I watched Our Lady be processed throughout the piazza of Fátima. I truly felt the power of God and felt on top of the world. It rooted me even further in my faith, and you couldn't slap the smile off of my face even after I came home. After that trip, I really started to become more involved with my relationship with God. I felt called to go to Mass and Adoration more often, which I can confidently say I've been taking every chance I can to go. I find myself always attributing everything in my life back to God. This trip is actually what led me to find my parish and find those friends I mentioned earlier. I didn't know that's what God had in store for me, but I am so ever grateful that it all played out like it did! So, in many ways, it was (again) absolutely life-changing! There's just something about a trip like that that fills you with such a grace to steer your life towards God, and the true joy you feel makes you want to live in that grace forever. It's what drives me to keep going— the grace and joy that I get from God.

It's never too late to start a relationship with God, no matter how far you feel you are away from Him. I had the opportunity just recently to help a friend of mine try to find God. She doesn't have a relationship with God, but she still took a step with me to pray within my church's chapel. I told her, "He will leave the other 99 [sheep] to go after the 1." It's easier to start now than it is later, and it can only grow as time goes on. You've got to start somewhere, even if it is just a simple Our Father, Hail Mary, and Glory Be right before bed. The fruit that can come from starting small like that is unimaginable. God can truly make all things possible.

Blank stares. Some looks of awe. Great. I'm definitely in awe of her.

What do you think? Are you thinking that she can't be 17? Are you thinking, "Wow, good for her, but I can't be like that?" Me too. I read this and think, "My faith at 34 isn't even as strong as hers." But, it's so important not to compare. I didn't read this to you so you could compare yourself to Yzzy. I read it to let you see what your faith can be, even at your age.

The main point I want to convey to you today is that your relationship with God *now* matters. It is the foundation for your future marriage. Then, with your husband, your relationships with God will matter when you complicate your lives with beautiful children. You can try to build a marriage and tackle parenthood without God, but it will be lacking. It will be lacking the strength that God provides. I'll say it again. **You matter.** Your eternal soul matters. When we zoom out on the length of our lives, what's our ultimate goal? Where do we want to be at the end of this life?

Look around the room. Some of them seem engaged. Is anyone brave enough to answer?

Student: "Heaven?"

Yes, heaven. That is where we ultimately want to be. That is where we want our husbands and children to end up, too, right? Did you know it is your job to help get your husband to heaven? *Every girl looks shocked. Some shake their heads no.* Yes, you heard me correctly. It is our responsibility as wives to get our husbands and our children to heaven. But, there is a caveat. We cannot force them to choose heaven. Marriage is about sanctification. It's ordered to us growing in holiness and preparing for heaven.

Hand raised. Oh, good! Some engagement!

Student 1: "Is it their job to get us to heaven too?"

Haha, yes. It's a mutual thing.

Student 2: "I don't think I'm understanding you. It sounds like you're saying *we* have to get our husbands... but that can't be right. That can't be what you mean."

You heard me correctly. That's exactly what I mean.

Student 2: "But... they should get *themselves* to heaven. We shouldn't have to do it for them."

Are you familiar with the term helicopter mom? Well, God isn't like that. He doesn't hover over us, making sure we do exactly what He's told us to, don't fall into harm's way, and dutifully follow His path. He loves us, but He gave us free will. He invites us to follow Him. It's an invitation and a free gift. This is how we approach our husbands and children. We invite them to have a relationship with God. You see, when you start this foundational relationship with God, you strengthen your connection to Him so that when you meet a young man who may or may not have his own strong relationship with

God, your faith doesn't waiver. When a man enters your life, you pray he can walk with you and complement your faith journey. It's really hard to be selfish in marriage. It's designed to give myself away, which is essentially preparing for heaven. The mission is for both the husband and the wife to love like Christ and to hand each other over to one another like Christ.

Think of it like a table. You bring one side. He brings the other. If both are built well, they make a flat, solid surfaced table to hold up your children. But, if one side of the table isn't sturdy, the table will not be balanced. There will be times when you are struggling, and your side sinks a little and vice versa with him, and it becomes unbalanced. In those moments, the legs of the table will hold you up. The legs represent the Trinity.

When you add children to your life, even if you have a wonderful, God-focused marriage, it adds complexities. You have to ensure that your foundation is rooted in Christ *before* you bring children into the world, and you can start that right now. Do any of you play sports? *Some nod yes.* Okay, so you practice a lot, right? Do you know the rules before you get to the game? They don't just throw you out in the court or field without any knowledge or know-how and say, "Good luck!" They prepare you for the game, right? This preparation is a bit different because you're not currently in a practice life; you're living your actual life, but it's essential to do this preparation work before you meet your future spouse and before you have children.

Please don't misunderstand me. A relationship with God is not some place of perfection; when we reach it, we stop, and it's not some game to win. Think of your relationships. Do any of y'all have boyfriends? *A few raise their hands. Some sly, shy smirks.* Okay. Okay. Don't worry if you don't. This exercise works with any relationship, one with your friend or mom or dad. Think about how when something happens to you, good or bad, you want to tell them about it, right? You got a good grade, did something fun, or got accepted to the college you want to attend, and you want to share the great news with them. Even the bad things you typically want to share. You got into an argument or a car wreck. You want to share it with them because you know they care about you. You know they love you, and they want to hear what you have to say. Now imagine, when you tell them these things, that they ignore you. They don't engage with you at all. They have nothing to give you, no sign to show that they care about you. That would hurt, wouldn't it?

Student: "I'd break up with him."
Me: "Haha, what?"
Student: "If my boyfriend ignored me like that, I'd break up with him."
The whole class laughs, and I smile.

Okay, but now, imagine you're the person who does the ignoring. Imagine that the one you're ignoring is **God**. Hits home a little, doesn't it?

I'm a cradle Catholic. I attended Catholic schools all my life until college. We were taught all of the prayers. We went to Mass weekly. But one day, I realized I didn't know how to pray. I could say I loved Jesus, but did I? Could I say it out loud and mean it? I tried it. "I love you, Jesus." I'm going to be honest. It felt a little cheesy. It kind of felt like those other countless denominations and how they approach God. I knew, though, that as Catholics, we aren't only supposed to love Jesus; He's supposed to be our everything. Our every waking moment should be dedicated to Him.

Have y'all ever heard of "offering it up?" *Shakes heads no.* I hadn't either. Offer it up? What do I have to offer to God? Well, everything. We have everything to offer him. Our entire day. Our joys. Our sorrows. Our every waking moment. It's that easy, y'all. When you wake up in the morning, before your head leaves the pillow, give Him your day. Offer Him your entire day. What does this mean in practice? It's literally one sentence. "Jesus, I offer you my prayers, works, joys, and sufferings of this day." That's it. The whole prayer is a few lines and is called the Morning Offering Prayer.

Okay, some of them seem to get it, but some look so lost. Let me try to explain more.

You may be thinking, "No way, that's not a prayer." I'm here to tell you that it is, and it's the easiest one to say and the hardest one to do. Why? Because of what it does. It orients your entire day, every day, towards God. You begin to question everything. Does this music bring me closer or further away from God? Does this show or video? Does this friendship? Does this thing that I'm choosing to do? Does my relationship with my boyfriend or my parents? Every single thing you experience. Every engagement you have with another person is transformed through this lens. Not to mention how it transforms you. Everything you do. Your entire outlook on this day, this week, this month, this year, this life points you towards God or away from him.

Did you know that good things could become idols? *Shakes heads no.* I didn't either. You're probably thinking that an idol is like the golden calf, right? I had that idea of idols, too. An idol is anything that takes the place of God in your life. Your grades, your sports, your relationship with your boyfriend, your relationship with your friends or family. They can all become idols if you aren't careful. These have all been my idols at different points in my life and aren't in themselves bad. In fact, they can be very good. It's the disorder of putting them before God that is bad. Our disordered attachment to these things, if we allow them to become our gods, is the bad part. God has to be first and foremost in our lives, in all that we are and in everything that we do.

I played travel soccer when I was in high school. There are games, primarily out of town, almost every Sunday of the season. I loved soccer and dedicated my life to it while in high school. Soccer in itself is not a bad thing. It can be a good thing, but the moment that I ordered my life in a way that soccer took the place of God, and when I allowed it to prevent me from going to Mass and honoring the Sabbath, it became my idol. And, what do I do with soccer now? Nothing, so was it worth being an idol? The answer is no. Nothing is worth taking the place of God in our lives.

Do you remember when we talked about zooming out on your life? Well, now, let's zoom back in to right now, to today. You probably had a test or a quiz today; if not, you most likely had some homework due. It's easy to think those don't matter in the grand scheme of things. You know, I had to change a poopy diaper today. Quite a few tee-tee ones, too. It's easy to think those things don't matter, too. But what would happen if I didn't attend to my responsibility of changing my daughter's diaper? It'd be neglectful, right? To leave my baby in her waste? It would not only be unjust and dishonoring her dignity as a person, it would be dishonoring God. Do you see the correlation I'm trying to make? Those small, daily tasks that may seem insignificant now at this moment are actually a part of God's calling for us in the *now* that is our lives. Your test matters, not because its grade will determine the rest of your life, but because it is a part of the chapter that you are in right now, the chapter God has put you in. These little daily tasks add up to whole chapters that add up to the entire story of our lives here on earth and ultimately determine where our souls end up in eternity.

Are they getting it? I hope it's making sense. Are they able to follow along? I tend to talk all over the place when I'm excited or nervous. I want to talk about St. Ignatius of Loyola's discernment of spirits. I can see the magenta book on my nightstand, "The Discernment of Spirits: An Ignatian Guide for Everyday Living" by Fr. Timothy M. Gallagher. Too bad I'm only twenty pages in. It's some deep stuff to digest while your 4-year-old is jumping on your bed dangerously close to kicking your baby in her face. Oh well, the 30-minute podcast of Fr. Gallagher on the topic I consumed this morning will have to do for now. Hopefully, some of the girls' curiosity will be peaked enough to look into it more.

A well-known American exorcist gives wonderful lectures online that I enjoy watching. In one of them, he said that besides sin, demons get a foothold in our lives, typically through oppression or obsession, because people in today's age do not know how to have a basic prayer life.

Boom. I dropped the demon card. This time tomorrow, I'll be relieved of my moral-teaching post after some angry parents wonder where I got the authority to talk about such things. Although, they don't look as shocked as I thought they would. That's interesting. They should be shocked that not having a basic prayer life can open you up to nasty players. I sure was.

Sounds too simple, right? A basic prayer life. What does that even mean? He explained how many lay people don't even pray the Liturgy of Hours (also known as the Divine Office) or the Angelus. Liturgy of Hours? Angelus? What are those? I've been a Catholic my entire life and never heard of those or didn't listen if I have. According to WordonFire.org, the Liturgy of the Hours is "the Church's official prayer, and the highest form of prayer after the Mass. It is an ancient, structured way of praying Scripture throughout the day, focusing especially on the Psalms. It hearkens back to the Jewish custom of praying at fixed hours, a practice continued by the early Church." Priests promise to pray the Liturgy of Hours every single day for their entire lives. The hours are 3 am, 6 am, 9 am, 12 pm, 3 pm, 6 pm, and 9 pm, and an Office of Readings, which I like best because I love the homilies and sermons it features. Religious orders and lay people pray it, too. And here I was, a cradle Catholic, and I had never heard about them or cared enough if I had. Here was the answer to not knowing how to pray!

I set reminders every hour and began my new prayer life, and it was great. Hard, but great. Father Mike Schmitz said in one of his 'Catechism in a Year' podcast episodes that he wasn't nervous about taking the vow of celibacy when he became a priest, but he was anxious about the canon law that priests are required to pray the entire Liturgy of the Hours every day. But then, he said, after a couple of years of doing it, he was walking in the woods while on a retreat. While he was walking, he realized he was praying. He was praying, without realizing, the Liturgy of the Hours. They had become engrained in him. The glorifying words had become a part of who he was and flowed out of him to God with such ease, whereas before, they had been somewhat of a burden. I wanted this, too. I wanted to know how to approach our Lord, so I fervently attempted every hour. It was rare that I could stop for five minutes strictly at the right time, so I'd compile them altogether when I could. Some days, I did every single one before I went to bed. It would take about an hour. I was constantly glued to my phone, reading the prayers from one of the many free apps that house them. This was much better than social media, but I was still looking into this black device instead of my children's faces.

But aren't we called to lead a life of prayer? I was slowly getting discouraged. Rest assured, beautiful things were happening in my heart, too. God had indeed become centered in my mind throughout my day. I thought of Him almost constantly, so much that when I was tired and grumpy one day and viciously yelled at my child, I immediately broke down into tears. In addition to the rule in our house not to yell at one another out of anger, no matter the circumstances, I hurt God. I saw the terrified look on my child's face when she saw the bitter anger in mine and heard the vileness of my tone. Sure, she wasn't on her best behavior. Yes, she needed an authoritative parent at that moment, but there was no excuse for my behavior. Before I started this prayer journey, my first thought would have been, "Easy, Kira. Slow down. She's four. You're just tired. Tell her you're sorry. That's not how we treat people, especially those we love, and then don't do it again." No. Now, I felt that sin to my core. Which was it? Venial? Well, at least it's not mortal! Wrong. Wrong way of thinking. I needed to get myself to the confessional. That was a new phenomenon after I'd done something wrong. To clarify, the Act of Contrition prayer may be said to ask God for forgiveness for venial sins, but the Sacrament of Reconciliation is a purification and an act of love unlike any other. If you are unsure as to the differences between mortal and venial sins, I encourage you to find a reliable Catholic source to learn more.

You see, we think we can't hurt God. He's God, right? The one who made the entire universe. What does our little sin do to him? He can't get wounded. But we're wrong. As a parent, I see this sin more now than ever before. How does it make me feel when another little kid is rude or mean to Piper, our four-year-old? One time, she tried to handle it like our six dogs do when they disagree, with her teeth. That was fun, but as her parent, it hurts me when she's hurt by somebody else, infinitely more than it hurts her. That part of parenthood is rough-going, and now here I was, hurting God. So, did the Liturgy of the Hours change my life? Yes, they did.

About this time, I found a spiritual director. You may be wondering what that is. Another Catholic secret I didn't know about that's not a secret. A spiritual director is a loving coach and attentive counselor for your prayer life. They help you grow in your faith by walking alongside you in it. I told my spiritual director about my prayer routine at our first meeting. It was way more than just the Liturgy of Hours and a bit over the top, to be honest. It was starting to make me neglect some of my daily tasks. I hated that my girls saw me constantly on my phone, even if it was for prayers. My spiritual director assured me that though a noble cause, I was doing too much. She told me about a quote from St. Teresa of Avila that said, "Our goodness derives not from our capacity to think but to love. God walks among the pots and pans. The important thing is not to think much but to love much."

Overthinking, the story of my life. I was trying too hard at trying, and it was getting in the way of my love for God and my love for my family by being present for them. I scaled back to either morning prayers (Lauds), Office of Readings, evening prayers (Vespers), and/or Night prayers (Compline). Still, I continued my daily devotionals and daily learning through books, podcasts, and videos. Thank you, God, for spiritual directors.

Student: "I've grown a lot in my prayer life with God this past year, but sometimes, it can seem like a checklist."

That's a good point, and I'm glad you brought it up. Remember how earlier, I told you my father suffered from narcissistic personality disorder? Well, for narcissists, love is often transactional. They will love you if you do x. They will love you if you do x better than that person. They will love you if you make them feel overabundantly appreciated and idolized. God is not like that. He loves us no matter what, but He still has expectations for us. This brings me to this: you may only see Catholicism as a church of rules. Many people can't see past the quote-unquote rules. Rules are constraining. You know, I don't much like "rules" either, but you know what I do like? Instructions. I like to know the guidelines when I'm trying to do something. I get anxious when there aren't any instructions. It brings me comfort to work within parameters. I used to think God and the Church had too many rules, too. Now, I'm so grateful that God didn't just put us here and say, "Best of luck figuring out how to get to heaven!" That wouldn't be fun, would it? It'd be daunting and scary.

I mentioned demons earlier. I assume you all know that demons are fallen angels. They don't hold a candle to God regarding power, but they do try to disrupt our lives. They are tempting us a million thousand times a day (*because that's a real number*). Tempting us to do what? Turn away from God. This is one of the reasons why it is so essential to work on our prayer foundation. St. Ignatius of Loyola came up with a way to discern whether or not something was from God or the devil. It's known as the discernment of spirits. He discerned 14 rules for becoming aware and understanding, to some extent, the different shifts that are caused in the soul. These rules help us discern what is good and safe to receive and those promptings that are bad in order to reject them. We don't have time to get into the rules today. Please seek out a good podcast or video with Father Gallagher. He's amazingly helpful, but it all comes back to that question, "Does this bring me closer to God or further from him?" This can be applied to the most minor everyday task up to something as significant as whether or not this young man is the one you should marry.

We'll get into that big one more next time, and we're also going to talk about community. Yzzy mentioned community in her letter to you. This past summer, she sat down with me and came up with all the topics we will talk about over the next few months. Being a young woman is tough, and these topics come up so often naturally in our brains. Community is important, y'all. When you get to college, you may have a group of friends or people you know, but you will ultimately be alone unless your mom follows you there, which would be weird. You'll likely be alone for the first time in your life. Working on your relationship with God now is imperative in preparation for that.

Oh, and I know we're running out of time, but I have to say it! You will not be able to grow in your relationship with God and prayer if you're holding onto sin. Confession is a beautiful gift that none of us utilize enough. Go there. I sometimes ugly cry. The priests don't mind.

There they go. I mention the word sin, and off some of them go to another world, one of indifference where sin is seemingly fun and harmless.

I watched some of you just zone out when I mentioned sin. I get it. You don't want to hear about it. I probably didn't want to either at your age. I'm not going to lecture you. I'm not going to chastise you. I don't even really know you, remember? But, it's the reality of the situation. You cannot truly grow in your love of God if you are holding on to sin.

I went to confession for the first time in eight years a few years ago. It was a big one. When I was done, the priest said, "Well, you were young and foolish." That made me feel good in the moment, but later, I thought, "young and foolish." Is that an excuse for mortal sin? I thought I was wise at the time. I knew I was living in mortal sin. I just didn't care. Father Mike Schmitz says sin is, "God, I know what You want, but I want what I want." Do you know what mortal sin is? It's what it sounds like, mortal. It's sin that can permanently detach you from God for eternity, so if I had died when I was "young and foolish," living in mortal sin, where would I have ended up? I know God is merciful, but I also know He is just. I don't really want to test his mercy. Do you?

And do me a favor! Download one of those free apps with the Liturgy of Hours and commit to praying just one of them a day until the next time I see you. Maybe it'll make a difference in your life! You never know. It's like an appointment with God. I know you're busy, but it's a great way to keep yourself on track. It'll help give you the words for prayer if you're struggling to find them.

Oh, oh, oh! And, please do send me good responses, y'all. Help me help you answer the questions you care about. I want to know what you got out of our talk and what questions you may have. It's anonymous, so you can ask those questions you may be nervous to ask. As much as I'd love to sit down with each of you in conversation for three hours, we don't have three hours, so this is how we'll have that conversation. For the class with the best answers, not just, "It was great" or "I hated it," I'll bring in a baby goat or food.... on the last day. "*BABY GOAT!!!!*"

I smile and leave feeling drained but satisfied. In fact, I feel a little heavy. This feels like a big responsibility, one I'm not sure I'm ready for. Are you sure I'm supposed to be here, Lord? Some of them looked like they wanted to kill me. Others were hungry for every word like they had been starved. There were a couple of questions about divorce at the end. Divorce?!? I'm here to talk about the beauty of the covenant of marriage, not the rules on how to escape it. Abuse within a marriage came up, too. I got a response asking more about life after death. I'm not equipped. Where's the priest? These young women are people with messy lives, just like me. What *am* I doing here? My husband says I'll ask myself that until the day I die. Ah, well. I'm here now. Thank you, Holy Spirit, for giving me the words.

What Did You Learn?

Four different classes sent in their responses and questions. Their responses are placed at the end of each chapter. Their questions are placed towards the back of the book.

Class One
This first class was allowed to email me directly after our first talk. Then, it was changed to a form for organizational ease, so the responses were a bit shorter overall.

- I learned that we cannot live in this world that is corrupting without God and him transforming our lives. We should be more grateful that we were raised to be Christian and that God put us here for a reason. He loves us so much that he died for us to live in eternal life with him and many don't really realize the impact that can have on the world. I was put on this planet to have a purpose and make a difference and I need to find that purpose.

- I thoroughly enjoyed the talk you gave our class and found certain aspects extremely relatable to my own life. I could especially relate to your 17-year-old sister, as I have divorced parents and had a very troublesome relationship. With that being said, I have also lived a very fortunate life and do not often go without, so it is hard to express without feeling like others do not understand or think I am blowing hardship out of proportion. Having difficult situations/circumstances in my early high school years left me confused for a long time, feeling like I had nowhere to escape and not knowing how to cope. I felt alone as an only child as my parents went back and forth, often using me as a weapon to use against each other. With this being said, I have come a long way with my faith and overall lifestyle. I learned quickly that moping in your own problems doesn't pull you forward, but it is impossible to rise above them without the "ship" of God. I loved your talk today because it engulfed the importance of having a relationship with God. Not just because it helps the mental state, but because it is VITAL for LIFE. I feel like this is often known, but the importance is not stressed. God does feel like a checklist. Learning the daily walk and the small prayers benefit every realm of living. Also, I have never thought about the importance of working deeply on myself now because of how many people will depend on me in the future. I loved all of the profound questions you asked because they truly made me reflect on my inner being in a new way, fully through the lens of death.

- I loved your talk and felt it was very relatable to the world we live in. I often think about what happens after death, and I am glad you brought that up because that is our reality. I am super excited to talk about your take on Godly-centered relationships. I am currently in a relationship and have also been in a serious relationship previously, but they are completely different. With that being said, I struggle with seeing what is right and wrong in a relationship. I am looking forward to hearing you speak to us again. I hope to come back and speak to students one day as well.
- I just wanted to tell you that what you were demonstrating to me was very motivational. You spoke the truth, and I feel like many needed to know this and begin to explore life of prayer and speak to God more. I am glad you came to talk today because I was literally thinking about my life with God in these past few days and how I can be a better Christian, loving, and motivated person.
- Your speech really stood out to me, especially when you talked about your parents being divorced and how your little sister went through a tough relationship. Well, I can relate to that, and just hearing that really made me feel better about the problems I have been through over the last year. I now realize that I can't control everything, but what I can control is lifting my problems to God and letting him take the wheel. Thank you again for this speech!
- I learned that even if your peers do not have a good relationship with God, a good prayer life, or even have belief in God does not impact what you do with your life. I also

learned that no matter how distant your relationship with God has gotten, how far you feel from him, and even past actions you made the choice to do, that you can always come back to God and have a relationship with him.
- I learned that having a relationship with God takes a lot of time, effort, and prayer.
- I learned how important it is to love God over everyone, even your future husband.
- I learned that I don't have to serve my future husband like a servant but to serve him in the way of God.
- I learned how to find Jesus.
- Even though it may be hard, we need to love God more than anyone else in our lives.
- We have to help our spouse get to heaven.
- That God has a plan for us, and we just have to let all our problems to Him, and to get close with Him.
- That you and your spouse help each other get to heaven.

Class Two
- I really liked how she talked about the center of every relationship being God. I learned that I should be prioritizing God in everything between friendships and romantic relationships.
- That you and your spouse are responsible for getting each other to heaven.
- That it is a woman's duty to get her husband into heaven.

Class Three
- That I should follow God's calling no matter what.
- I learned that is our responsibility to get our spouse to heaven.
- I have learned that prayer life is extremely important. I have begun praying more recently and discovered how much it can change your perspective on anything, and I love it.
- It is never too late to start your relationship with God.
- To trust God.

- I learned that other people feel the same way about how the Catholic Church teaches you about their prayers but then does not always teach you how to help your personal prayer life.
- God is with us.
- Prayer can be a simple Hail Mary, but it can also be a song or just a simple conversation with God. It is not easy all the time to just choose God, but it is a journey.
- I liked/learned how Mrs. King related God's care for us to being the opposite of a helicopter mom. I liked how you said that God is a chill mom who looks out for us but lets us make our own decisions. *Note: I did NOT call God a chill mom. Haha*
- A life of faith is achievable for a teenager.
- I learned that I am responsible for guiding my future family to heaven.
- I learned that I can find what God meant for me to be closer to him. I also learned that the reason I was so close to God and had fallen out of good habits was because of demons. *To clarify, demons may have played a hand in the temptations you faced to fall out of good habits, but the choice was ultimately made by you.*
- I learned that just giving up my day to God can jumpstart a prayer life with God.
- Daily prayer helps to keep demons away. *Catchy.*
- Starting a prayer life is crucial. You will be responsible for getting your husband's and kid's souls to heaven.
- I learned that my relationship with God should be more stable.
- I learned that it's common for people to start a slow relationship with God, and prayer life takes time, but you need to be disciplined.
- I learned that you can always improve on your faith even if you take baby steps you are still improving your relationship with God.
- That it is not unattainable to have a strong faith and prayer life at my age.

- One thing I really took to heart was saying, "Lord, I give this day to you." in the morning to start your day.

Class Four
- Marriage is a partnership with the goal of getting your partner to heaven.
- How God can impact my day and how a strong prayer life is something I should work for.
- I learned that a mother is responsible for her family's faith. It really opened my eyes to if my prayer life is strong enough for something like that.
- I learned about how important God is in a relationship and in our daily lives. Being close with him is super important, and devoting your day to him is a great thing to do.
- I learned that a wife's job is to get her husband to heaven and be accountable for him.
- When I am married, my purpose is to help my husband and children get to heaven.
- The Liturgy of the Hours is an amazing way to pray. You can say it at any time, anywhere, and you can even find it online.
- That the goal of marriage is to help one another get into heaven.
- As a wife, we are responsible for ensuring our family goes to heaven.
- I learned that God loves us, and we all matter. He gives us gifts and expects us to use them. When we do not take advantage of them or recognize His blessing, we upset Him.
- That women are responsible for guiding their husbands and children into heaven.
- I learned that the journey with God will only get stronger and deeper but you do have to give him some of your time a day to build up this connection it won't just appear without putting any work or energy into it.
- That I matter even when I don't feel like it.
- Marriage is about getting your husband into heaven
- Women play an important role in a family.

- I learned that the goal of a Catholic marriage is to get your husband to Heaven.
- That I matter.

You will find the questions and answers for Chapter 1 on page 276.

Let Us Pray

Conversing with Jesus

This time of prayer focuses on the Morning Offering. Pray the Morning Offering two times: the first time for understanding, the second time from the heart. Follow the steps that are listed below.

Begin your prayer with the Sign of the Cross.
(The Sign of the Cross affirms our belief in the three Persons of the Triune God and that we are saved by Jesus' death on the cross.)

In the name of the Father, and of the Son, and of the Holy Spirit. Amen

(Pray together aloud when praying with others)
Jesus, please give me the grace to quiet down inside so as to become aware of Your love for me. Jesus, I want to spend this time with You. Help me to give You my full attention & to pray from my heart.

The Morning Offering Prayer

O Jesus, through the Immaculate Heart of Mary, I offer You all my prayers, works, joys, and sufferings of this day in union with the Holy Sacrifice of the Mass throughout the world. I offer them for all the intentions of your Sacred Heart: the salvation of souls, reparation for sin, and the reunion of all Christians. I offer them for the intentions of our bishops and of all Apostles of Prayer, and in particular for those recommended by our Holy Father this month. Amen.

❖ EXPRESS silently your sorrow for any sins you committed, remembering that all sin offends God.
❖ PRAY the Morning Offering a second time, silently from the heart, more slowly than the first time.

❖ CHOOSE a word or phrase from the Prayer that stood out for you. Silently think about it, speak with God about it, and share it aloud with those with whom you are praying.
❖ THANK Jesus in your own words for a blessing received. (Share this aloud.)
❖ ASK the Lord for any request that is in your heart. (Share this aloud.)

Close this time of prayer with the Sign of the Cross.

(Source: Office for Catechesis and Evangelization, Diocese of La Crosse)

Chapter 2

Community & Finding the 'One'

"O my God, teach me to be generous, to serve you as you deserve to be served, to give without counting the cost, to fight without fear of being wounded, to work without seeking rest, and to spend myself without expecting any reward, but the knowledge that I am doing your holy will. Amen."
–St. Ignatius of Loyola

Come, Holy Spirit. Please give me the words these girls need to hear. I'm glad it's raining. We need it, though I had to leave the baby a bit earlier than I would have liked to be on time. "Hi, my name is Father Mike Schmitz, and you're listening to the Catechism in a Year Podcast... This is day 320... We begin by talking about the truth... What is the truth?... And, how are we called to live? We're called, in fact, to live in the truth. And to not only live in the truth but to bear witness to the truth." Bear witness to the truth. Thank you, God, for this podcast. Thank you, God, for Father Mike. That man has changed my life, and I'm sure many others, too. He's going to be a saint with a capital S one day. "Bear witness to the truth." Lord, I'm trying. Please help me.

Hey, y'all. How's it going? Has anyone tried praying the Liturgy of Hours since I last was here? No? Some yes? Okay, well, it's not homework, but I'd love to see if any of you notice a difference in your life if you commit to praying just one of them a day. It's up to you. It's a beautiful place to start when you're struggling to figure out how to talk to God. Even only praying Night Prayers before bed can be life-changing. Alright, we're going to start with a prayer today.

In the name of the Father, the Son, and the Holy Spirit. Amen.

Mary, Mother of the Church, I come before you in the spirit of St. Maximilian Kolbe, who consecrated his Franciscan life and work to you without reserve. You accepted Maximilian's self-offering; accept me. You led Maximilian to Christ; lead me. You formed Maximilian into a mirror of Christ; form me. Your union with Maximilian provided the backdrop for his works of evangelization and heroic acts of charity.

Please grant, through the intercession of St. Maximilian, that I might fully collaborate with you and the

Holy Spirit as an instrument for the upbuilding of Christ's Church. Amen.

In the name of the Father, the Son, and the Holy Spirit. Amen.

I'll tell you why I chose that prayer in a little while. Today, we're going to talk about community, and then we're going to talk about the topic that most of you are interested in, finding the 'one.' A lot of y'all are wondering, "How do I find my future husband? Is he the one?" We'll get into that a little bit, but today, we will build on what we've already talked about. We focused on prayer first because I wanted you to start looking inward. What does it mean to look inward? What is our relationship with God? And, how do we go forward? It was vital for you to hear that first talk on prayer because we will build upon that today. I can't talk to you about the other things we will discuss until you understand that prayer is the foundation for everything. Having a loving relationship with God affects everything else, everything that we will discuss.

Is everyone planning on going to college? *Almost everyone raises a hand.* Okay, great. College is not everyone's calling, and that's okay. If you are going to college, you may be going off to a small school, or you may be going off to a big school. I went to the University of Georgia, a pretty large school. No matter where you end up, there will probably be a Catholic Church around you. It's such a blessing. How are you going to find friends? I went up to UGA with thirteen other girls from high school. There are 40,000 people at that school. Do you think we could hang out or see each other all the time? We tried in the beginning, but life happens. You go where you have to go. Even now, my mom has a core group of friends that she made at St. Vincent's Academy. I had a great group of about thirteen close friends here, but we all went to different schools and separate ways. Friendships are weird. Some you can put down for a while and pick up right where you left off, and others that you think will last forever slowly dissolve.

So when I went off to UGA, which side note: If you're going to school anywhere north of here, pack a jacket. I didn't think I'd need a jacket until October in Athens, and I was wrong. I was freezing trying to make it to my 8 am classes that first semester. For anyone who cares, Athens is always about ten degrees colder than Savannah. Anyway, I digress. I went up to UGA, and my mom pushed and pushed me to make new friends. "Okay, Mom. How exactly do I do that?" I grew up in Savannah. I went to Catholic schools all my life. I had built-in friends. I didn't know how to make "new" friends. Well, what did I do? I'd go to the dining hall, and if none of my St. Vincent's friends could come with me, I'd look around the room. My mom had said, "Just sit by someone."

I'd look around the room and see a table of girls or a girl off by herself. Maybe some of you are comfortable approaching girls you don't know, like, "Hey! Will you be my friend?" No, not really. But like, "Hey, may I sit with you? I'm Kira, and I'm from Savannah. Where are you from?" You know, stuff like that, but I was uncomfortable doing that with other girls at the time, so what did I do? I sat next to guys. Well, that's helpful when you have a boyfriend you've had since you were 14. I had a serious relationship, and here I was going to sit next to random guys. My boyfriend didn't go to UGA Freshman year, so I couldn't sit with him, but at least in that setting, if you just randomly sit next to a guy, they tend to think you're interested in them, like to date or possibly more. I remember this one time I sat beside a guy eating by himself. We were both eating waffles, and he said, "Um, what are you doing?" I said, "I don't know. Trying to make friends." I have no idea what I'm doing!

So, the question is, what do you do? You'll naturally form friendships in your classes, but when you're in the core classes at a big school, there are 300 people in those classes. You're all just trying to pay attention and get good grades. And unless you sit by someone you connect with, there isn't much time for friend-making. Where is that community? Where are all these "new" friends? You can feel alone. It can get very lonely. I'm sure you can see where I'm going with this.

You have a community. It's built-in to who you are. It's built-in to how you were baptized. It's built into the network of the Catholic Church all over the world, and it is available for you right there. You have something even at the smaller schools where you might not have a Catholic center on campus. That's the beauty of the Catholic Church. There is usually a church within an hour or so of you at all times, at least in the United States. This gives you a stepping stone to finding a community.

When I got up to Athens, I utilized the Catholic Center for a time but did not utilize their Sunday evening spaghetti dinner. That spaghetti wasn't very good. I'd find something else for dinner. At the time, I failed to see that it wasn't about the spaghetti. It was NOT about the spaghetti. It was about the community. And, maybe I wouldn't have connected with some people there, but perhaps I would have. Maybe, for those of you looking for a nice Catholic boy, your future husband might be at that spaghetti dinner! You never know!

I had friends, but they were from Savannah. That's totally fine, but you're in this new place, in this new experience, with all these other people who are having a new experience. That makes a huge difference. Have any of you been to World Youth Day or Grad Night? *Shakes heads no.* We went to Grad Night in Disney World when I was a senior in high school. It was one of the coolest experiences because we were all running around and having a good time when, at some point, we realized that everyone around us was in the same moment in life. That's a rare occurrence. It was so cool. Every one of us was about to graduate high school. Every one of us was trying to figure out how to get ready for college and how to live away from our families. We had our differences, but overall we were all in the same, exact moment in life. Every one of us was just excited to be there and be alive. You have this feeling of belonging in moments like that. College is similar. You're all relatively in the same moment in life, so you already have a commonality that you otherwise wouldn't have in other circumstances.

So, what are you hearing from me? "Go to the Catholic Church, and you will definitely find community and the man you will marry." No. No. No. Here's what you're hearing from me. We talked about talking to God and growing your prayer life. What I want for you. What I hope for you. What I pray for you is that your prayer life isn't just a side note to your life. Your prayer life needs to become a part of who you are because that's ultimately what being a Catholic Christian is. It's not, "Oh, this is just my religion." When I say I'm Catholic, it's not just because my parents baptized me Catholic. No. I am a child of God. You are children of God. Being a child of God makes up our identities. It is who we are.

Do you know how when you go around town in your uniform, people know that you're a St. Vincent's girl, and people have good or bad connotations about that? Just like they do about being a Catholic or Christian or what have you. But, you probably find some comfort in the fact that you fit that label. Does that make sense? You find solace in the fact that you *are* a St. Vincent's girl. Your parents love you so much that they sent you here to be educated. That's a big deal. Not everybody has that opportunity. It's a big sacrifice, and the same is true for Catholicism but on a much larger scale.

When you walk with God now and start building that foundation, you will *want* to be in the Catholic center on your campus. You're going to want to find your FOCUS missionary on campus and check out their annual SEEK conference, where many young adults in your age bracket go and talk about God. They *want* to talk about God. It's not some faux pas thing or in keeping with that old-age etiquette rule, don't talk about religion, politics, or money, all that stuff that unfortunately hardly anyone listens to anymore but basically how to have good manners. You will want to surround yourself with people who unapologetically talk about God. And Jesus. And Mary. And Confession. And the Sacraments. And marriage. And babies. Things that matter as children of God and people who walk with God. You may be thinking, "I don't need a missionary. A missionary is for someplace like Haiti or some third-world country that needs help." We do. We do need people who will witness to us their faith, but the point is you already have a built-in community. As you go forward in life, and you start feeling kind of alone, because it happens, you don't have to be lonely. Does that make sense?

It's such a simple but complex concept to grasp. I hope they're getting it on some level. Save yourself some lonesome hardship, girls.

Okay, great. In that built-in community, what do you do? Well, you look at their events calendar. Check out their retreats. What do they have available? At UGA, the dining halls are closed Sunday nights, so the Catholic Center has a 5:00 pm Mass and dinner afterward. I didn't utilize that enough, and I wish I had. If you go to a smaller school and don't have a church on campus that holds events, find something. Find a Christian group or another event you're interested in. What if you can't find something? This is where we return to the prayer at the beginning of our talk today.

Does anybody know who St. Maximilian Kolbe is? Has anyone taken the Holocaust class they provide here? *Some shake their head yes.* It was one of my favorite classes I've ever taken, next to the horseback riding classes I took in college. Yes, I got graded to ride horses. Do any of you know how Kolbe's story is interlaced with the Holocaust? *Some yes.* He died in it, right? He was a martyr, but we're not going to talk much about his death today. We're going to talk a bit about what he did in his life. St. Maximilian Kolbe was a young priest in Rome in the early 1900s, around the same time as Our Lady of Fatima was appearing to the shepherd children in Portugal, when Freemasons marched through the Vatican towards St. Peter's Basilica in angry protest.

St. Maximilian Kolbe saw their blatant lack of respect for God, the Blessed Mother, St. Michael, and the Church, and it bothered him.

I'm not going to touch a lot on this point of others openly disrespecting God, but I just discovered that some people think Catholics aren't Christians. That was shocking to me. How could anyone think we aren't Christians? Especially considering Christ started the Catholic Church! You may one day meet or already have met some people who have stereotypes about Catholics and Christians. It can jar you if you're not rock solid in your love of God and walking with Him in your faith. It can shake you up.

St. Maximilian Kolbe saw this gross display by the Freemasons and thought this was not okay. They're going to march an army into the Vatican. He thought we should have an army, too, a spiritual army.

Now, I'm not asking you to start a spiritual army, though that would be cool. Here's the part that pertains to you. He started something called the Militia of the Immaculata, and it grew. And, it grew. It was a dedication to Our Lady. Just by walking in his faith, St. Maximilian attracted hundreds to join. It's not like he went door to door knocking and asking people to sign up for a fun, new group. It just grew. It grew because people were drawn to St. Maximilian Kolbe's faith and his love for the mother of our Lord. It still exists today. I just watched a video with interviews of members of the Militia of the Immaculata, the same one that St. Maximilian Kolbe started before the

Holocaust. Some members were your age. I consecrated myself to Jesus through Mary this past year (and after this talk officially joined the MI). This spiritual army is still actively praying for lost souls.

St. Maximilian Kolbe probably didn't foresee this group still going strong over a hundred years later. Maybe he did, but people from all over the world still flock to it. Why? Because they're attracted to having a loving relationship with Jesus through Our Lady. That's what we talked about last time—starting that loving relationship with God.

St. Maximilian Kolbe ended up dying in Auschwitz when he volunteered to take the place of another man in the starvation bunker. His life is amazing. Our lives can be amazing, too. We don't have to die in a starvation bunker. Our lives can be amazing, too. The world does not have to know our names.

So, if you don't have something available to you, start it. Are you thinking, "No way! That sounds hard and scary. How do you even do that?" I thought that, too. A couple of years ago, my husband and I started a ministry for millennials and Gen Zers. We had run into this exact situation, in a way. We went to Mass and prayed daily, but we were still missing a close-knit, God-loving community. Our parish had Bible Studies and Youth Groups available, but we didn't fit into the age categories. The Bible Studies provided were typically for older men and women at midday, and the Youth Group obviously didn't fit our needs.

We're in this weird middle-ground age. We're in between, and we didn't know what to do. So we talked and talked and talked about it. I mean, we spent hours at the dinner table figuring this out. It sounded daunting at first.

Like, who are we? What makes us qualified to start a ministry? My husband's not a priest. I'm not a nun. It turns out we don't have to be. We just have to love God and love others. We've met so many great people through this ministry that we began. They come to our house for dinner every other month. We live on a little farm, so we called it Farm to Jesus, a play-off of farm-to-table dining. We pick a topic on God and our faith and talk about it while the kids play. Then we all eat a delicious, home-cooked meal together. Eventually, we hope to help others through Farm to Jesus by growing food for those in need as a group. We hope to expand it as a prayer group, too (through the Militia of the Immaculata). We needed community. You need community.

But, how do you find people if there aren't already planned events for you to attend? Well, look around after Mass for someone who looks around your age. Ask the Holy Spirit to give you some courage, and invite someone to get together for coffee or to go for a walk or something (somewhere public for safety purposes). They might say no, but who cares? Give it a try. You don't have to only talk about scripture or God, but it's a great jumping-off point with people you just met.

Oi. My feet are going to sleep. I have to stand up and walk around. Nope. Nope. Too many eyes. Too many faces. Nope. Sitting back down. It's a conversation, not a presentation. Conversation, not a presentation. Come Holy Spirit. Give me the strength.

Y'all lived through Covid and I don't know how it affected you, but one thing I think that the world figured out through the pandemic is that having friends is really important. It doesn't have always to be a ride-or-die until I'm old and grey kind of friend. It can be just a seasonal friend, but you must have friends and mentors. Friends are supposed to help you, right? As a friend, what are you doing? What's the definition of love? According to St. Thomas Aquinas, it's willing the good of the other. Isn't that what you're doing as friends? Or trying to do? If you're a good friend, that's what you're doing, willing the good of the other. You're not trying to cut them down. You're trying to help them grow as a person and vice versa, even if it is just a seasonal friendship based on a common short-term goal or only based on fun.

We've gone over how to meet other people. You're going to find them in your classes. You're going to find them at events. You're going to find new people through existing friends. Let's now move on to what kind of friends we are looking for. Probably not that single guy eating waffles you sit next to in the dining hall, right? He's probably not going to be the friend that's going to walk with you through this chapter. He might be, but that is a discussion for later. It's essential to find someone who will help build you up, to help you grow in virtue.

Do they have to be Catholic? No. I'm not going to sit here and say, "You're only allowed to have Catholic friends." That's ridiculous and not realistic. I am going to tell you that it's going to be a lot easier to go to Mass on Sunday if you have someone to go with you. I am going to tell you this. It's going to be a lot easier to say "no" to many things that will not bring you closer to God if you have someone to do it with you and with whom you can talk it out. Yes, you can call your St. Vincent's friends, and yes, you can call your parents. Absolutely, but in that moment, when you wake up Sunday morning and you were at the football game late the night before, you're tired and don't want to go to Mass, what are you going to do? You can go by yourself. Of course, you can, but it'll be a lot easier if you have a friend texting or calling you to say, "Hey, I'm so tired. Are you going to Mass? Alright, cool. Me too." This is also why a lot of on-campus Catholic centers have afternoon Masses; it can be hard to get up and get motivated in the morning in college.

My husband and I have a saying. If someone is not positively influencing your life, then why are they in it? It sounds harsh, doesn't it? It sounds kind of cut-throat, like get out of my life if you're not helping *me*, but it's not like that. Do you see things coming out of a friendship not in keeping with what God wants? We all know what that looks like. Your initial thought may be, "No, what are you talking about?" But, really think about it. You know what that looks like. If someone is being unkind. If someone is cutting other people down. Drinking until you or they pass out or throw up. Treating others disrespectfully. There are objectively grave sins like sexual sin and idolatry. These things and more are not in keeping with the will of God, right? We have that natural and learned ability to feel when something isn't right. Well, Jesus says it way more eloquently than my husband and I do.

"You will know them by their fruits. Are grapes gathered from thorns, or figs from thistles? So, every sound tree bears good fruit, but the bad tree bears evil fruit. A sound tree cannot bear evil fruit, nor can a bad tree bear good fruit. Every tree that does not bear good fruit is cut down and thrown into the fire. Thus you will know them by their fruits." (Matthew 7:16-20)

What's He saying? He said, "You will know them by their fruits." JESUS says, "that some trees bear evil fruit." Do you think He's talking about trees? He is not talking about trees, y'all! He's talking about people. He's talking about choices. We got that much, and you can apply what He said to everything in your life. Does this fill-in-the-blank bear good or evil fruits?

We're talking about friends first because, ideally, you start dating a friend. Ideally, your boyfriend now or your boyfriend in the future, your future fiancé, your future husband is your friend. Ideally, your friendships bear good fruit, and so do your choices. From discerning the fruits, you can build upon your prayer foundation and your relationship with God.

Y'all will get tired of me saying this, but remember when we talked about your prayer foundation being like a table? Remember how we talked about your future spouse being half of the table? If he can't meet you in the same place or on the same level, does that mean he's not worthy of you and your time? If your friends can't meet you in the same place as you are in your relationship with God, does that mean they aren't worth you or your time? No, but please recognize that your love *cannot* force them to be where you want them to be. Just because you love them does not mean that your friend, your boyfriend, or whatever relationship you put here will reach where you'd like them to be spiritually or morally. It's not saying, "You're not on the same level as me. You're not in a close relationship with God, so I don't have time for you." It's saying that we must love everyone anyway, even those who bear bad fruit, but we don't need to or have to walk with them if the fruit is rotten. Does that make sense?

Some of them aren't following. I can see it. How do I explain that faith isn't just belief in a creator? How do I explain that faith isn't just religion? Faith is our very being. It affects all our relationships.

Y'all are in high school. I am sure you have been in a situation where you knew something wasn't right. You might have even stood up and said, "I'm done. I quit. I'm out. This is not right." But, how many times have you not done that? *I raise my hand.* I've done it. I've stayed. I've watched. Thought it was funny. Sin often is funny. That doesn't make it right.

We're going to progress through this a bit. I had friends in college who would frequent fraternity parties. I did not. I had a full-time boyfriend and no use for those parties. By the way, you don't have to do that. You don't have to go to college and go to parties, drink excessively, and go to bars. There's a whole network of people who don't do those things and still have a perfectly wonderful and fun college experience. Anyway, friends called me from the frat house multiple times in the middle of the night. "Will you come get me?" "Yeah, I'll come get you," and off I'd go into the night to try and figure out which mansion was the fraternity house they were stuck in. I had a friend call me at 6 am one morning. I'm sure we can all guess why she was still there at 6 am. I went and got her. What was I going to say? "What are you thinking? We went to a Catholic school. What *are* you thinking?" No. That first time, I said, "I love you, and I will come get you as often as you need me to. I mean to a certain extent. I'm not going to be like your taxi for sin. I will love you through this, but I'm not going to say, 'Good job.'" I was so sad for her, but I didn't lecture her. I didn't pass judgment or criticize her. She did quit calling me to come get her eventually because at some point I ever so nicely said, "WHAT ARE YOU DOING?! Why are you doing this?" Our friendship, which I thought would last a lifetime, slowly faded, and it hurt.

I always tried to be open to helping one of my friends get out of a sticky situation in a healthy, non-condescending way, but there's a limit to helping someone when mortal sin becomes a habit. Sometimes, you're the one in the sticky situation. Who will you call? You'll ask, who will treat me like I want to be treated? Which one of my friends will love me as God loves me? Sometimes we need to be that friend, y'all, and sometimes *we* need that friend who looks at us and says, "What are you doing!? Where is God!? Have you forgotten He existed!?" God is a loving god. He's also a just god. We need that accountability. It's not just sexual sin and partying I'm talking about. Everyone's thoughts always seem to go there first, and I know my example didn't help, but I'm talking about everyday life kind of things too. You need to hold yourself accountable, and you need others around you who will help you do it.

Now, let's get into the boyfriend part. Some of you have boyfriends now, right? Is he going to be the one you marry? *Some heads shake yes. Some shake no. Others look so confused.* No? Do you want to marry him? Yeah? Some of you are thinking about it. Some of you might know for sure that he's the one you want to marry. Some of you might be thinking, "Eh... probably not." Why are you dating them if you're not trying to determine if he's the right one to marry? Is it for fun? Or entertainment? Is it so you're not alone?

Student: "To get to know someone."

Absolutely. You have to date someone before you marry them. You have to learn more about a person and whether or not you are compatible. You should grow and mature as a person while in the dating world.

Student: "I mean, I think that's a broad question to ask a teenager."
Teacher: "Some people will answer immediately."
Student: "I mean, I love my boyfriend and everything, and I'd liked to think that we'll get married one day, but like, I don't know if that's going to be the case."
Me: "Well, to clarify, I'm not telling you that you should get married right now."
Awkward laughter.
Teacher: "Some people will have that feeling immediately. Some people will not, and that feeling will come later after you've been in the relationship awhile."

Thank you for the backup, Mrs. Teacher!

I received many questions about how to know if he's the one. I did not know for a long time that my husband was the one. And for the record, God does not make one human being on the planet the 'one' for you to find on one great big scavenger hunt.

I started dating my husband when I was 14 years old. We went to Blessed Sacrament School and had been going to school together since we were four. Our grandmothers were friends. We are NOT related. *Giggles.* You gotta make sure of that in Savannah! Everybody's related. We took two breaks. One was in the middle of high school. There was a lot of deep stuff going on with both of us. We were both dealing with some heavy family stuff, like really heavy. I got scared, threw up my hands, and said, "I need a break." And by break, I mean we talked every day and still hung out all the time. Quote-unquote break, right? In that break, this sounds horrible, he never wavered, but I went and talked to other guys because he was my first kiss. I needed to date around or thought I did. Everyone else said I did. I was not Arthur's first kiss, and he knew he wanted to marry me one day, even then. Somehow, he knew, but I was not as sure. I went to church every week but did not grace the confessional often. I did not walk with God as I should have. I did not love Him as I should have. I did not see my life with the clarity of the love of God.

When you walk with God and have a relationship with Him, it becomes much easier to discern things. I'm not saying easy as in simple. God doesn't say, "Oh, you should definitely do this or that. This boy's definitely the one you are meant to marry." No, but you start to see things that you otherwise would struggle to see clearly. This harkens back to what we talked about last time. Does this bring me closer to God or further away from God? That summer after my sophomore year of high school, my relationship with my now husband was blurred. The whole thing was grey, and I had no idea. I needed to step back and take a break. Well, hello, we're in high school. What did we do?

After the summer, we got back together because we're "KirandArthur." Everyone knew us as "KirandArthur." One word. That's what we were supposed to do: get back together. A lot of times in relationships, if you do not lean on God, what can happen? If God is not your foundation, what do you do? You lean unhealthily on each other. You make your relationship an idol. You depend entirely on each other for confidence and comfort. Do you know what that is called? When you lean unhealthily on your friend or boyfriend? (They're interchangeable here, though we'll keep talking in the boyfriend realm.) That would be called co-dependency.

Everybody in Savannah knew "KirandArthur." Kira and Arthur were never apart. It was never just Kira or just Arthur, except at school. Thank God he went to BC (Benedictine Military School), and we didn't go to the same school. I don't think we would have made it. Our relationship was a little codependent. I got in trouble one time, and my mom gave me the punishment of reading a book on codependency. I read it, gave it back to her, and said, "I am not codependent, Mom." Well, she was right, and I was wrong. So, we went to college. We were still codependent. I loved him dearly. Obviously, to this day, he is my very best friend. He can make me belly laugh like nobody can which you know, what's life without joy? He sees all of my strengths and all of my flaws and still adores me. I adore him too, but for a long time, I loved him with a shallow, earthly love. I just didn't know it. I wasn't aware.

I had all this confusing friend stuff I was going through when I got to college. I hate to say it, but I eventually quit going to Mass. I stopped walking with my faith. Did I talk to God? Sometimes. Did I pray? Yes. Regularly? No. Was I in a state of mortal sin? Yes. Do you remember the last time when I talked about how when you are in a state of mortal sin, the devil has jurisdiction over you? Grave sin is not just sexual sin, y'all. It can be intentionally skipping Mass on Sunday. I didn't know that. Did any of you know that? That skipping Mass just because you feel like it, not for some legitimate illness or unforeseen circumstance, is a mortal sin? *Shakes heads no.* I don't mean to bring up sin in a condemnation way. It's the truth. It's the reality. That's why we discussed the devil last time and how he gets a foothold in our lives. If you're in a state of mortal sin, the devil has a claim over you, and your walk with God is that much more challenging because you're not in a state of grace. You've turned your back on God.

Listen, side note. If y'all want to come pray with me on Tuesday afternoons at St. James and go to confession, let's do it. If y'all want to meet me and my family at Mass on Sundays, if you don't for whatever reason go with your families, at St. James for 11:30 Mass, bring it on. I'm all about it. We sit near the choir so our 4-year-old can stare at the Sister who sings, and our baby can yell louder than William Wallace in Braveheart at the priest during his homily. Don't get the reference? Look it up! We normally run her out to the narthex. It's chaos, and we love it. So, there's that invitation, and I do mean it. Y'all are welcome to join us, especially those whose families don't attend Mass and who don't want to go by yourself. We'd love to have you.

Anyway. Train of thought... let's get back to it. Where were we? Codependency. Right. So, I took another break from dating Arthur in college. My now husband, then boyfriend, knew he would marry me. He just didn't know when or where. Thank God for his loyalty. Me, on the other hand... I struggled with, "How do I know he's the one? I'm only 19 years old." So, what did I do? I went to Florida for the summer after my first year of college. My dad lived in a beach community in the panhandle, and I worked at the pool for the summer. What did I do there? Surprise, I hung out with guys. That's what. I became friends with one girl who worked at the pool with me, and we only hung out with guys all summer. That's probably good, right? That's a recipe for goodness. (*Please note the sarcasm.*) Through that experience, though, for the first time in my life that I had noticed, I experienced use. I didn't have Arthur. I didn't have St. Vincent's friends to fall back on. I didn't have anybody besides my family and random people that I met. For the first time, I saw the truth of use. St. Pope John Paul II said that the opposite of love is... fill in the blank.

Student: "Hate."

You'd think that. No, the opposite of love is not hate. It is use. Arthur and I used each other in all sorts of ways without realizing it, not just in the way that your mind is immediately going to, but in all kinds of ways, sexual and non. We did. We loved each other, but that's what codependency is. Use. We used each other emotionally. It didn't negate the fact that we loved each other, but it did devalue that love into something not in keeping with God and His will. It was disordered.

I know I keep saying that. God's love. God's will. Relationship with God. You might still be thinking, "WHAT IS SHE TALKING ABOUT?" It's why we spent the entire first talk on prayer. Our relationship with God is not part of our lives. It is our life. Last time, one of you asked, "How do you balance your marriage and your faith?" I don't because it's one and the same. It's one and the same, and we'll get to that in the marriage talk. It is easy to think faith is just a box you check. It's not a checklist. It's the innermost being that you are, and that affects everything. It affects **everything**.

Discerning whether or not someone should be in your life is something you can start doing right now. You don't have to wait until after high school. How are you going to know bad fruits? Well, because you're going to know God. Get rooted in a faith life now so it can help you make decisions that align with God's will for you. The discernment will be that much easier. That's my hope for you. That's why I'm here. Our moral basis is rooted in our faith. That's how it should be. A lot of people don't have that foundation, but we do because we're Catholic.

When I was in Florida that summer in college, I encountered a boy there who really liked redheads. He was attracted to me only because I had red hair, and it was creepy. Listen. You're not going to be everybody's cup of tea. I learned that a long time ago. There are boys out there who don't like redheads just because they're redheads. Okay. It doesn't matter, but this boy only liked me just because I was a redhead. And, it felt SO weird. He started trying to date me. He was older and was a baptized Catholic but didn't practice. Arthur and I were always Catholic. We were just Catholic. Our religion was a part of our identity. I didn't know it was going to bother me that someone who wanted to date me wasn't Catholic or didn't practice their faith.

And yes, there are interfaith marriages. Some of your parents may be in an interfaith marriage. There are some beautiful couples with beautiful, fruitful interfaith marriages. Yes, it can work out wonderfully. However, there are substantial differences between Catholicism and other denominations. Think about that right now. Are some of your boyfriends of another denomination? Are you planning on making them Catholic? Because you can't. Remember we talked about how it's our job to get our spouses and children to heaven, but we can't force them. We have to invite them. There are a lot of couples who make interfaith work and have figured out how to bridge the differences in interfaith marriages. There are a lot who have not, and some have even put their kids through hell because of it.

Back to the story. There were many other things that this guy did that I'm not going to mention because it's not worth the time and/or is inappropriate. He was nice enough, but I quickly realized this wasn't it. You know you always think the grass is greener. The grass was NOT greener in my case. Sometimes, in other cases, it is for other people. Sometimes, you're in a relationship you shouldn't be in, and the grass truly is greener with someone else. That's where you need that God-based discernment and why I mentioned St. Ignatius of Loyola's discernment of spirits. Looking through this lens of God's love, everything will open up to you. Is this of God or not of God? Is this a temptation by the devil, or is it just my human nature getting in the way of things? Does this bring me closer to God or further away from Him? You will begin to see more clearly.

How do I personally know this is how life is supposed to be? That God's design does, in fact, work? Here I am a hypocrite, right? I had a friend this past week that I was talking to about coming here say that she wishes someone could speak to y'all that walked the perfect road. They could say, "I did everything right. Y'all follow my path. It's clear and free. I've listened to and loved the Lord the entire time, and my life has been smooth sailing. Everything's good." That's not life, and that's not my story. The road will always be bumpy. There will always be ups and downs. So, how do I know the fruits of a close relationship with God? I know because I implemented it at some point in my life. I've reoriented my life to love God. I thank Him for all my joys and sufferings and ask Him to help me with even the most minor tasks of my day.

I've seen its fruits, and they are good fruits. I've implemented this love into my family relationships. I've implemented this love into my friendships and within my marriage, and I've seen the fruits. I hope someone can give you a near-perfect testimony sometime in your life. I still struggle. I did not take the smooth road, so what am I doing here? To tell you not to follow my path? No. So you know that at the very base of life is, "Are you talking to God?" That affects ALL the rest of your life because our souls are ETERNAL. Our very make-up is designed to be in loving communion with God. He LOVES us. We just have to participate in that love. You matter, infinitely.

Student: "I went to a conference a couple of weeks ago, and I wouldn't have understood what you were saying fully before that, but now I do."
Me: "That's awesome!"

Student: "But like, I'm kind of getting it now. I feel like I didn't treat religion seriously. Now I feel like the Bible is the actual living word of God. Me two weeks ago would have been like, "Oh yeah.... I need to pursue a relationship with God. I need to read my Bible more." But now, I'm seeing how it's supposed to be a personal, intimate relationship with God. Literally, I feel like my life changed two weeks ago."

Me: "Isn't that so cool?! You have these moments where you go, "Oh, wait! All of a sudden, I get it. I get it now!" It clicks."

Student: "I didn't have the want or urge to read my Bible. I was like, "Why?""

Me: "Remember that the Liturgy of Hours is the highest form of prayer next to the Mass. When the Bible seems overwhelming, start there. Read one prayer a day. Just one. Focus on one word, one phrase, one psalm, scripture, or prayer within it that speaks to you, and sit with it. See how it affects you. It can be just one word. Maybe the whole thing affected you that day, but it can be just one word that suddenly just hits you like, "BAM!" You have that moment of clarity, and you're like, thanks God! Thanks for opening my heart to see. You never know. It might have been right there, in that exact moment, that God was waiting to give you the grace to understand something you couldn't grasp before."

Back to the "how do I balance my marriage and faith" question. The answer is you don't because it's not a question of balance. They are one and the same because our faith is engrained in us. It's who we are. It's not, "Oh, we're Catholic, and it's over here separate from the rest of my life." No. I am Catholic, which means that I was baptized as a child of God, which means that I walk with my faith. If someone looked at you and you weren't in your school uniform, would they know you were Catholic? Maybe you're wearing medals/sacramentals, which is excellent. Some of them, like the St. Benedict and Miraculous medals, have built-in prayers. But, if someone looked at you, could they tell by the way you walk with God that you were Catholic? Could they tell by looking at your life that you talk to God? Could they tell by what you do that you're a Christian? Could they tell by how you treat other people? I'm not talking about preaching it from street corners or yelling at people. I'm just talking about what you do in your daily life if someone looks at you. Are you a witness to your faith? Do you love others as Jesus loves them? Do you worship Him? Do you love the Lord? Do you honor and glorify Him with your actions?

I was recently listening to a priest's lecture where he challenged the listener to grow in virtue. How? He said to say out loud to your guardian angel, "Show me my defects in virtue." So, I did, and I kid you not, that night, I picked up a book I had had on the shelf for a while that I hadn't gotten around to reading yet. I got 100 pages in when there they were, my defects. There was a list of attachments to sin in four neatly organized sections by category. I went down the list... I struggle with this one, and that one, and that one, and that one. Aw, man. Thanks, Guardian Angel. I have a lot to work on. This is not to focus on, "sin sin sin sin sin sin. All the church and God cares about is sin." It's not like that. Again, God gave us guidelines to get to heaven, and really, we ought to be so grateful, right? He gave us the ability to receive special graces and virtues to help us become holy, to help us become saints.

What is an attachment to sin? It's wanting to sin even when we know it's wrong. Sometimes, the only thing preventing us from sinning is that there's a 'rule' that prevents it. Sometimes, we may even yearn to be free of this attachment, but the seduction of sin is still there. As disciples of God, we're not called to avoid sin because it's a rule. We're called to avoid sin because *we* detest it. We're called to do what is genuinely loving and pleasing to God because *we* WANT to. This brings us back to that invitation He extends to us, right? The invitation to love Him. Think of it like breaking a bad habit. Have you ever had a habit that you really knew you needed to stop, but for whatever reason, you just struggled to? Something like gossip. You knew it would be better not to have that habit, but your will struggled to overcome it. You may be sorry that you tend to gossip. You may have even confessed it, but it still lingers. We must learn to say "no" to these impulses even if they mean suffering losses. In the case of gossip, we could lose friendships based on gossip or feel like we're missing out when we don't join in on a gossip conversation. If we recognize these attachments to sin, we can slowly begin chipping away at them with God's help. Just like we can ask our Guardian Angel to show us our defects in virtue, we can also ask him to help us say "no" to our attraction to sin and to help us grow in virtue.

Did I answer everyone's question about finding the one you should marry? Yes? No? Let's run through it again quickly. Does your community help you in your quest for holiness? Will your boyfriend potentially help get you to heaven? Will he help you get your future children to heaven? No. Can you help him get to heaven? Maybe not as-is right now. Do you think that y'all can grow together in your love of God?

That's what happened to me and Arthur. I look back at 20-year-old Kira after that summer in Florida, and I had grown. Not only had I learned that the grass wasn't greener, but I had also worked on my issues and shortcomings. I went back to Arthur and said, "Alright. I'm ready. We can get back together now. You're the one." He slowly responded, "I'm not ready," and my heart deflated. What!? You were always there. You have always loved me. You know that we're going to get married. What do you mean you're not ready? I just had to figure out if you were the one because I'm an idiot. And, he repeated, "No." I was devastated. Then, like twenty minutes later, as I was crying in the middle of some chain Italian restaurant (I liked their lobster ravioli), he couldn't bear my pain any longer and said, "Okay, okay, let's get back together."

Thank you, God, because now we're married with beautiful children. We had to do things a bit differently this time around, though. We had to be able to stand on our own to stand firmly together. We had to be strong by ourselves to lean on each other healthily, the way that God designed a man and a woman to lean on one another. We had to do more than just love each other. We had to complement each other and trust one another. We had to strengthen our wills and grow in virtue. We had to make sacrifices for one another. We went to individual counseling and tried to better ourselves but still failed to see then that we needed to put our relationship fully in God's hands. Only He could transform it into what He designed it to be.

So, I did not technically have to play the dating field to find my spouse, but that's where finding a community comes in. Surround yourself with people who help you attain holiness. You may be thinking, "Kira, not all the holy boys are cute." Figure it out! Yes, you need to be physically attracted to a man. Yes, you want to marry someone who will make cute babies with you. My babies are adorable. My husband is precious, and our second daughter has his eyes. My eyelashes are blonde, so without mascara, I look like a ghost. Girlfriend has dark, long eyelashes that arch up to her eyebrows. They're beautiful. So yes, of course, you want attraction. Is attraction alone going to get you to heaven? Probably not. Does God want you to be happy? Yes. There's some misconception out there that God doesn't want you to be happy. That's not true! He gives us guidelines to get to heaven. If He didn't want us to be happy, once again, He'd be like, "Good luck. We'll see if you make it to eternal happiness." He doesn't do that. He loves us, and through that love is how we're supposed to love others. By knowing His love, we know how to love others. So, do you need to be physically attracted to somebody? Yes. Does he need to be the fill-in-the-blank guy you know of who is unthinkably cute? No. (I don't know your generation's cute guy. My go-to was always Brad Pitt, but he's old now.)

Physical attraction is a beautiful gift that brings us towards one another, but it is only the first step. Is your potential partner going to have faults? Yes. Is he going to be perfectly faith-filled? No. But, are you? Y'all will both have struggles, but can you stand together in them? Can you grow? What does he or your friends say when you go to Mass? When you pray? Do they say you're weird or make fun of you in a nasty way, not a playful banter way? They're probably not good fruits for your life then, right?

I have a friend who is not Catholic. She doesn't know God. She wasn't raised with faith. I don't preach. I don't look down on her. Sometimes, I'll say things like, "The Holy Spirit gave me this idea," and she'll say, "What does that mean?" It means that I suddenly had an idea that wasn't mine. I don't know where it came from, and here we are, which is how I got here to talk to you, by the way. She doesn't make fun of me. She isn't condescending, and I'm not condescending back. "You idiot. How could you not know about God?" I try not to shove my faith down her throat, and she doesn't ridicule me for my faith. We can be great friends because we have similar morals and values. She respects my faith, and I respect that she doesn't know God. Now, do I slide in some things into conversations like, "God loves you. You matter." Yes... I do because that's what we're called to do as Christians: share the good news.

One of you asked, how do I make my friend a Christian? You can't, but you can walk as a Christian. They may see you. How do I make my boyfriend a Catholic? You can't, but if he sees you praying, going to Mass, loving others, and walking in your faith, he may think that's pretty attractive. If he loves you and respects and/or admires your relationship with God, then you're on the right path, right? It's not that hard. Everyone stresses, "How am I going to find the one I'm supposed to marry?!?" You don't. God finds them for you. How does He do that? Ask Him to help you and start making decisions that will open you to His love. Not your future spouse's love. God's love. When you open yourself to God's love, you're opening yourself up to a world where God works miracles in your life. Again, there's not just one guy out there for you that's the one. The one. Yes, there is the one you're going to marry, but there isn't some magical *one* out there waiting for you to find him. Ask God to reveal him to you.

We have a throwaway culture. You're not cute, swipe. You're not popular, next. That's use. We are not supposed to use people. I got down to Florida that summer and devised a motto, "Entertainment is entertainment." It didn't matter if a boy was cute, which I mean, I worked at the pool. I worked at a *pool*. I could clearly see if a boy was cute or not. It was very apparent. But, my friend and I would scope out the pool during the day to find guys we could hang out with after I got off work that night or while I was working. Entertainment is entertainment. That was our motto! Y'all, that's awful. I look back and think, "Oh my gosh, you were using these boys to cure your boredom." "Well," you may say, "you were just having fun." You're right. I was having fun, but I was using them for entertainment. That's ridiculous. I wasn't trying to know their hearts. I wasn't respecting them as a person. I wasn't treating them with dignity. I'm not saying you should dive right into a deep relationship and share all your most profound thoughts when you first meet someone, but I wasn't even trying to get to know them as people. I was like, let's go swimming or drive around all night on the golf cart! Let's drink and do all these things that avoid us getting to really know one another and just have "fun."

Are those things bad in themselves? No, of course not. Are they bad in the way I did them? Yes. Why? Because I was using another human being for entertainment. I didn't care to know them or see their worth as a human person. I reduced them to their physical attributes and what they could do for me. Again, not sexual sin. Use is not always sexual. It often can be, but use is manipulation. It's lies. Use is the throwaway culture. I've met you, don't care to love and honor you as a human person, and am looking to get something solely for myself out of this. Use is emotional. It's the means of objectifying someone else to reach a selfish end. People are not objects. I think we can all agree on that, right?

Do you know how the Eucharist is kept in the Tabernacle on the altar? We all know that Jesus' body is in the Tabernacle. Did you know that when we consume the Body of Christ, we become walking tabernacles? Did you know that? How cool is that!? Jesus resides in us as walking tabernacles. That is super cool. Knowing this, you would think we'd know how to treat another human being with love, respect, honor, and dignity. You would think we'd know how to treat another human person like they mattered, but we forget that, especially when we don't frequently receive this gift. We forget to be Jesus to other people.

So, what's my point? The point of the last chapter was it's time to begin and strengthen your prayer life if you haven't already. Start to know God so that you can love Him because to know Him is to love Him. The point of this chapter is that your prayer life and relationship with God should become integrated into who you are as a human being. It's not a purse that you pick up sometimes, throw on your shoulder to go somewhere, and then put down and walk away. Some people see you wearing it and might think it's a nice purse. Other people think it's ugly or don't see it at all. Some people know I have morals and can say "no" to certain things and "yes" to others. Other people

73

don't. Some people ridicule me for my faith. Others admire it. Either way, I can hide it away when I need to or want to. This integration of God in your daily life will affect your friendships and romantic relationships. It will affect your finding of the 'one' and discerning whether or not he is the one.

When you find a friend group, whether or not they're Catholic, do they respect you as a human person? Do they respect you when you say, "Yes, I'm going to do this?" Do they respect you when you say, "No, I'm not going to do this?" Do they care about you? My friend who isn't a believer, whom I love dearly, respects my faith because I walk in it or try my best to. I may say things about God that she doesn't understand in a conversation, but I might have planted a seed. Or, more correctly, the Holy Spirit planted the seed. And, I'm not trying to convert her to Catholicism through our friendship, but if it is a fruit of it one day, that's not a bad fruit. And, if she never converts to Catholicism, the fruits of our friendship are mutual love and respect. It's the same thing with any relationship. It's the same thing with a guy. Look at your relationship. Why are you dating? To get to know one another. Why are you trying to get to know one another? To see if there is the potential for friendship and if they're the one you want to marry. To see if they're the type of person that will get you to heaven and one you can help get to heaven. Because that's a huge deal (especially if your boyfriend isn't a Christian). Then you add your children for whom you will literally die. Is he one day going to be able to help you get them to heaven? Because if he's not, then **what are you doing**? I can't say that Arthur and I have always been in this mindset. I can't because that wasn't my story, but it is now.

Student: "Is kissing a mortal sin?"

Haha, no. We will talk about intimacy at some point because we're going to touch on Natural Family Planning and marriage and all, but we're not going to focus too much on sexual sin. We're going to focus on the beauty of sex and intimacy in marriage. There is such a beautiful side to it that is so skewed and twisted in our culture.

When you walk with God, these things we're talking about seem so big that they become a part of your nature, and it's not a big deal anymore because you just do it. It just happens. It becomes who you are.

Student: "I wouldn't have understood this talk two weeks ago. I know that sounds weird, but now, on the other side of that conference, I can listen to what you are saying and feel it."

Right!? Okay, so I used to play year-round soccer. In the winter and summer months, I would play with the guys. I had Arthur, so I would join his indoor soccer team. I would literally sign up as a guy to play. When I got to my fall soccer practice with my girls' team after one of my summers playing on the guys' team, I had a real snarky British coach. I don't know what he was doing coaching teenage girls. We're playing 6 v 6 in that first practice, and I'm flitting around the little field and scoring like it's no problem. All the players around me looked, to me, like they were in slow motion. My British coach was shocked and yelled all sorts of obscenities at me for "holding out on him." Are you following my analogy? I had gotten so much stronger in my abilities as a soccer player that what had previously been a challenge was no longer much of one, which is what the challenge is for your prayer life. Get so strong in your prayer, your love of God, and your relationship with Him so that all the challenges that might come at you aren't as hard to face anymore. You live your life without them knocking you down.

Student: "I feel like a lot of people might not understand because faith can feel like a checklist. You're trying to say we should have a relationship with God, but you're also saying that we should have a relationship with the Spirit. I feel like there's a difference between someone who just says I'm a Catholic or a Christian and someone who walks with God and walks with the Spirit. I feel like that's what you're trying to say, like pursuing a relationship with God, but I feel like some people aren't getting it because you're not saying to walk with religion or Christianity in name but to actually walk with God."

Yes! Oh, thank you, thank you for this insight! This disconnect between quote-unquote religion and a true, loving relationship with God is sometimes so hard to get across.

Yes! And, I never bring up sin to say, "You bad people. How dare you." Because helloooo. I'm a sinner. I'm not a perfect person who can say, "Follow me, and do exactly what I did or do." But, I am coming here to say that all you have to do to talk to God is say, "Hello." Just start by saying hello. Try it! However, if you *are* in a state of mortal sin, which again is not just sexual sin. It can be skipping Mass on Sunday just because you don't feel like going or receiving communion while not in a state of grace. If you are in a state of mortal sin, then your walk with God is skewed, greyed, and is just that much harder because the devil has jurisdiction over you. We must be in a state of grace. Why? Because we want to be in a loving relationship with God. We want to surrender ourselves to His divine will. He will never steer us wrong, and our lives come into focus through Him.

You have to find your people, y'all. It's really important. Last time, we talked about finding yourself. This time, we talked about you growing in virtue and finding your community because you will find your husband through that community and growth in virtue. How do you figure out if he's the one? We'll get more into this next time, but you can start right now. There are 64 virtues. Work on them. Pick one to focus on today or this week. You're looking for self-growth but not self-reliance. Your self-growth will come from relying on God. Ask the Lord to help you grow in virtue, and lean on Him. Get closer to God. Our utmost desire should be to be like Christ and to be in heaven with Him one day. That starts right now. Start praying for your future husbands right now, too. Hopefully, he's praying for you too! When you walk the path God lays before you, if marriage is your vocation, your future husband will be on His path for you.

Thank y'all so much. You're in good running for that baby goat prize. Thank you for your feedback. I so wish I could sit down with each of you and have a conversation, but there's just not enough time.

Student: "Baby goat! Here?! What?! What's its name?"
Me: "I don't know. It's not born yet!"

Once again, I smile as I turn to put up my chair. Who knew the bribery of a baby goat would be the way to their hearts? Pickles & Ginger better keep those babies in until the spring. Wow. That one felt like a doozy. Friends and boyfriends are hard, but it will only get harder from here. If they just understand the love of God. If they just understand that all He wants is our love. We can't even attempt to broach marriage and motherhood without this understanding, but I only get to see them a handful of times. We only get a few hours in total to cover these gigantic topics. Oh, Holy Spirit. Please plant the seeds. I know you are. Thank you.

What Did You Learn?

Class One

- I learned a lot about how our faith is a rock in our lives. Mrs. King talked about her sister, who is our age and has so much faith. This taught me that I should try to strengthen my faith as much as possible to create a foundation of religion in my life.
- Using people for entertainment is not worth it, and you should stay with the people who benefit your life mutually.
- I learned about starting to find a community early on and finding my people that are similar to me.
- That we need to be stronger in our faith and that we should have a good friend group to look up to, the ones who bring you closer to God.
- I learned that not everyone gets that 'he's the one' feeling about a boy.
- I learned that faith is not always just doing the right steps and never forgetting to go to Mass, but it is also the depth of your relationship with God.
- I learned that through community and embracing our foundation in Christ, we will be led towards our husbands and a walk with God. Our life comes in seasons and sometimes experiencing the hardships of seasons brings us closer to God.
- That not going to Mass is a mortal sin.
- We need to start our walk with Christ now. We shouldn't keep putting it off until we "want" to. The sooner we start walking with Christ, the sooner our lives can come together. If we aren't distracted by worldly things and sin. Also, we should find our community, and it's really important for me to find that as I grow, so I'm so glad you talked about that topic.
- It is important to try and keep a stable relationship with God throughout college and throughout trying to find a partner.
- I learned today that I need to grow more within my faith and get more involved in my church. Because of Covid, I kind of

stepped back with my faith and was lazy about it which you should not absolutely do because I was drawn away from God. So like Mrs King said, I need to act now and start now to grow my heart towards God and let him in because that will benefit me when I get to heaven and live in eternal life with God.

- I really liked when she said, "The world doesn't need to know your name." It really hit that you can make an impact through the simple things, not having to achieve what society deems as great. I also liked how she talked about finding community and gave relevant examples.
- There's a community out there for me.
- Marriage should be based off your relationship with God.
- It is important to understand yourself as completely yourself and not be attached to anyone else.
- Ways to find a community.
- It is imperative to be okay with being alone.

Class Two

- I learned that my spiritual life should not be separate from my marriage when I get older.
- Today from the discussion I learned that good friendships are so important in our spiritual walk with God. After Mrs. King spoke on this topic, I immediately had a Bible verse come to mind. "Sweet friendships refresh the soul and awaken our hearts with joy, for good friends are like the anointing oil that yields the fragrant incense of God's presence." Proverbs 27:9 *So beautiful! Thank you for sharing.*
- I learned that the opposite of love is using.
- I learned that you have to surround yourself with people who bring you closer to God.
- I learned how to make friends in college. So grateful. *:)* *"Friendship is the source of the greatest pleasures, and without friends even the most agreeable pursuits become tedious." - St. Thomas Aquinas*
- I learned about relationships and how to find God through them with your partner.

- I learned that we shouldn't try to look for the one. Take the time to build a relationship with Jesus before taking the time to build a relationship with other people. It's okay to lean on others but lean on God. There's a difference between using people and loving them.
- That it is okay for your partner to know and you not to know, that is normal.
- I learned that if you actually grow your relationship with God and ask God if the person you are in a relationship with might be the person you end up with, God will help you decipher it by getting you to be in tune with him and to listen.
- I learned that while having a religious life that you practice in will take you very far in life.
- That dating just for fun is not in the way of God, but it's okay to have to take time to figure that out. *Dating can and should be fun! Especially if you're dating a wonderful man that you may possibly marry one day. A fun, loving relationship without unhealthy conditions and attachments is the recipe for a beautiful marriage one day. I know this firsthand. :) And, it's 100% okay to take the time to figure it out. Just don't let fear stop you from the figuring it out part.*
- I learned what being co-dependent on someone can do, and how it can affect your life and the people in your life.
- That the person you're with should bring you closer to God, even if it's a boyfriend.
- I learned that your boyfriend has to be good to you and benefit you in order to get to heaven. *Your husband ultimately has the responsibility to get you to heaven in addition to your own responsibility to get yourself to heaven, but surrounding yourself with people who will help you become holy in a number of different ways is always a good thing!*

Class Three

- That Catholics have a built-in community, and I will always have someone- Jesus!
- That there is always a way to get to God no matter where you are.
- I learned that we can always pray for our future husband or children, which I forget a lot. We were born into a community when we were baptized, and the community is reliable when we feel alone in the world.
- You can form communities through the church.
- I learned that you can still find a balance in social life and faith in college. In Catholic school, we have built in time for religion, but it is up to us to build in that time in college. It is also up to us whether or not we want to surround ourselves with faith-filled people and people who will positively uplift our lives. Marriage is made so that we can get to Heaven. Being married to someone in the church helps you get to Heaven by influence and spiritual guidance.
- When asking God questions, he may not immediately or directly answer them but he will find his own way to guide you.
- That I need to become friends with those who believe the same thing as me. I also learned that there is a community that will always be there I just have to reach out and try it.
- I learned that we need to start praying for our husband and kids now, and that hopefully, our husbands are focusing on improving their vocations right now as well as me!
- I learned that I need to think differently about how society wants us to think and that walking with God and knowing/ loving him will help you to get to heaven.
- It is important to have a community!
- If you are struggling to find your people in college or life in general, either attend a Catholic community or start one. Also, if a person in your life isn't adding anything positive to it, remove them.
- I learned that marriage is meant to be a pathway to heaven.
- I learned that if there are problems in my life to look toward God.
- - surround yourself with a good community

- change can be scary
- your job to get your husband to Heaven
- your boyfriend should help you on your path to seek God
- It's harder to be a Catholic than you think.
- No matter where you are, there is a Catholic community that can be there for you and that you can join!!

Class Four
- How to surround myself with people who have the same beliefs as me even if I may be in a situation where they aren't right in front of me.
- It is important that you keep God in your life in college.
- I learned that the Catholic church is surrounded all around us and we are able to connect with God everywhere.
- Sometimes, you have to build your own community.
- That I can find Jesus anywhere. Even at college, there are places to reach out to communities like me.
- I learned that sometimes friendships and relationships need to end if they aren't enriching our lives and/or bringing us farther away from our faith. It can be difficult but there is no point in being in difficult relationships or friendships that are very toxic and not adding anything to our lives positively.
- That I would be welcomed by any church if I just made an effort.
- There are so so many options in college to stay close to God.
- You find the One in community.
- I learned that a Catholic Church is always within a 2 hour drive of anywhere we are. This means that God is always around us, and he is never too far away for us to reach.
- Your community can largely affect you, even if you think it can't.
- I learned that there's a Catholic church within an hour from me anywhere I go. Also that God is very forgiving and confession will help us confess our mortal sins.
- Community matters.
- I learned that it is a sin to receive the Eucharist after you missed Sunday Mass (without just cause).

- I learned that if I marry someone, I am responsible for leading them to Heaven.
- There are far more mortal sins to be conscious of than I previously knew.

You will find the questions and answers for Chapter 2 on page 295.

Let Us Pray

Angelus
(Most often prayed at 6 am, 12 pm, 6 pm)

V/. The Angel of the Lord declared unto Mary,
R/. And she conceived of the Holy Spirit.

Hail Mary, full of grace, the Lord is with thee;
blessed are you among women, and blessed is the fruit
of thy womb, Jesus. Holy Mary, Mother of God,
pray for us sinners now and at the hour of our death.
Amen.

V/. Behold the handmaid of the Lord,
R/. Be it done unto me according to your Word.
Hail Mary...

V/. And the Word was made flesh,
R/. And dwelt among us.
Hail Mary...

V/. Pray for us, O holy Mother of God,
R/. That we may be made worthy of the promises of
Christ.

Let us pray. Pour forth, we beseech you, O Lord, your
grace into our hearts: that we, to whom the Incarnation
of Christ your Son was made known by the message of
an Angel, may by his Passion and Cross be brought to
the glory of his Resurrection. Through the same Christ
our Lord. Amen.

(Source: Excerpted from Catholic Household Blessings and Prayers, revised edition © 2007 United States Conference of Catholic Bishops.)

Chapter 3

Catholic Marriage: Discernment & Commitment

"He will provide the way and the means, such as you could never have imagined. Leave it all to Him, let go of yourself, lose yourself on the Cross, and you will find yourself entirely."
—St. Catherine of Siena

Lord, it's the first time I'll be speaking to all of them together instead of to individual classes. Please give me clarity and strength. Please open their hearts to your love, and please calm my anxiety about the short time frame and the mountain of material we have to cover. You always give me the words they seem to need to hear, even if they aren't the exact words I had planned. Be with us now, Lord, at this time, in this place. I trust in you.

Hey, y'all. How's it going? We've had a lot to think about so far, getting closer to God and how to do that, seeking a community that will help sanctify us, figuring out the difference between love and use, and desiring growth in virtue. All of these topics could be year-long classes in themselves. We've only just touched on some of the main points, but I hope it's given you the hunger to dive further into each of them on your own. It is ultimately your responsibility to learn more and grow in your faith. You're not alone, though.

Today, we will cover how to discern whether or not the man you've found is the 'one' and what a Catholic marriage looks like. What does it mean to be in a Catholic marriage? First, please listen to this little disclaimer. There is no "perfect" marriage. There isn't a strict rubric for you to follow that will guarantee a perfect life with your future husband and children. Also, I'll be using some examples from my own marriage and relationship with my husband, which are just that, examples. Everyone's relationship is unique to them. However, we can all strive to put Christ at the center of our relationship. God should always come first in our lives, even before our spouses. That is why we began with prayer as our first topic. It is imperative to remember that our relationship with God is the foundation for every other relationship in our lives and how we live out those relationships.

Okay, so keeping that in mind, I will pick up where we left off in my personal journey. I was twenty-two years old when I graduated from college. Arthur, my then-boyfriend, was a year behind me, so he wasn't due to graduate for another year. Slacker. Just kidding, he just took a little longer. That threw quite a large wrench into my wedding, career, and life plans. We weren't engaged at the time, but once I returned from that summer in Florida my sophomore year and realized that Arthur was, in fact, the "one," I started pushing engagement pretty hard. I admit my tactic was a bit too forceful. It was to the point where I reminded him he wanted to marry me a few times a day. I wasn't sure what he was waiting on, but... I did want that perfect vintage ring and that perfect big, Savannah Catholic wedding. I obsessively watched all the wedding drama shows that showcased the perfect dress and perfect reception. I was wedding-obsessed. Notice the word wedding and not marriage. Y'all, I even went and bought a wedding dress that was on sale at a cute boutique downtown that was closing. I wasn't even engaged yet! Well, Arthur wasn't phased by this wedding obsession of mine. In truth, it turned him away from wanting to propose to me while we were still in college.

In addition to failing to control my future nuptials, I began to panic about graduation and my future career, and I do mean panic. Have any of you read *Tuesdays with Morrie*? It's a good book with numerous insightful one-liners about life. I had never read the book, but I came across one of the quotes somewhere, and it stuck with me.

"As you grow, you learn more. If you stayed as ignorant as you were at twenty-two, you'd always be twenty-two. Aging is not just decay, you know. It's growth. It's more than the negative that you're going to die, it's the positive that you understand you're going to die, and that you live a better life because of it."

I was twenty-two. I wasn't planning on dying any time soon, but I was actively on the search for a better life. Because that's what we're doing at college, right? We're there to educate and prepare ourselves as best as possible for our future careers and lives. We can often think that college holds all the answers. When I was your age, I had one big goal: get into the University of Georgia. I accomplished that, and then what? I don't know... find something I want to do for the rest of my life—no big deal. No pressure. False. Huge pressure! I jumped around a few majors, finally settled on Public Relations, and thought, "Great. I've got my major. Opportunities and a "better life" will soon be in focus." Wrong again. I had already had some pretty big successes in public relations.

Arthur and I had started an online cooking show in our sophomore year, and it had what was considered relatively significant success in the year 2010 on an up-and-coming platform called YouTube. (It's still on there. It's called Cookin' For College and is very entertaining, in an old home movie, cringe-worthy kind of way.) Fox News had flown Arthur and me up to New York City to be on their morning show. He was a guest on Paula Deen's show on Food Network. Did all of this attention and little fame give me fulfillment and purpose? No. I had turned away from having a loving relationship with God. No accomplishment or achievement was going to take His place in my life.

Take a walk with me real fast, and bear with me. I know this is kind of corny. Let's venture down the road and imagine we're leisurely strolling around the grounds of the old Catholic cemetery. What do we see on the headstones as we casually stroll along? Do you see, "Beatrice Bubbles, (*Good pretend name, right? Can you tell I have a four-year-old?*), Great Lawyer" or "Posie Poppycock, International Career Woman"? No, absolutely not. What do you see? You see, "Beloved Wife. Beloved Mother.

Beloved Daughter Of Christ." You see vocations on the headstones. You don't see resumes. Why? Because when we zoom in on our lives, our daily tasks *do* matter. Those little daily things fill up the pages that turn into the chapters and ultimately turn into the whole story of our lives. But, when we zoom out onto the big picture of our lives and look at the entire story, our life's vocation is what matters most. Our lives are created by our daily tasks, even the monotonous ones. The little moments of our day are opportunities for holiness. Strung together, these moments make up our vocations. Those few words etched in stone, underneath the date of birth and the date of death, tell the entirety of someone's life.

That quote from *Tuesdays with Morrie* shook me. Acknowledging aging was not just decay but growth made sense, but growth to where? Growth how? In my last month of college, after being a lifelong student, something I was pretty good at, I basically had a life crisis. How was I supposed to achieve this promised better life? Where was I supposed to find fulfillment? My boyfriend wouldn't propose to me when I wanted him to. I couldn't find the perfect job. I didn't know where I was going to live. What was my future? Where was my purpose? I didn't find the answer then, though it was a straightforward one if I had just thought to seek God. I ended up using a dry-erase marker to fill up my entire back sliding glass door with *Tuesdays with Morrie* quotes to ponder during the last few weeks of my college career. Then, I practiced some college self-care 101, working out and drinking away my troubles, the latter of which I do not recommend. Thankfully, Arthur didn't think I was crazy. Well, not too crazy. No more than usual.

Let me interject something right here for those of you who don't have boyfriends, have never dated, or are nervous to. At 13 years old, I was going through a lot of dark family stuff on both sides of my family. I was in a rough spot. I vehemently prayed the same prayer every day that year. I asked God to send me a man (technically a boy at that time) who loved me for me. The very next year, He answered that prayer with Arthur. I am incredibly blessed. He has always loved me for being me. Don't forget to pray, ladies. Ask God for help in finding your future spouse.

Anyway, I graduated college and moved home to my parents' house to figure out my life. You see, our culture puts such an emphasis on having the perfect wedding, marrying the perfect man, having the perfect, lifelong career, living in a perfect house, and having the perfect 2.5 children. This is so wrong for two reasons: A. It sets the bar of perfection infinitely too high. B. It takes the place of God in our lives. God doesn't ask us to be perfect. What does He ask of us? He asks us to love Him, worship Him, and love others. Our culture tells us to love ourselves in a disordered way, to worship ourselves, and to, at best, tolerate others or tip-toe around them. Can you have a career *and* a husband *and* children? Of course, you can. Many women work while being wives and mothers. There will be sacrifices and hardships you will have to endure, but it can be done. It's imperative to keep what matters most though always in the front of our minds: God, His infinite love and mercy, and His divine will for us.

Y'all have sent me a lot of questions. I'd say your top two are: 1. How do I find the man I'm going to marry? 2. How do I know he is the one I should marry? Hopefully, you find your future spouse in that loving community that will help you attain the holiness that we discussed. Hopefully, you and your future spouse develop a beautiful friendship and turn that friendship into a romantic relationship. My husband is my very best friend. Some relationships can operate without a deep friendship, but I honestly don't know how. Friendship is at the very core of a loving relationship. Furthermore, hopefully, you and your future spouse enter into a committed relationship, one built on mutual respect and attraction.

Once you've found this man that you think you want to marry, how do you know he definitely is the one you want to spend the remainder of your life with? That seems like a monumental, impossible question, doesn't it? It can often bring about a substantial amount of anxiety and fear, but it doesn't have to.

When you get married in the Catholic Church, the priest will ask you both, in front of everyone in the church on your wedding day, whether that be two witnesses or five hundred, if you are entering into this marriage, "freely, totally, faithfully, and fruitfully."

Giggling.

Yes, fruitfully, something for you and your significant other to talk about while discerning marriage, but not something to practice. We'll get more into this in our intimacy talk.

What do these mean? Are you and your future husband entering this marriage of your own free will? You are not being forced into it by an outside source or under false pretenses. Neither of you has conditions in place for your love. Remember that true love does not have conditions.

True love is not narcissistic or transactional love. Are you and your future husband entering this marriage totally? You are committing yourself entirely to each other, knowing the implications of this commitment. Through God's design, you are giving yourself entirely over to the other.

I asked my cousin to proofread this book, and she said, "Make sure you mention self-respect, self-dignity, and self-love!" That reminds me to tell you this. You cannot fully and totally love another human being until you love yourself and see yourself the way God sees you. Please stop and slowly read that sentence again. You cannot fully and totally love another human being until you love yourself and see yourself as *God loves you and sees you*, not as the world does nor in a disordered, egotistical way.

I know it sounds terrifying to give yourself over to someone else entirely, even if it's in God's plan for marriage. Opening ourselves up to potentially be hurt can be frightening, but we must remember that this promise of freely, totally, faithfully, and fruitfully is a mutual promise. Both you and your future husband will be taking this vow, and similar to how you can start talking to God now and growing in virtue right now, you can also start placing your trust in God in all that you do. It is His trust that enables us to give of ourselves fully to another person in marriage.

Back to the faithfully. Are you and your future husband entering this marriage faithfully? You understand that it is your duty to help each other attain sanctity in heaven and to abide by God's will here on earth to do so. Are you and your future husband entering into this marriage fruitfully? You both promise to be fully open to welcoming children into your lives. As I mentioned, we'll get more into this later.

When pondering whether a man you are dating is the 'one,' ask yourself if your relationship meets these four requirements for a true marriage, one that mirrors Christ's love for His Church. Christ died for our salvation. He did so freely, totally, faithfully, and fruitfully. A true, loving relationship flourishes in the same call to love.

Some of you asked, "When will I know I'm ready for marriage?" This is the Catholic Church's answer. Are you both mutually ready to take this vow? When you're in a committed relationship and discerning marriage, talk about these things with your boyfriend or fiancé. Discuss each one in length. If you agree that your love and future marriage are ready to be free, total, faithful, and fruitful, then you're ready for marriage.

Here's another list of some words to think about during your discernment, and full disclosure, I jotted these two lists down as I was brainstorming how to break down the self-giving and sacrificial love that Christ and the Church teach. This list is not directly from the Church.

5 Selves of Good	5 Selves of Bad
Self-Giving	Self-Absorption
Self-Control	Self-Complacency
Self-Sacrifice	Self-Indulgence
Self-Denial	Self-Reliant
Self-Surrender	Self-Interest

The Five Selves Of Bad versus The Five Selves Of Good. Clever titles, right? What do you think about them? Do you see a common theme in each list? The Five Selves Of Bad are all me-focused but in a disordered way, a way that goes against everything Christ told us to do and did do for us. If you really think about it, none of us like to be around someone with the kind of character made up from the Five Selves of Bad list.

Let's unpack the bad selves. What is self-absorption? One is obsessed with one's own life. Obsessed meaning they could typically care less about other people and their lives. They may appear to, but it's a facade. What is self-complacency? When someone lacks the ambition to grow in virtue and truly better themselves. They are completely fine with exactly who they are, character flaws, and all. They lack any desire to become who God intended them to be or to grow in virtue. What is self-indulgent? When someone does exactly what they want no matter the consequences. They make sure they get what they want or their way and don't care if others get bulldozed in their path. What is self-reliance? When someone rejects fellowship and a reliance on God by pridefully depending entirely on their own abilities. And self-interest, someone who is only out for their own good. They're only interested in themselves and their lives.

We can agree, I think, that it's not fun to be around these types of people, but more importantly, it's not fun to be that type of person. It may appear fun or feel fun fleetingly, but it's only on the surface. Deep down, a person who lives a life made up of the Five Selves of Bad is interiorly screaming for help and for their pain to be seen. We live in a world of people obsessed with themselves who struggle to look outside of themselves to the needs of others, let alone love and serve others as Christ calls us to.

The Five Selves of Bad list is kind of our world's norm now, isn't it? We may not realize it, but many of us fall into at least one of these and quite possibly all of them at different times in our lives. I know I do. Our culture is a mess. It's true, but praise God that we have Christ's words and the Church to show us another way.

When you're trying to figure out if the man you're dating is the one you'd like to marry, ask yourself, "Does my boyfriend/fiancé's character possess these "Selves of Bad" more often than not? If yes, then it's probably a red flag. You must pay attention to red flags, hopefully towards the beginning of your relationship and not in the final days leading up to your wedding. Some people do have the courage to look at their relationship for what it truly is and wake up and see the red flags before it's too late. What happens when you get infatuated with somebody, and you're so attracted to them, and you're so in love, and blah blah blah, the red flags are the things you'll overlook. You'll look at them and say, "Well, he can change. He loves me enough to change." We can even do this to ourselves. "We'll grow up and mature in love one day. We'll love God and others how we're supposed to *eventually* when we're older."

Yes, you do naturally mature as you age. You do grow as a couple and individually as your relationship advances, but what we've been talking about are tools and things we can work on right now. Deepening your relationship with God and growing in virtue are two such tools. Look at your own life. Look at our culture. How many 'likes' you get determines what? How important you are? No. We've already established that you matter, right? Everybody remembers that from earlier? I'm going to repeat it a thousand times. YOU MATTER. You have dignity as a human person and as a child of God, but it is still up to you to choose love. Use your time now to mature in the ways of love that you can. Start with your family, friends, and boyfriend if you have one. Try loving them as God loves them. It won't be perfect, but it'll be intentional, bringing us to the "how" of loving in this way.

Moving on to the "5 Selves of Good." You may look at this list and say, "Well, duh," but this is not well-known in our world now. We think life is made up of milestones, but there isn't a magical age where you're suddenly ready to be married. Doing groundwork now and setting that prayer foundation with God now will help you to become ready to get married, but you're not going to hit age 23 and be like, "This is it!" At 22 years old, I was ready. I had a committed relationship. I had the dress. I checked all the boxes the world told me needed to be checked to be ready to marry. I'm telling you right now. I was not ready. I got married at 23, and I thank God that He bestows on us grace and mercy and that my husband and I were able to mature in our love. We loved each other at 14 when we started dating. We loved each other that summer when we were 19 and took a "break." We loved each other at 25 when we were grinding to build a life together, but it was a shallow love. We didn't know it then, but we still used each other. Our love was nowhere near what God was calling it to be. Remember what St. Pope John Paul II said in *Love and Responsibility*. The opposite of love is use.

What is true love? What is love in divine communion with God? How do we do actually will the good of the other? What does it look like? Well, look at Christ. What is the Sacrament of Marriage? Why did God give us marriage? We could have just procreated like animals. We didn't have to be married for the human race to live on. So, why did He give us the Sacrament of Marriage? The answer is to infuse grace. If we look to Christ as our example of sacrificial love, it's totally self-giving.

Let me pause here to preface what's coming with this. Am I telling you that your dignity as a person diminishes by the giving of yourself to, in this case, your future spouse? Absolutely not. Your dignity, as a child of God, *never diminishes*. I may repeat that a lot, but I want it to be ingrained in your brain. Now, though God always loves us, we do have to participate in His love. It's our choice. God loves us no matter what, but we must acknowledge and reciprocate His love. Christ gave His life for us. There is no greater sacrifice than Christ's dying on the cross for our salvation.

So, what do the "5 Selves of Good" look like? Right now, they're just words on a chart. You may have started losing interest by now, and I get it. Looking inward at our flaws is hard. I totally get it, but what we're building with these talks are the blocks that will be the foundation for you and your future marriage. Again, you cannot love another with any of the words off this list until you love yourself as God loves you and until you love God.

Let's go down the list. Self-giving. Am I able to give entirely of myself for the true, eternal good of the other? Entirely is a big word. Self-control. Am I able to practice restraint for the good of the other? Am I able to keep my emotions, my actions, and my desires in check? Self-sacrificing. Am I able to make uncomfortable accommodations and let go of my wants and desires for the good of the other? Self-denial. Am I able to say "no" to myself if it's for the true good of the other? Am I able to deny something that may boost my ego? This comes into play a lot in marriage, a whole lot.

You have to die unto yourself in marriage, and that sounds like too much. I don't mean physically. In 99% of marriages, you don't have to physically die for the other unless you're in a traumatic situation. Self-surrender. Am I able to totally subject myself to God's divine will? Am I able to surrender to the vulnerability and the trust that marriage is calling me to? In short, am I able to be Christ to the people in my life, especially to my significant other? Am I able to follow and fully trust God's will for me, my life, and my future spouse's life and trust that it is for the greater good?

This is the meaning of love. This is the meaning of willing the good of the other. If we surrender to God's will, and marriage is the mirror of God's love for us, then it's safe to say that we need to surrender to our spouse in marriage, right?

You might be thinking, "No, I'm going to do that. That leaves me vulnerable. That leaves me unprotected, and I won't do it." I understand that. I really do, more than you know. It took me years, *years*, to become vulnerable and fully trust my husband, and he's a wonderful man. What if it turns out you don't have a wonderful man as a husband? We won't be covering what the Church says about abusive relationships, but if you'd like to know more details about that, please look at the Catechism or reach out to a priest. There are completely free apps with the whole Catechism, and there is also the 'Catechism in a Year' podcast with

Father Mike Schmitz that I highly recommend. It helped me answer hundreds of questions I had about the Church.

Truly loving your spouse with the love God designed for marriage will be one of the hardest endeavors but also one of the most rewarding you will ever do. Jesus never said following Him would be easy.

So, how do you know if he's the one you should marry? You and your future spouse will never reach perfection, and that's okay. Again, God doesn't ask us to be perfect, but He does ask us to walk with Him. He does ask us to love Him. Your relationship can help you attain holiness. It can help you become a saint one day in heaven, or it cannot. Does the man you are dating have characteristics from the Good or the Bad Selves list? What about you? Which list do you fit into most? And, I assure you. I am not sitting here saying that I'm perfect, and y'all have some work to do. Not at all. I fall into these temptations just as much as you do. We all possess one if not all of these awful qualities at different points in our lives. Look at the two lists again. Where do you have room to grow? Never lose fervor for growth in virtue, and never forget that prayer is a powerful, divine relationship with a father who loves us and wills our ultimate good. We need help shedding our selfish egos, and He wants to help us.

Now, if you have gotten this far, and you're saying, "Kira, this didn't answer my question. I've listened to what you are saying, and I still have no idea how to tell if he's the one or not." Well, here's another suggestion that I hope will be easy to remember in five to ten years when you're like, "What'd that lady say about discerning the one?" Let's turn to 1 Corinthians 13:4-8. You've probably been to weddings where this scripture was a reading. I don't know who originally said this or when, but I've heard what I'm about to tell you multiple times before in my life. It's always been impactful. When you're discerning whether or not a person is the one you should marry, put their name in the place of "love" in 1 Corinthians 13:4-8.

"Love is patient, love is kind. It is not jealous, [love] is not pompous, it is not inflated, it is not rude, it does not seek its own interests, it is not quick-tempered, it does not brood over injury, it does not rejoice over wrongdoing but rejoices with the truth. *It* bears all things, believes all things, hopes all things, endures all things. Love never fails."

Those of you with boyfriends you hope to marry one day put his name in "love's" place. Now, all of you, put *your* name in there. How does it sound? Does it line up with his character and behavior? What about yours? How does it feel to put your name in the blank? No one will perfectly exemplify this scripture passage because we're humans with the stain of original sin, but this is the meaning of true love. Does your boyfriend/future fiancé come close to matching this? Not entirely because he won't be perfect. He's not Christ. You're not going to be perfect either, but if your boyfriend resembles this scripture passage and there's mutual respect, then he's the one, y'all. If you have mutual physical and emotional attraction and this kind of love within your relationship, then he could very possibly be the one God is calling you to marry.

What do you think? Are you thinking that that's not attainable? That would be the first thing that came to my mind, I think. That this isn't possible. It is. Why is marriage a Sacrament and not just a piece of paper at the courthouse? So many people nowadays don't marry in the Church. Why? Because it means this, and this looks really hard and scary. So, what's the purpose? Why would you get married in the Church when you can have a wedding at the beach or some mountaintop with a view?

Well, what is a Sacrament? A Sacrament is an infusion of grace.It's an outward sign of an inward reality instituted by Christ to give grace. It's the way that God has chosen to convey His life to us and His help to us. That's amazing. Truly incredible! Can God's grace come to me without a Sacrament? It can, but it's similar to the vast difference between me talking to God on my own and me going to worship Him at the Mass. Going to Mass transforms how I talk to God. My prayer then becomes a form of worship and communion. It's the highest level of worship available to mankind. It's a bit more than me just saying, "Hey God, what's up?" It's the same thing with marriage. Yes, people get married and have natural marriages all the time. They get their piece of paper from the courthouse, their contract that says, "I'm married," but that marriage is not the same as this marriage. I don't mean that in a hateful or condescending way at all. Marriage existed long before Christianity, but God gave us the Sacrament of Marriage as a gift through Christ's gift of himself. He gave us this as a Sacrament when Christ came into the world, so sacramental marriage is how Christ gives himself to us. Lived in that light, it's also a way that God conveys His grace to us. The first marriage ever in Christian history was the marriage of Adam and Eve. God gave us marriage as a gift, to share with us the grace He intends to bestow on us through the Sacrament of Marriage.

When I was twenty-two years old, panicking about graduation and trying to force my wedding plans onto my boyfriend, I didn't know what true love was. I didn't know how it could shape my entire life, from the most significant decisions down to the most minor things. Making ourselves vulnerable by being totally self-giving can be seen as one of two ways. 1. Vulnerability and complete trust in another is too scary to endure and leaves us open for heartache. OR 2. Embrace the vulnerability and complete trust and see it as participation in God's design for love. For a long time, I chose to shy away from trusting in God and putting complete trust in my significant other. It felt like the opposite of everything my human nature for protecting myself wanted to hold on to. I held on to a lot of shame and pride. Praise God, He tore down the thick walls around my heart.

As you get older, you will hopefully find wise women in your life who are older than you and can be mentors to you. We talked about finding a community amongst your peers. Also, strive to find older Catholic or Christian women. They are an incredible community. They can help you navigate and give you support. I had one such woman. She and I would go to lunch every week. She suffers from early-onset Alzheimer's now, but I love her dearly. She told me at some point, "You know, you and your husband are a family now." Confused, I replied, "No, we're not. We don't have children yet." She continued, "Yes, you are. The two of you are joined in marriage and are a family now." She was right. It's called the domestic church. What does that mean? It is within our family that we learn who God really is and prayerfully seek His will for us.

Let's go to Ephesians 5: 21-33.

"Be subordinate to one another out of reverence for Christ. Wives should be subordinate to their husbands as to the Lord. For the husband is head of his wife just as Christ is head of the church, he himself the savior of the body. As the church is subordinate to Christ, so wives should be subordinate to their husbands in everything. Husbands, love your wives, even as Christ loved the church and handed himself over for her to sanctify her, cleansing her by the bath of water with the word that he might present to himself the church in splendor, without spot or wrinkle or any such thing, that she might be holy and without blemish. So [also] husbands should love their wives as their own bodies. He who loves his wife loves himself. For no one hates his own flesh but rather nourishes and cherishes it, even as Christ does the church, because we are members of his body. "For this reason a man shall leave [his] father and [his] mother and be joined to his wife, and the two shall become one flesh." This is a great mystery, but I speak in reference to Christ and the church. In any case, each one of you should love his wife as himself, and the wife should respect her husband."

St. Paul tells us that Christ is the bridegroom, and His Church is the bride. What does that mean? This truly could be a year-long class in itself. It means that in your marriage, in your relationship, one day, your husband represents Christ. Does it mean that he's God? No. Please don't mistake me, but he represents Christ in your marriage. So, what does that mean? You see in Ephesians 5 that St. Paul also says, "Wives submit to your husbands." Does that mean servitude? Does that mean slavery? No, because Christ was not tyrannical, was He? What does His love mean? It means what we've already covered earlier in this chapter. Christ's love was and is a sacrificial love, a self-giving love. It is divine love. You might think, "That's too much. I can't put that on another human. They can't provide that for me." And you're right. They can't, fully, but through the Sacrament of Marriage, with the infusion of grace from God, that is what husbands are called to be. St. Paul didn't tell husbands to *kind of* be like Christ. He told them to be their wives' head and to love their wives as Christ loved the Church and handed Himself over for her. In Ephesians 5, verse 32, St. Paul says, "This is a great mystery," and it is similar to how the transubstantiation is a great mystery in the Mass when the bread and wine become the Body and Blood of Jesus Christ. Both are mysteries, and the mystery doesn't change the fact that both are true.

In the domestic church, our husbands represent Jesus to us, and if the calling arises, they are literally called to lay down their lives for us, just as Christ did for His Church. Is that common to physically die for your spouse? No. Not unless we are in very traumatic situations, so what does it mean on a day-to-day basis? It means husbands practice self-giving, sacrificial love for their wives by going to work, providing for their families, being the spiritual leader of the household, and leading lives of selfless service to their wives and children.

I know every piece of you that is looking ahead to your future careers is screaming, "No! I don't need a man to take care of me!" But that's not what it means. That took me a long time to figure out in my marriage. You're doing this together. This is *mutual* love and vulnerability. This is a *mutual* trust. This is mutually coming together to participate in God's divine love and design for marriage, and that's what makes it different than a piece of paper from the courthouse, from a civil union. This is what makes it a covenant as opposed to simply a contract. Contracts can be broken. Covenants cannot.

Someone asked, "What if I eventually get tired of my husband?" St. Paul didn't say respect your husbands *if*... There are no conditions. He simply said to respect your husbands and to be subordinate to him as to the Lord. What is submission? It means to be under the mission of, and what is the mission that we know our husband has because we've already talked about it? To get his wife and children to heaven. God gives us marriage as a way of sanctification or a way that we can grow in holiness. Marriage is an institution ordered towards helping us to grow in holiness. To learn what it is to love and to be loved, in preparation. We are called to help get each other and our children to heaven. That's not all that bad of a mission to be under, is it?

Before we move on, let's take a moment to address interfaith marriages. My great-aunt and uncle were married for 67 years and were not of the same faith. He was Catholic, and she was Lutheran. They had a beautiful marriage, so can it be done? Absolutely, but know that there are challenges. When a baptized Catholic desires to marry a baptized Christian of another denomination, the interfaith marriage requires the permission of the Bishop of the diocese you reside in. He may grant this permission if you, as a Catholic, promise to do these two things. One, continue practicing your faith; two, promise to baptize and raise your children Catholic.

That is a conversation you will have to have while you're dating if you're in a long-term, committed relationship with a non-Catholic with whom you see a future. "In my faith, I promise to raise our children Catholic. If that's a problem, then we probably shouldn't get married." It's a big deal, but people overcome it every day. The non-Catholic in the relationship may consent and agree, which would be wonderful. If they don't, you may need to rethink your relationship. Now that being said, in your day-to-day life with them, how will you worship? How will you pray? My grandmother was married to my grandfather, who wasn't Catholic, and after he passed away, she married another non-Catholic man. My grandfather would sometimes go to Mass with her, mostly on holidays. Her second husband did not. She would go to the early Mass by herself and then attend his church's service. He never went to hers, and it hurt her. It did. She was a devout Catholic woman. She loved the Lord. So, just keep that in mind. Can interfaith marriages work? I just told you 67 years, until my great-aunt died. Absolutely, they can work, but you have to recognize that there will be some challenges to overcome and definitely some conversations that need to happen before you get married.

Back to Ephesians 5. If our husbands are supposed to be Christ in our domestic church and we are supposed to be the body of Christ, what does that look like? Our home, our family unit, is called a domestic church because our love is and should be participation in God's divine love. Our husbands have the call for sacrificial love, and we must respect that, but what does that mean for us as wives? We already talked about how it's not slavery or servitude. So then, what is it? It's devotion. It's devotion.

We do not worship our husbands. That's not what I'm saying, but it's not uncool to be devoted to our husbands. It's actually extremely fulfilling. Quite honestly, my husband and I didn't know these things when we got married. I had never heard of a domestic church. I didn't know the goal of marriage. I was poorly catechized. When we started spiritually maturing together, learning more and understanding our family as a domestic church changed everything. Everything. It changed the path that we were on in our lives. It changed what we were doing daily and what we focused on. It changed everything.

Now, I don't mean that in a way where it halted success, something our culture deems so important and necessary. We've both experienced success in our careers, but when we adopted what St. Paul advises us for our marriage, it took away the focus on that success and put our fulfillment in God. Not in our own accomplishments. Not in ourselves. I no longer looked to Arthur to fulfill me, which is what I did for a long time, and guess what? He came up short because he's a human, and so am I. We do our best as God calls us to do, but we're not God. You can try making your spouse your idol, but you won't find ultimate fulfillment in your spouse. You might think, "Oh, I'm going to get married, and it's going to be perfect!" It's not because we aren't perfect, but we can try to reach holiness together, which is the ultimate perfection.

At the end of the day, what are we doing? We're trying to get closer to God. We're trying to lean on Him for the foundation of our marriage. We're striving to become saints. All of this matters when we get to the intimacy and motherhood talk. You think you know what self-sacrifice is? Just wait until it's the middle of the night, you're real tired, and your baby is hungry. All of this sounds really hard, and our culture says, "Don't do hard. Why would you do hard?" The answer is because it brings us the ultimate fulfillment. It brings us purpose, meaning, and hope. It brings us to God. It brings us to heaven.

Thanks y'all. This was a long one to get through. I miss our smaller groups and longer discussions. I feel like I'm yelling at you now, and I hate it, but this is what we have to work with. Please know I am still reading your responses and questions and carrying on the dialogue with you that way. Your questions are so good. Thank you for sharing them with me.

No one had anything to say today. Having such a big group definitely changed the dynamics of things. It feels like I'm talking *at* them instead of with them. I hope they don't feel the disconnect like I do. If just one person learns something from all this that helps them in some small way, God will make it all worth it.

Oh, one of them has stayed behind to talk. How exciting! She approaches and says, "These talks are a direct answer to my prayer. Like God is answering my exact prayer by you being here and talking about these things. I think God sent you here for me." Oh, sweet young woman! Thank you! Thank you! I was feeling so discouraged that this new format was ruining everything. She continues, "I prayed and prayed for God to please help me and my boyfriend with our future, and here you are. I didn't have anyone to turn to with my questions." I won't share the rest of our exchange because much of it was personal and about her past, but here she was, the one person. Praise God. You are almighty and ever-knowing. Thank you.

What Did You Learn?

The questions and responses were no longer homework and were sent in voluntarily from now on.

Class One
- I learned that it is ok to be a different denomination and still have a successful marriage.
- How to determine when I'm with the right person to marry.
- Marriage is about uplifting each other.
- I didn't learn anything from the discussion. *Oh, good.*
- I learned that it is ok to be married to someone who is not of the same denomination as you.

Class Two
- That we need to find someone who will bring us closer to God and not away from Him.
- That in a relationship your mission is to guide each other towards God.
- Marriage is a commitment.
- Think about what your s/o does for you and if they treat you right. *We must remember that marriage is about mutual commitment to serve one another.*
- I learned how to know if he's the one.

Class Three
- I loved replacing "His name" in Corinthians 13!! It helped me envision what a future husband should look like!
- How to know if he's the one.
- There isn't a certain time when you are ready to get married.
- Submitting to your husband.
- I really enjoy the talk on marriage, it is important for the foundation of our future. Marriage is a blessing!

Class Four

- About love.
- Submit to your husband.
- How to maintain a healthy relationship.
- God is always there.
- That relationships are not perfect, but we must continue to work together to keep a loving relationship that lasts.
- I learned that you should get married when you're ready, not when you feel like you're supposed to.

You will find the questions and answers for Chapter 3 on page 327.

Let Us Pray

Litany of Humility

O Jesus! meek and humble of heart, Hear me.
(After each petition, respond with "Deliver me, Jesus.")
From the desire of being esteemed,
From the desire of being loved...
From the desire of being extolled ...
From the desire of being honored ...
From the desire of being praised ...
From the desire of being preferred to others...
From the desire of being consulted ...
From the desire of being approved ...
From the fear of being humiliated ...
From the fear of being despised...
From the fear of suffering rebukes ...
From the fear of being calumniated ...
From the fear of being forgotten ...
From the fear of being ridiculed ...
From the fear of being wronged ...
From the fear of being suspected ...

(After each petition, respond with "Jesus, grant me the grace
to desire it.")
That others may be loved more than I,
That others may be esteemed more than I ...
That, in the opinion of the world,
others may increase and I may decrease ...
That others may be chosen and I set aside ...
That others may be praised and I unnoticed ...
That others may be preferred to me in everything...

That others may become holier than I, provided that I may become as holy as I should...

(Source: Cardinal Rafael Merry del Val (1865-1930), Hallow Prayer App)

Chapter 4

Emotional & Spiritual Intimacy and Unexpectedly, Redemptive Suffering
Part 1

"Where there is no love, put love, and you'll find love."
- St. John of the Cross

Today feels different, and it's not because I only got four hours of sleep last night. I could not turn my brain off. It's the only time I'm quiet enough to hear the Holy Spirit, I guess. Today is the day we start looking at the practical implementation of everything we've talked about. Blessed Mother, please take this anxiety from me. Please help soften their hearts so they can hear your son's message. I give it all to you.

Hey, y'all. How are you? How many are in your class? Seventy-nine? Okay, then, can you tell me why I only got twenty responses from our last talk on marriage? I know it's not technically homework anymore, but come on, y'all. This is a conversation. I'm up here talking to you and only have 20 minutes now, but you have ample time to talk back and engage with me.

Student: "You were very thorough, so we didn't need to respond."

Is that so? Is that why one of you wrote that you learned nothing? *Laughter*. Yeah, so you've got this right? Come on up and handle the rest of our talks, and I'll go home. Listen. I don't dumb down any of this material for you. Please don't dumb down your responses to me, and if you still have hardened hearts to the message, at least remember that I've bribed you with baby animals. I have a baby goat named Parma, like Parmesan cheese because she's all white, and a little piglet named Cora (long story to how we have an unplanned piglet) to bring into the class with the most thoughtful responses. For those of you who carried on with our conversation, thank you. I appreciate you.

In this talk, we're going to cover emotional and spiritual intimacy. What is intimacy? In his book, *Spousal Prayer,* Deacon James Keating defines intimacy as "a form of communion that comes about as a result of a spouse offering himself/herself as a gift to his/her beloved in a reciprocal exchange." How beautiful is that? In the last chapter, we discussed marriage as unending, self-giving, and sacrificial love. Intimacy takes those large concepts and breaks them down to the day-to-day, moment-by-moment interactions between you and your spouse. Though some, not all, of the things we will cover can apply to a committed relationship outside of marriage, at this point in our journey, we're imagining that you are in a loving, Christ-centered marriage with 'the one.'

When I was in high school, our history teacher had some friends who were ballroom dance instructors. This was the era of Usher, and I assume that she would have rather us dance more elegantly than we intended to rap, so she asked her friends to teach us ballroom dancing. They came to the school on Sunday afternoons for nine weeks. We had never ballroom danced, but Arthur and I love to dance, so we were like, "Heck yeah! Sign us up!" It was actually a lot of fun. If you don't know, in traditional dancing such as ballroom dancing, the man leads. The steps often require the woman to go backward, which is difficult to wrap your head around, whereas the man is moving forward. Moving forward is more natural, so it only makes sense for him to take the lead. It took me around three to four dance lessons to let my now-husband lead. I did not trust him to remember the steps, let alone glide us along to music. I mean... I'd only been dating him three years at that point. (*Note the sarcasm.*)

Eventually, I relinquished control, and something wonderful happened. We floated all over the floor. By week nine, we were so graceful and much further along than any of the other couples because we had accepted each of our roles within the dance. The instructors even invited us to their Friday night free dance, where couples got together to just have fun and dance. They said they enjoyed watching us dance so much that we could come free of charge. I wish we would have taken them up on that invitation, but alas, we didn't, and our ballroom dancing skills became a thing of the past.

Today's world tells young women that they must fight for control. You must handle it, or no one else will. I know relinquishing control, especially to a man, is a scary thought to some of you. It was to me too even in something as simple as dancing. I understand that your initial reaction may be, "Well, yeah. If he won't rise to the occasion, then I'll handle it." Some of you may come from backgrounds with trauma where if you didn't handle something, then literally no one else would. You had to handle it. I have had some similar situations. I promise I can relate, but please keep an open mind as we move through this. What we're about to discuss was revolutionary to my marriage. In a safe, mutually trusting, mutually vulnerable marriage, letting go of all of the control and letting the man you love and trust lead you, especially spiritually, is okay. It's not only okay. It's life-altering. You have the green light to honor and respect your husband in a safe space, and your marriage reaches new heights.

Father Mike Schmitz is a hero of mine if you haven't been able to tell so far. I came across a talk he gave at a conference in 2022 at some point where he dove deeply into the creation story. One of his themes was love versus respect. He started breaking down the creation story in a way I had never been privy to. He read Genesis Chapter 3 line by line. He said that often, people think of the devil appearing to Eve as a harmless little green, garter snake, but that the Hebrew word that was originally used meant sea monster. A dragon approached Eve in the garden. What was Adam's job in the garden? What was the role that God gave him to do? It was to cultivate and guard the garden, including his wife Eve, so where was Adam while a *dragon* was talking to Eve?

Student: "Work?"

Good one. He was right there, y'all! Have you ever thought about it? I hadn't. Here's Eve conversing with a dragon while her husband stood by and watched when he was given the duty to protect her. So, what did Eve do? She took control! She handled the situation. Poorly, as it turns out, but she saw that Adam was cowering from his responsibility and handled it. How often do we do that in our lives, even when it's not our situation to handle? How often do we approach someone or something with the intent to take control? Control brings us comfort. We think if we can control it, then what? We won't get hurt. We think we can control the outcome to be in our favor. Adam failed to show his wife that he loved her by protecting her, so she lost all manner of respect for and faith in him.

And, because of the stain of original sin, this trickles down to us today. It is in our very makeup as women to desire love just as it's in men's natures to desire respect, and even better if we can do so within our marriages. It's so easy to get caught up in this game of, "If he loves me, he'll do this." And, "If she respects me, she'll do this." But, this isn't a game. This is your marriage. This isn't to say that both parties don't enjoy and desire being treated with both love and respect, but deep within our natures, women ultimately desire love, so much so that it is placed above our desire for respect. While men ultimately desire respect even more so than their need for love. These natural desires do not negate the need for the other, and knowing this helps us to operate in a way that serves one another.

Everyone here probably knows communication is critical to any successful romantic relationship. Even the secular world knows that, and there are a ton of resources out there on how to communicate with your spouse effectively. Communication is an imperative tool in marriage, but what does it mean in our context? Can you talk to one another about God and life? Even now, those of you with long-term boyfriends, can you have a conversation about real life? Not just superficial or shallow things. Like real, authentic life. Can you? Because if you can't, then it's not real good when a conflict comes up, is it?

The day you are married, the day you say, "I do," is the easiest day to be married. Yeah, there might be wedding drama, and that can be hard, but on that day, it's super easy to say "yes" to marriage. You're excited, but in ten or twenty years, sometimes that "yes" is a little bit harder to say. The "I do" becomes harder to live out, not across the board. Not always. There are days and moments of absolute joy. My husband travels for work, and when he walks in the door after traveling a lot, my heart still pounds. Filled with gratitude, I think, "There he is. He made it home safely." I get so excited, still, after ten years for him to be home, for him to be with me. The excitement you feel on your wedding day doesn't have to fade, but it will mature. As your relationship matures, your love will mature, and your communication will mature, too.

Often in a relationship, when conflicts arise, you begin to see your significant other as your opponent. A conflict can be for something as simple as who did the dishes last to something as complex as which family to spend Christmas with. When you get into a conflict, your instinct is usually to win. You've met opposition in the quest to get what you want, and you formulate a plan on how to reach your end goal. In marriage, you have to remember that your husband isn't your opponent. He's not your enemy. This isn't a game. If I win, it means my husband loses. I don't want him to lose. We're in this together. We're trying to get ourselves and our children to heaven *together*! You're not against each other. You're with each other, and because your relationship ideally mirrors God's divine love, you don't want to hurt your spouse or beat him in an argument. Remember when I said that my husband cannot fulfill me? Only Christ can. My husband represents Christ in our family and domestic church, but he's not Christ. Christ is the foundation for everything in your marriage, including communication.

What does communication look like? Can you talk about God and life? Can you talk about the joys and the hardships? Can you plan? Can you work through conflicts? Can you speak truth to one another respectfully and out of love?

My husband and I both come from divorced families. We knew we didn't want divorce to be part of our story, so we made a rule. We never ever use the d-word. We don't joke about it. We don't threaten it. We don't talk about it all because no matter what happens, it's not a card on the table. We made an unbreakable covenant with God, and we intend to hold up our side of that covenant. We know He'll hold up His side. One of the saddest questions I've gotten so far was what if I fall out of love with my husband, can I divorce him? No. Why? Because marriage is more than a contract. It's a covenant. You both said vows. I'm not talking about abusive relationships. I'm talking about literally getting tired of each other. No. You said, "I do" to that person, and he said, "I do" to you in the safety and comfort of Christ's love.

Student: "You can't control how you feel. You may love him at one time and then slowly fall out of love. That's what happened to my parents. I don't think it's a sad question. It's the most realistic one nowadays. Divorce is so common."

And, I am so sorry that's a part of your story. Divorce is common, which is a problem, right? Feeling love is a fruit of marriage. It is a part of it, yes, but it is not a requirement. Love as a feeling is not the ultimate goal. This is what all of our talks have been leading towards. Our feelings come and go. True love that is wrapped in Christ's heavenly love does not.

When my husband and I went into marriage prep with the priest before we got married, we did the FOCCUS questionnaire. It's not a compatibility test, but it's similar in format and helps you both work through some of the questions or situations that come up in marriage. We answered all of the questions similarly except for one. "If my spouse cheats on me, will I leave?" We both answered yes. The priest gently but very slowly said, "Wrong answer."

And, there they go. Almost the entire class is up in arms. Wow, they're loud.

Why is "no" the answer? Because if we look for the exit route, especially if we premeditate it, it cheapens marriage. You can't cheapen what we talked about in our last talk. You can't cheapen what God designed for marriage. You can't, and if you do, then that's exactly what happens. It becomes a piece of paper and not a true commitment in communion with God.

Fifteen hands raise.

Oh gosh, yeah.

Student: "If you can't say that you would leave, then what also keeps it premeditated that your spouse wouldn't cheat knowing the fact that you would not leave? How would you know that your spouse, like in time, wouldn't cheat?"

You don't. You don't know. What's to say you won't cheat? You don't know for sure. It comes down to mutual love, trust, and vulnerability. I understand that everything we're talking about sounds extreme because it's not normal nowadays. I do understand that.

Student: "Infidelity is not only physical betrayal. It's also emotional betrayal. So, what's to say that if you can't trust someone again and can't build it back up, then the end goal changes? If that other person emotionally and physically betrays you, it means that they're not living their life in Christ. They don't have the idea of living for Christ, so why would you stay with them if you're supposed to lift each other up and they aren't?"

My great-grandmother had six children. My great-grandfather came into a lot of money after the last child, my grandmother, was born. His father owned a shipping company downtown, and when he died, my great-grandfather inherited a large sum of money, and he bounced. He abandoned my great-grandmother and his children, including my grandmother, who was a baby. He went up to New York City, got with another woman, and lived with her for the remainder of his life. My great-grandmother took her pain and sorrow to the foot of the cross because that's what Christ calls us to do in that situation. She was one of the most holy women in my family that I know of. She lived a chaste life for the rest of her life. Was it easy? No. Was it ideal? No. But that's what Christ calls us to do, to align our suffering with His.

Student: "With all due respect, I think what that describes is forgiveness, and I understand that forgiveness is healthy and that Christ calls us to forgive. But, Father Mike Schmitz said in one of his talks that forgiveness is key but that forgetting isn't required."

Forgiveness is key. She didn't forget. I feel certain that she was in pain every day. They did not get divorced. My great-grandfather's abandonment affected my grandmother's entire outlook on life. She had extreme trust issues.

Oh, Lord. There's so much chatter that it's hard to hear any one of them. I don't want to focus on divorce. I'm not even well-versed in the Church's teaching on divorce. I've never cared to know much about it. I'm here to talk about the beauty and gift of marriage. Lord, please help them understand.

I know there are a lot of questions on this, but please let me get through what we had planned today. My parents divorced when I was one. Arthur and I decided early on that divorce was not an option for us. It would never be an option. It doesn't matter if, for whatever reason, he loses his mind and goes and cheats on me. It doesn't matter because that's what we signed up for. Not the cheating but the commitment. The covenant we made with God.

Student: "What's the benefit in staying in a marriage when you know that your significant other has chosen someone else?"

Suffering. Your suffering will sanctify you if you allow it to. (Better known as redemptive suffering.)

A roar of noise rises to the 16-foot ceiling of the old convent classroom.

I know it's not a cool idea and that this might be the moment when some of you check out and never listen to another word that comes out of my mouth. I do understand that, but please go look at St. Monica, St. Augustine's mom. Her husband was a pagan. He cheated on her all the time. She prayed for him immensely throughout their entire marriage. Nearing his death, he converted to Christianity.

Student: "If the husband cheats on the wife and the wife realizes she hates the man now..."

Well, Christ told us not to hate.

Student: "What about like kids, though?"

What about them? My grandmother was just a baby when her father abandoned them.

Student: "Wouldn't it be like better for the kids to have like two parents who were separated rather than two parents that hated each other and argued all the time?"
Student 2: "Yeah, because then the kids are not given a good example of what love is..."

Everyone is getting louder and louder, and things are starting to snowball.

Listen, I understand that this is not a popular opinion. I promise I didn't make it up.

Student: "What if my husband like murders someone?"

I don't know. You'd have to look into what the Church teaches on annulments.

Student: ...

I literally can't hear her. They are so loud.

Please speak up. Y'all, please. I'd like to hear her.

Student: "If I'm with a man and I know I'm not going to leave regardless of what he does and he continues to cheat, isn't that an abuse of power?"

That would be something to talk to your priest about.

Student: "She did not just say talk to your priest about this!?!"

I'm standing right here. *You don't have to yell.* Yes, I did actually just say that. Why wouldn't you want to talk to your priest about something like that?

Student: "Because that's ridiculous!"

Why?

Student: "There's nothing that a priest can do to fix it, or if you're from a different faith background, then what's the point!?"

What's the point? What's the point of all of this? We're trying to get to heaven. We're trying to be like Christ. That's the point. When you make the vow to get married, this is what you're saying. I understand that this is hard. I come from a divorced family. My husband comes from a divorced family. I get it. It's not easy.

Student: "If you don't mind me asking, would you have rather been raised with your dad in the household? Or with just your mom?"

My stepdad came into my life when I was two. I don't remember a time without a dad in the household, so I can't answer that question. I don't know.

Student: "So you're supposed to guide your children to heaven and guide your spouse to heaven; if you don't take your children out of an abusive situation, is that still guiding them to heaven?" (Disclaimer: *I didn't hear this student use the word abuse in person. It had gotten a bit loud.*)

[We're not talking about abusive situations. We've been talking about a marriage where both the husband and wife have good intent.] What happened to St. Augustine? He's a doctor of the Church. He was a non-Christian living a robust life of sin and even had a child out of wedlock. St. Monica prayed and prayed and prayed, offered up her suffering, and St. Augustine became a *doctor* of the Church. He converted before her death. She saw her prayers answered, and St. Augustine is one of the most brilliant Catholic minds to ever live. What I'm saying is not something that hasn't been done before.

We have to move on.

I know all of this is not popular. I do understand that. It's kind of the reason I'm coming to talk to you. This challenges everything the secular world tells you and everything in your being that says, "I'm protecting me. It's about me and me, and I'm going to handle it." I get it. I'm so sorry, y'all. I'm sorry if some of you haven't been taught this until now. I am. I hope that some of you have parents who have a beautiful, loving relationship and who can show you the true meaning of marriage. *Loud tuts of disbelief.*

Oh, girls. I really am sorry. I know it's not fair. I wish someone had told you before now. I didn't know either. I'd never heard of redemptive suffering either. It's mind-bending.

I didn't come here to give you the sugarcoated version of marriage. I came to tell you the real version and give you practical tips to have a successful, God-centered marriage. That's what all of our talks are about. How do we have a successful marriage even if something horrible happens? I didn't say, "I do, until..." That's not how this works. Let's please move on.

How in the world are we supposed to move on? This is not part of the plan. There are some of them, though, who aren't staring at me with pure hatred and who want to know more about intimacy. We have five minutes. We'll get through what we can.

Being of service to one another is a beautiful thing. There are a million different ways to be of service to our spouses on any given day. My husband is naturally thoughtful. I've said that we always loved each other but that it was a shallow love because we used each other. We didn't realize that for a long time. Without even meaning to, I used his thoughtfulness. I guess this could go under the physical intimacy umbrella, too. When I'm pregnant, he provides everything I need within arm's reach, without me even realizing I need it first. When it would take me 5 minutes to lift myself off the couch, he'd come running over to assure me he could get what I needed. To which I'd sometimes reply, "Honey, you can provide a lot of things for me and this baby, but you can't pee for me." He's a great cook. He truly loves to provide what he can for others.

When we were first married, I took full advantage of his natural thoughtfulness. I didn't even mean to, but I'd sit there on my high horse while he literally served me. It took a year or two for me to realize, "Wait a second. What am I doing to serve him?" And, I don't just mean physically. I mean emotionally and mentally. "How am I of service to him?" I had to look inward at my weaknesses, take a deep look at him and his needs, and figure out where I could help and where I could be of service to him. We do that even now. We check in with each other to see where the other could possibly assist and lessen the burden off of the other.

He works for a company that deals with a lot of huge international companies. He sells food, and this one time, a cheese deal he was working on fell through. Yes, you heard me correctly. Cheese. Well, he was so upset. He'd been working on that deal for over a year. I could have very easily told him to get over it. It's just cheese, but it wasn't about the cheese. It was about the amount of effort he had expended. And so, at that moment, how could I serve my husband? I could be supportive. I could say I'm sorry. We could talk through his disappointment. I couldn't fix the problem for him, but I could be there emotionally to serve him.

There's not much time left, but there is another practical tip that I want to tell you about today. Gratitude in marriage is so important, y'all. It's so important in a marriage. When you say thank you to each other for everything, you feel the love and mutual trust in a daily setting. About five years ago, my husband started a habit of gratitude that I wasn't expecting. He started saying, "Thank you for marrying me." I'd say, "Of course, you asked me to. I love being married to you." He'd say it at the most random times and often in moments of chaos and stress or when we were working through a conflict. It didn't take long for me to start saying it back, and I quickly started understanding the power hidden in that short sentence. Thank you for marrying me. Thank you for dedicating your life to me. Thank you for your "yes" not being cheap and your "I do," meaning that our marriage is in loving communion with God. Thank you *so* much.

I only have two minutes, but let's quickly run through some of the spiritual intimacy. Praying with and for your spouse is going to help you both. It's going to help your marriage because it's going to remind you that your marriage is based on everything that we've already talked about. God is the foundational block for your marriage. Not yourself. Not your spouse. And please remember to pray for your spouse, even now. If you feel marriage is the vocation God is calling you to, pray for your future spouse. You can start that prayer today. Attending Mass together and both of you going to confession is extremely important. When I go to confession sometimes, and I confess not having charity towards my husband or not being the best wife I'd like to be, my priest reminds me that spouses who both go to confession stay together. Why? Because they're able to look inward and say, "These are my faults." They're able to give them to Jesus and say, "Help me. Help me to grow, Lord." Confession helps you to grow individually and together with your spouse. Lastly, offer up your marriage. Give your marriage to God for safekeeping.

Before you leave, I'd like to read you a quote. I told you I'm not dumbing things down for y'all, and this quote is no different. Please, if the bell rings, don't get up until I've read through it.

"As life goes on, they become not two compatible beings who have learned to live together through self-suppression and patience, but one new and richer being, fused in the fires of God's love and tempered of the best of both." *The bell rings, and they are standing and making a mad dash to the door. Quite literally mad, but I'm going to finish reading the quote. Maybe some of them will hear it.* "One by one, the veils of life's mysteries have been lifted. The flesh, they found, was too precocious to reveal its own mystery; then came the mystery of the other's inner life, disclosed in the raising of young minds and hearts in the ways of God."
- Ven. Fulton J. Sheen, *Three to Get Married*

Thanks y'all. That was a tough one today. I'll see you next time.

And that dear reader is how the first talk on intimacy went. The d-word derailed all of the good that we had covered previously and most of the good we had planned for the day. I left completely disheartened, feeling like the devil had won this round. I felt sorrow at the state of things in our world. Our poor Lord. I stopped by the principal's office on the way out to let her know there might be some angry phone calls. She was in a meeting, so I waited outside her door next to a beautiful statue of Our Lady of Fatima. I leaned against the cold stone wall and hung my head while tears swelled up in my eyes. I can't stand crying. I know it's not, but it always feels like a sign of weakness. For me, tears come quickly in moments when I'm tired, angry, or don't have hope, or in this case, all three.

The vice principal came to check on me, and I couldn't hold them back any longer. As she was trying to get the story out of me, I croaked out, "How is this news!? How could this possibly be news to them? Why would they *want* to get divorced?" She gently ushered me into the office, where she and the principal listened to what had happened. It took them a minute to realize that I wasn't upset about how the girls acted. They were upset, but it wasn't totally out of hand. Most of them were still respectful, and one even came up afterward to voice her support. (You know who you are, thank you!) No, I was at that moment crushed by the weight of these young women not believing in God's love, not believing true love between spouses was even possible, and not believing in or loving themselves. If I felt this despair at the state of things, what did our Lord feel? How could the devil have such a hold on marriage in these girls' minds? The principal and vice principal could not have been more wonderful. They asked me not to quit. No chance of that. I had made a commitment and intended to see it through, but I told them if they needed to fire me as a volunteer, they could. I'd understand. As I turned to go, they assured me that wasn't going to happen. "The girls need this message," they collectively said. I walked out into the brisk, winter air of the open hallway, put my sunglasses on so no one could see my red eyes as I left, and went home to my family.

I later posted a video to the social media account I had made to be a resource for them and their parents. It felt a bit immature to carry on the conversation this way, but we only had twenty minutes together, and I knew this was a way to carry on the conversation through a media they were familiar with. I also thought some parents would like to know who I was. They probably had some questions about me before, but most certainly did now if they hadn't before. I was told later by a student that every senior girl, some parents, and some students from the other grades saw that video and that it caused quite a stir. Angry parent phone calls made their rounds. The video was shared and shared. Strongly worded emails were sent to the principal. Yes, that video caused quite a stir, and I'm glad. The principal publicly commented on it that I was amazing and was changing lives. Arthur had to remind me of that public show of support when I watched it for the twentieth time to make sure I hadn't stepped out of line. In the video, I walked through our journey together.

Talk One: YOU MATTER. Are you talking to God? Do you have a basic prayer life? Where can you improve?

What daily habits can you build that bring you closer to God? Start by offering Him your day.

Talk Two: How do you find a loving community and ultimately the 'one'? Do the people around you and the decisions you're making bring you closer or further away from God?

Talk Three: Why is marriage a Sacrament? What makes it different than a legal, contractual marriage? Why did God give us marriage, and what does a marriage in communion with Him look like? What is self-giving, sacrificial love? How do you know if the man you're in a committed relationship is the one you should marry? What does freely, totally, faithfully, and fruitfully mean when pledged in Catholic wedding vows?

In the video, I talked about the pressure points so far, such as getting our spouses to heaven being our job as wives (and theirs as husbands) and how I thought there'd be a lot of pushback on the covenantal marriage versus contractual marriage but was surprised to not meet much opposition. I addressed some of the questions from the day, such as the one about love as a feeling that comes and goes, and I equated premeditating divorce to boarding a sinking ship. It logically just doesn't make sense. I even went as far as asking if the people who died on the Titanic had fun the few days they were on the ship before it sank and if it was worth it. I was honest about how little I know or care to know about the Church's teachings on divorce and mentioned Élisabeth Leseur, a woman who offered up her life for the conversion of her husband through intense and undistracted prayer. Just before her death, she wrote a note to her husband, a staunch atheist, that said, "In 1905,

I begged Almighty God to send me sufferings with which to pay the price of your soul. The day I die, that price will be paid. There is no greater love to be found in a woman than when she gives her life for her husband." I explained how we weren't to go looking for suffering by marrying a man who was all wrong for us or us for them, but if suffering (not abuse) became a part of their story, they could endure it through Christ.

We can do ALL things through Christ, not just the pleasant things. Don't believe me? Go read through some of the Saints' stories and look at how they handled suffering with God's divine assistance. There's a short dialogue in one of my favorite movies, *A Walk to Remember,* that lives rent-free in my head. Mandy Moore's character says, "Without suffering, there would be no compassion." Shane West's character, Landon, snaps back, "Yeah, well, tell that to those who suffer." We all have unique stories of suffering. However, not enough of us know that though suffering may be unbearable for us, Christ can endure our pain and our hurt. We can offer our suffering to Him for the glorification of His Father and for the good of others. I know it's a hard concept to wrap your head around. It took me a while to even attempt to understand it, and I admit I have barely scratched the surface of that understanding.

I'm trying to teach it to our 4-year-old early so she understands redemptive suffering better than I did. She got a blister on her foot recently and started howling when the water from the shower that night hit it. I said, "Hold on! Hold on! I have a blister, too. I know they hurt, but do you know what we can do? We can offer God our pain for the good of someone else. Who would you like to offer your blister pain up for?" She pondered for a moment and exclaimed, "Mrs. Laney! (*Her name has been changed for privacy.*)" Surprised that she thought of my close friend who wasn't raised with faith, I said, "Mrs. Laney? Why?" In her sweet little child's voice, she replied, "So that she knows God." Dear reader, I offered my blister pain up for you that evening. It's not much, but it's something. A few minutes later, when our daughter went to complain again, she stopped herself and asked, "God can use my pain, right, Mama? To help Mrs. Laney?" Smiling wide, I softly replied, "Yes, baby. God can use anything we offer Him for His greater good." This is a tiny, seemingly ridiculous example of how redemptive suffering works, but it's true. God makes everything good. Just as we believe in faith, when we pray for others, God hears our prayers; redemptive suffering is an act of faith. It's a mystery. Remember when we talked about offering Him our day and all its joys and sorrows? It doesn't matter how big or how small something is. When we intentionally offer it to God, He transforms it for His good.

As I was talking on that live social media video, the Holy Spirit was working on me. I had a repairman out to the house that afternoon after the talk but before the social media video. He's a Catholic man that I've known my whole life, and when he saw that I looked like I'd been run over by a truck, he asked what was up. I filled him in a little bit, and we got to talking about it. He's a few years older than me, but we agreed that our millennial generation knows next to nothing about God's design for men, women, and marriage. He said, "The Church needs to do something about that." To which I replied, "WE are the Church! We have to do something about it."

While I was talking on that video, God was working on my heart. This message isn't just for young women on the brink of their adult lives. It's for me. It's for my generation, for the one behind mine, and quite possibly the one ahead of it. It's for women who aren't yet married and those who have been married for twenty-plus years. Somewhere in the last 100 years, through all of its wars and economic crises, there has been a complete and total breakdown of the family and what it means to be in a Catholic marriage. This is not to say that there aren't wonderful, God-loving families in the world, Catholic and non-Catholic, but overall, the cultural battle on marriage is real, and the culture is winning.

My sadness and despair from earlier in the day quickly turned to strictly anger and frustration, not at the girls, but at Satan. How dare he try to rob these young women of a wonderful life. How dare he spit lies of distrust of a man they might not even know yet and of God into their ears. How dare he sneak into their hearts the lie that they aren't good enough for a true, loving, Christ-centered relationship. How dare he try to keep them, their future spouses, and their future children from heaven. He's the worst.

You're right, repair man friend. The Church has to do something about this, which led me to the planning of the first Catholic Wives Workshop at my home. It didn't matter if one woman showed up or 500. I was over Satan's attack on marriage. I was fed up with couples believing his deceptions that they aren't worthy of marriages in communion with God. Arthur and I believed his lie for half of our marriage. Not only did we believe a true marriage in Christ would be boring and archaic, but we didn't know it was even attainable! That was for older generations who, for whatever reason, still went to weekly Mass and were "good" Catholics. Not us.

We were wrong. Unequivocally wrong.

When I was in high school, a movie came out called *Coach Carter*. For all its faults (fornication, abortion, bad language, gang violence, etc.), I loved that movie. It came to mind while my daughter and I were praying the rosary the next day. In it, Coach Carter requires that his high school basketball players go to classes and maintain their grades to play. It's a true story. The school was in a poor district riddled with crime, and for many of the players, basketball was all they had. When Coach Carter set grade and attendance guidelines, parents and players alike were furious. When the players failed to meet these expectations, Coach Carter put a padlock on the gym, and his then-undefeated team took their first loss by way of forfeit. There's a scene where Coach Carter has to stand before the school board to defend his actions. The board and the parents were in agreement that these boys could not possibly meet the parameters that he placed on them in order to play. When the board moves to end the lockout without the parameters being met by the players, Coach Carter stands in front of everyone and says, "You really need to consider the message you are sending these boys. I'm trying to teach these boys a discipline that will inform their lives and give them choices."

Now, I'm not standing in front of a board or a mob of angry parents. At least not today, Praise God, but the anger that rose up in that classroom of young women over perceived injustices of the hypothetical decisions of their potential future spouses was palpable. Not everyone was angry or upset, but it was apparent that I had lost all credibility in the eyes of the ones who were. I can only imagine that in their minds, I had told them that their lives were destined for unhappiness and male dominance. In their minds, I had said to them that they weren't worth loving. This scene from Coach Carter came to mind, not because of an angry mob, but because of the message.

What are all of our talks about? What is their message? To glorify God. St. Paul tells us to "do everything for the glory of God." (1 Corinthian 10:31). You are not too young or too old, too lost or too broken, too immature or too intelligent, or too unworthy to glorify our Lord. Glorify Him with your day, your friendships, your future marriage, your future children, and with your entire lives. Glorify God with everything that you are, everything that you have, and everything that you will be in this life. Our talks have this message woven into their very fabric, and even though you may not be getting married now, you can start glorifying our Creator right now—this very moment. By doing so, you are opening yourself up to living in accordance with His will for your life, and when the time comes for your wedding vows, you might just be ready to say, "I do," freely, totally, faithfully, and fruitfully, and actually mean it. At that point, you'll be open and willing to place your trust in your spouse because you will know and trust in God's divine love. You will already be in a close relationship with Him, and you will see the fruits of His love touch every corner of your life.

At some point that evening, while folding clothes, I threw my hands up in frustration. "None of this matters!

What *am* I doing there? Why did God ask me to do this?" My husband silently looked on as I threw my small temper tantrum, as he usually does, to allow me to work through to the conclusion on my own. I realized what he was doing, gradually looked up at him, and quietly whispered, "All of it matters. These are human souls. This is all to glorify God." Arthur said, "Yeah, and to help the girls." To which I boldly replied, "Yeah, by helping them to glorify God!" I've been slapped over the face by the Holy Spirit more times than I can keep count during this whole process, and this is a small example of one of those times. Not twenty minutes after my mini pity party, I received a text message with a meme from the principal. It read as follows, "The "do what makes you happy culture" is so toxic for Christians. We are NOT called to do what makes us happy. We're called to do what glorifies God. Christianity isn't always sunshine and happiness. It's hard work and dedication to Him, not us. Do. What. Glorifies. God." Thank you, Holy Spirit. This is the right path. I told her I have full trust in Him and thanked her again for her trust in me.

Do you know what I realized? What the Holy Spirit revealed to me in all of this? Through all their anger, they were listening. Some were most definitely attentive before (thank you!), but many had hardened their hearts to God's love. Now, God had their full attention. Anger, we can work with. Apathy, we cannot. I thought we had teed the ball up so perfectly to dive into the day-to-day practicality of marriage. When the ball went the complete opposite of the direction I had intended, I thought the devil had won. Oh, ye of little faith. God has much better tactics than me. My plans are nothing compared to His. I called a priest for help, and we went back to the school together to spread God's message.

Lord Jesus Christ, Son of God, have mercy upon me, a sinner.

What Did You Learn?

Class One

- I learned how important marriage is and how much your vows actually mean, and your "I do" is forever, not I do till things get hard. Some people make marriage seem casual now, or it's all about the dress, the venue, whatever else. And while that is so fun and amazing, you are committing to your husband forever, and it is the biggest day. I loved how you and your husband say, "Thank you for marrying me" when times are chaotic or stressful, I am 100% implementing that into my relationship!
- Communication

You will find the questions and answers for chapter 4 on page 334.

Let Us Pray

In the name of the Father, the Son, and the Holy Spirit. Amen.

> Christ Jesus, when all is darkness and we feel our weakness and helplessness, give us the sense of Your presence, Your love, and Your strength. Help us to have perfect trust in Your protecting love and strengthening power, so that nothing may frighten or worry us, for, living close to You, we shall see Your hand, Your purpose, Your will through all things. Amen.

(Source: St. Ignatius of Loyola, Prayer Against Depression)

> Heavenly Father, please be with me today. My heart hurts. I feel overwhelmed, and it's difficult for me to see the joy that only You provide. Still, I trust in You and place my problems in your hands. I pray that you can open my eyes to the ways in which Your love is embracing me. Amen.

(Source: Prayer for Hope, Hallow Prayer App)

In the name of the Father, the Son, and the Holy Spirit. Amen.

Chapter 5

"There's no such thing as Catholic divorce."

"The fruit of silence is prayer, the fruit of prayer is faith, the fruit of faith is love, the fruit of love is service, the fruit of service is peace."
—St. Mother Teresa of Calcutta

God has this, not me. God has this, not me. This isn't my message. It's His. God has these young women and me. Why is it so hard for us to put full trust in the <u>almighty</u> God and surrender to His will? For the first time in my life, I've finally given up control and let Him guide me, and I don't even recognize my life anymore. His plans for us are so much bigger than our own. Is it seriously taking me three attempts to parallel park? I must be nervous. There's a line of cars the length of two blocks waiting behind me. Fabulous. Holy Spirit, please give me

145

the strength. Please be in my words today. Please open their hearts to God's divine love. I'm begging you.

Me: "Thank you so much for coming."

Father Barnabas: "Yeah, of course, so what are we doing?"

Me: "We've gone through prayer, finding a community, the Sacrament of Marriage, and we were starting intimacy when divorce not being an option was mentioned, and some of them got upset."

Father Barnabas: "So, should I let them come to me with questions or just like talk about marriage?"

Me: "They have a lot of questions, but it's probably best if you start talking and see what questions come up then."

Father Barnabas: "Yeah, I'll ask them which they prefer too. What class is this?"

Me: "This is homeroom."

Father Barnabas: "Homeroom?!"

Me: "Yeah, about eighty girls squeeze into this room. I've stolen their homeroom time, which I think they're less than thrilled about, too."

Father Barnabas: "Eighty??"

Me: "Yeah, some of them have to sit on the floor. It's less than ideal. I was coming to four different religion classes to talk, but because of scheduling, it had to be moved to homeroom."

The girls start trickling in. It's been four days since our last talk, but some are still visibly angry.

Me: "I'm telling you some of them are ready for a fight."

Father Barnabas: "Like I said, if they start swinging, especially for the sake of time. I'm used to it with my boys' school, so you don't have to defend me."

Me: "Oh no. I'm gonna let you go."

Father Barnabas: "My hope is not to leave with resolution but rather with a sense of pastoral peace."

Me: "Exactly. Agreed."

Father Barnabas: "What I'm going to do today is tell the truth but also give some pastoral care."

Me: "That's perfect. Thank you."

Hey, y'all. We didn't get through everything we had planned for the last talk. The rest of the talk on emotional and spiritual intimacy will be its own chapter in the book I'm writing for you.

I listened to Bishop Barron's homilies the past two weekends, and he said a few things that made me think of you, so I wanted to share them with you now.

"What makes our lives properly ordered is the worship of God. The other relationships aren't going to amount to anything unless they're grounded in a relationship to the Lord. Unless we're rooted in prayer, all our practical activities are going to amount to nothing or devolve into something that they ought not to be. God is love, therefore the more you are in touch with God, the more devoted to love you will be- or better, the more that divine love will start flowing through you into the world. We who are members of his mystical body, we're supposed to be other Christs. Through our love and our service, we reach out to a hurting world."

THIS is the love that we have been talking about. This is the love that God invites us to participate in. I can see that some of you may still be upset or angry, and you know what? I'm glad. I would have never planned for that to happen, but I'm glad you're angry. You know why? Because you're listening. You're listening. God's got your attention.

We've been going through a journey, haven't we? We've been talking about your now and into your future and what you can do now that will affect your future. We started with prayer and what your relationship right now with God looks like, what you can do to get closer to God, and why you matter. Then we started envisioning your future together, didn't we? We went through college years and how to find a loving community and eventually the 'one.' That was one of your top questions for our talks. So, you've found the 'one.' You're in a committed relationship, and now what? Let me interject here that not every one of your vocations will be marriage, but there is wisdom in all of our talks because they're all oriented toward God. Then, in your committed relationship, discerning whether or not he is the 'one.' What does that mean? At this point, you've said, "Yes." A man asked you to marry you, and you said, "Yes, I'd love to marry you!" So, we got to the Sacrament of Marriage and why is it a Sacrament? When you say, "I do," what are you saying, "I do" to? Freely, totally, faithfully, and fruitfully. Then we got to intimacy, the day-to-day living out of those vows. What does a day look like in a Catholic marriage? And we had to slam on the brakes. That's totally fine. That happens sometimes when you're driving. And, then we got in a wreck. Not anticipated, but still something that can happen out on the road. But then, a tornado came, and sharks ate us all. We went from real, concerned questions to "what if he's a murderer, and I hate him" questions real fast. We made quite the jump to the extreme.

Pause to breathe. Breathe, Kira. Don't let them hear your voice shake.

What I saw through your anger and your concern was your hurt, your pain, your wounds, your distrust of a man you might not even know yet, and your distrust in God's love for you. I posted that video on social media for you. I made that account for you and your parents. I knew you were upset. In it, I wanted to make one thing clear. Marriage is not a flippant milestone. It's an invitation by our God to enter, with your husband, into communion with Him. It's good. It's true. And, and it's breathtakingly beautiful. We're talking about a marriage that is based on God's love, based on the love of the Holy Trinity. That's what we've been talking about this whole time. Remember the table analogy. Our husbands and we make up the two sides of a table that is sitting on three legs representing the Trinity. The Holy Trinity is our foundation. As Father Mike says, "Our holiness isn't up to us; other people see God through us."

I'm glad God has your attention. Now, I don't know all the Catholic Church's teachings on divorce. I've never cared to learn them because I'm not planning on needing them, but when I do need spiritual guidance or help, I turn to our earthly fathers and friends, our priests. So, I've asked Father Barnabas here today to answer your questions, and he graciously answered my call for help. Please be respectful.

The following was said by Father Barnabas O'Reilly, a Benedictine monk residing at Benedictine Military School in Savannah, Georgia.

Will you say a prayer with me?

In the name of the Father, the Son, and the Holy Spirit. Amen.
Come Holy Spirit.
Come Holy Spirit.
Come Holy Spirit.
In the name of the Father, the Son, and the Holy Spirit. Amen.

Alright, what's the best way to use this time right now. You guys were here for this conversation before. You're starting to get into hard things. My whole life is talking to people about hard things, so what is the best way to use our time right now? Meaning I can like give you my spiel or you can ask some questions. I do this with my boys all the time, so I'm used to it. What would you like to do?

Silence.

You want my spiel? Okay! So, as a priest, even last week and now, I'm getting phone calls from people about their marriage and to marry them. A part of that is doing marriage preparation. I sit down with them or do video calls where I have to talk to them about helping them prepare for marriage. Most people, what happens when you get engaged is like you're planning a party and getting really stressed out, so I like to give them some encouragement and teach them about marriage.

So, what are some things that you would say if you told me like, "Make sure you tell the couple this"? To prepare them for marriage. Give me like three things. Ready.

Number one. You. What's one good piece of advice for marriage?

Student: "Um. To place it on a firm foundation which is the Lord."

Good. Number two. You. Give me another piece of advice. I literally have a phone call next week with a couple. I'll share with them what you say.

Student: "Maybe like communication."

Yeah, that's huge.
Number three. Right there.

Student: "Respect."

Respect. Respect.

So, let me tell you this much. Any time I talk about marriage, I always know that, guaranteed, I don't know any of you, but I know guaranteed that about half of you are hurt by a lack of respect in a marriage of their parents, a lack of communication, or a foundation that wasn't firm. So, I just acknowledge that, and a lot of times, people get scared about marriage in general if they come from a family where they saw it fall apart. So, let me just give you a question. Why should we even get married? Do you know what a civil union is? A civil union? *Crickets.*

Come on, ladies. We've talked about this.

Student: "What's a civil union?"
Laughter.

So, instead of two Catholics going to the Church and getting married which sometimes cost a lost more money, you can just go with your future husband to a court to sign a piece of paper, like a court of law...

Student: "Oh yeah, we have talked about that."

And, then afterward, you just have your party. Why not just do that? What's the difference between the two?

Student: "Is it wrong?"
Student 2: "Well, it's not in the church."

Well, let's just leave the church out of it for a second too. I'm all about the church. Look at me. *As he holds up his habit. Laughter.* Let's just talk straight-up philosophy right now. Straight up like truth. Why is marriage different than civil union?

Student: "In civil union, you're united by law, but in the Church, you're united as one person by heart and soul."

Oh, so now we're getting to it, right? *Starts writing on the board and messes up spelling marriage. Laughter.*

Whoops. My boys would jump on this right away and be like, "Can you even spell? Did you go to school?"

As I teach philosophy, we have to understand definitions first. Let's understand this.

Contract, *written on the board.*

How many people know a civil union is a contract? Raise your hand. *A little over half raise their hands.* Good. What about marriage? Is marriage a contract? Raise your hand. Or is marriage something else?

Student: "It's like a union of two people but not by law."

Right. It's by something else.

Covenant, *written on the board*

Oh, the priest is talking about covenant and like Noah's Ark and all this stuff. No. So, the difference between these two is this. A contract is like if you call up somebody to cut your grass, and you're like, "Alright, you'll be the guy that cuts our grass. We'll sign this piece of paper. You come once a week to cut the grass. I will pay you." What happens if he doesn't come cut the grass?

Students: "You don't pay him."

I don't pay him. Why? The contract was broken. What happens if a covenant gets violated? That's the question. That's the question. So, this all comes down to this. Is it appropriate for me to tell people in marriage preparation, "Listen, this is a lifelong union, but we have another option. You can get married now for like seven years, and then we'll check in again and see if we want to read up on this." Does that sound like something that could solve this issue of divorce and difficulties in marriage, do you think?

Student: "It's like a free test drive."
Student 2: "That's a long test drive."

Yeah. What would be the problem with that?

Student: "A lot. It would not be sustainable if you don't go in with the mindset that it's not long term."

And, why should it be long-term? Like how long should it be?

Student: "Lifelong. For life. If it's placed on the right foundation, no one goes in looking to get out."

Yeah. Precisely, but why? Here's my little cheat sheet book right here. These are the words I use when I stand there and marry people. And just side note, marriage is the only Sacrament that you don't actually need a priest. Well, technically, you do need a priest by tradition, but the ones that give each other the Sacrament are the man and the woman who say the words. What do the words say? Let's take a look. Once I say these words, you can tell me, what is the thing that they are promising to do? Because both a contract and a covenant have a promise to it. So, let's figure out what marriage's promise is. *He opens his book and reads.*

"I, <u>Bob</u>, take you, <u>Stephanie</u>, to be my wife. I promise to be faithful to you in good times and in bad, in sickness and in health, to love and to honor all the days of my life."

Very simple couple words, but there's a lot right there. What is it that you promise to do?

Student: "To love."

Now, let me ask you. I just talked to my sister. She's married and has a couple of little kids. I told her I was coming to talk to high school girls about marriage and the difficulties around that. What do I say? She said, "Remember love." Good to go. I was planning on that. What's the best version of love?

Student: "What do you mean?"

What do I mean? If you could conceive up on romantic love, what's the best version of that? What are some things that could make it the best? For instance, I'll give you a hint. Are you cool with like a guy cheating on you?

Students: "No."

Does anyone have to explain to you why that's a problem?

Students: "No."

You just know it. That's called natural law. There's something in your heart. Nobody has to explain to you why cheating is bad. What's another thing that's the best version of love? Meaning how long should it be. Yes?

Student: "Unconditional."

Unconditional, but we have to identify what that means so let's get back to the time. How long is the best version that you would want to be loved?

Student: "Forever."

Forever. Let's just keep God and the Church out of it still for now. I haven't talked about God and the Church yet. Let's just go with what we know from our human experience. From our human experience, how long is forever?

Students: "Until you die."

Until you're dead. As far as we know, that's forever, so the best version of love is to love until you can't love anymore. I would propose it's beautiful when I meet some like old guy who's still in love with his wife and like visits her grave every day. That's beautiful. Alright, so it's til death. Everyone tracking?

So, with that in mind? What are some problems that come to mind that threaten it being lifelong?

Student: "Commitment."

Commitment, yeah. For instance, you guys know what a prenup is?

Students: "Yes!"

What do you think about prenups? Are they a good idea, just in case? *Chatter.*

Student: "Well, I guess not."

Whenever I do the marriage prep interview, I ask the couple if they intend to sign a prenup. Now, let me ask you this. Where does a prenup fit? Here (Covenant) or here (Contract).

Students: "Contract."

Here, right, so I, in good conscience, can't marry the couple that's right here (contract). Why? They don't have the forever in mind, or maybe they do, but there's still an out. And, if there's still an out, then it's not here (covenant). I think it's easier to argue, "Well yeah, no one wants to go into their marriage with a way out. You want to be all in, but things happen over time that make you question the all in." Let me tell you this: after working and talking to married couples, even the best, most wonderful married couples start to question at times. I like to ask my boys this, and it's funny to hear their response. For the sake of time, I can't ask you for your answers, but do you think that when you get married, you'll never see another man as attractive? Or even, like, your heart starts to unwind? Like, "Wow, I'm more attracted to that other man than I am to my own husband." Do you think that if you get married, it's possible that you could "fall out of love?" You don't feel that anymore towards your husband. These seem like scandalous things, but let me tell you this. This is a part of the game. You think me as a priest who took a vow to do this, like every day I want to do this? That's a good question. The point is this (contract) is based off of, "If you're cute enough, if you don't cheat on me, if you like do what you're supposed to do and don't piss me off, we're good." This (covenant) says, "Even if you don't be cute, even if you cheat on me, even if you piss me off, I'm staying." Now, why? Why?

What am I saying? I'm saying this (contract): when it hits difficulties, it's easy to just say, "Nope! On to the next one." This one (covenant), when it hits difficulties, if you just keep grinding and keep fighting, you could come through this. Now, as I say this, I know many of you probably have parents who are divorced, and you may be like, "Yeah, that's not possible for my parents." So, what does the Church say about this? You know there's no such thing as Catholic divorce. What does that mean? It means that you're all in, but there are situations where you say, "I can't live with this person. This is too bad." All those situations you posed up here, so you need to get separated in that situation. I'm not saying this is good, but it's reality. Let's say that you say, "Man, I need to be fully separated, even legally, so we file for legal divorce." The Church acknowledges that these things happen. At the same time, I have to be honest with you, and I tell people, if that's the case for a couple, it's because that's the best remedy for bringing some type of peace and healing. But, you're not free to get remarried. Why? Because you're still married. You can't break the covenant. When a covenant is violated, it doesn't mean it's broken. It's been wounded, but it's not broken. A contract gets broken, but if you say the words (of the covenant) and mean them from the beginning of this, it's not broken.

Now, what's annulment? Annulment means you said the words, but you didn't mean them. You said the words, and you didn't mean them. For instance, you marry some dude who was cheating from the beginning and didn't tell you. And you're like, "I wouldn't have married that dude if I had known that was going on." You married a dude, and he had an addiction to drugs, pornography, whatever, and he didn't tell you before. It rears its head and is calling trouble, and you're like, "I should have known that in the beginning." You marry some dude, and there was something important withheld. The Church would investigate and determine if this marriage never really happened because something that makes it a marriage was missing in the beginning. Sometimes, it's about a couple not having the true freedom to decide on marriage or not understanding the obligations of marriage beforehand. There are grounds for annulment even there. Annulment is not divorce, but it's like, "Listen, this wasn't completely understood to begin with, at the root." So, the Church can say, "This is annulled, meaning it was never fully understood to begin with."

Now, hard questions would be like, what if it was fully understood and one of them still messes up or does something that very much harms? Once again, I'll get back to the question of love. Love is lifelong. Love is faithful. Even when those things get broken, love still gives, even if it has to be separated for a while. Love still remains in some mysterious way. And, I know this seems very hard, but all I'll say is if you're in a family where there's been divorce, there's probably something in your heart that says, "Yeah, divorce is not good." Also, two parents staying in the same household and losing their minds is not good. Sometimes these things have to happen. The point, it seems of this, is it's better for us to tell you the truth, to set up shop, and find a man who can keep up with you in your desire for love. If you've been hurt by these things, I'm very much sorry. If you're in a family that's been divorced, that makes you no less qualified or able to be a part in a wonderful marriage. A lot of people get scared of this, like, "My parents got divorced. My grandparents got divorced. Whatever." This doesn't mean anything on you. It means you need to be healed. A part of healing comes out with anger and sadness, right? But, there's a need for healing.

A student asks a question regarding the situation in her family.

The Catholic Church recognizes two baptized Protestants who got married as a Sacrament same as any other Catholic. Catholic has extra subtleties to it, but you are married in the eyes of God because you made a covenant. You can't separate one flesh that's been bound. This (contract) just makes that a contract. This (covenant) is made of blood. What does that mean? It means maybe there's hope in a situation of coming back together and redemption. Maybe there's no hope, and somebody's mental health is like crazy, then I'd say two things. One, what does it mean to be divorced and still be married to someone? It means you're not free to get remarried because you can't marry more than one person. You're still married, but two, I'd say, "Let's talk." How long was this going on? Was there suspicion of this at marriage or beforehand? Just to see if there are grounds for annulment. Pastorally, what I like to say is that as important and as beautiful as marriage is for help, one of the more important things when there's trauma like that is to address the need for healing in general. Once you can establish healing... *Holds up habit.* This doesn't just mean I didn't need to get married to find happiness. It means God can actually fulfill what we're looking for. This doesn't mean like, "Yeah, I never wanted to get married." This meant like, hey, when you get married, don't make your husband your idol. Don't make him God. He cannot be. This (*his habit*) means that God can be God.

I could seriously listen to Father Barnabas talk about God and life all day. That went well. God's got this. God's got them. And, God's got me. Thank you, Lord. Thank you so much.

Let Us Pray

Litany of Trust

In the name of the Father, and of the Son, and of the Holy Spirit.

Ask Jesus to deliver you from the various fears and insecurities that hold us back from fully trusting Him.

After each petition, respond with "Deliver me, Jesus."

From the belief that I have to earn Your love
From the fear that I am unlovable
From the false security that I have what it takes
From the fear that trusting You will leave me more destitute
From all suspicion of Your words and promises
From the rebellion against childlike dependency on You
From refusals and reluctances in accepting Your will
From anxiety about the future
From resentment or excessive preoccupation with the past
From restless self-seeking in the present moment
From disbelief in Your love and presence
From the fear of being asked to give more than I have
From the belief that my life has no meaning or worth
From the fear of what love demands
From discouragement

Place your trust in Jesus, knowing that He will always wrap you in His arms.

After each petition, respond with "Jesus, I trust in You."

That You are continually holding me, sustaining me, loving me

That Your love goes deeper than my sins and failings and transforms me

That not knowing what tomorrow brings is an invitation to lean on You

That You are with me in my suffering

That my suffering, united to Your own, will bear fruit in this life and the next

That You will not leave me orphan, that You are present in Your Church

That Your plan is better than anything else

That You always hear me and in Your goodness always respond to me

That You give me the grace to accept forgiveness and to forgive others

That You give me all the strength I need for what is asked

That my life is a gift

That You will teach me to trust You

In the name of the Father, and of the Son, and of the Holy Spirit. Amen.

(Source: Sister Faustina Maria Pia and the Sisters of Life)

Chapter 6

Emotional & Spiritual Intimacy
Part 2

Blessed are the pure in heart, for they shall see God.
– The Sixth Beatitude

This is the chapter where we will circle through the topics we started two chapters ago. Thank you for your patience while we worked through some other things.

Have you ever watched a chicken family? Like not just the hen, but the rooster, hen, and biddies all together. We live on a little homestead and have a lot of birds- chickens, geese, guineas, ducks, turkeys, etc. It took us a few years to gather up the courage to get a rooster. Roosters have spurs on their legs, sharp little weapons, and we thought a rooster would be aggressive and a nuisance. It really wasn't about the noise. It was about the potential to do us harm. I read about them though, found a docile breed, and decided to plunge into bringing a rooster to the farm. I had read that they could help protect our hens from aerial predators such as hawks and owls. We had lost a few birds to predators, so it sounded like a good idea. Shortly thereafter, Reginald, a beautiful white silkie roo, came to live on the farm. Then our dog killed him, and we went and got his son from the same family, and Reginald Junior came to live on the farm. He is still a rather proud resident on the King homestead and is now called Reggie Jr.

Our favorite hen is a tiny jungle fowl named Batman. Long story short, she got mixed in with a set of guinea babies one year, and we thought she was a rooster. One spring, Batman disappeared. We couldn't find her anywhere for about a month, until one day, we heard some peeping under the lawn mower. Batman had set and hatched her and Reggie's babies. They were the smallest, cutest little chicks you've ever seen, about the size of a Lego man. Reggie had been a good rooster to our flock. When a hawk would fly over, he'd do his alarm call, puff his wings up, and shepherd our hens to the bushes for safety. When Batman brought their babies out of the nest, Reggie's protective demeanor increased tenfold. He was constantly on watch, always by their side, and guarding them to keep them safe. He'd scratch up the earth and point with his beak to yummy treats for the babies and Batman to enjoy. He took his job very seriously.

Out of the four biddies, two ended up being roosters, and two were hens. We named them after the Teenage Mutant Ninja Turtles. What can I say? We grew up in the 90s. The roosters are gorgeous. They're decked out in shiny red and gold plumage with long emerald green tail feathers, but fully grown, they're about the size of a softball. They terrorize their father sometimes but take the role of protecting the flock to heart. One day, a rather large, red-shouldered hawk boldly landed on one of our metal gates. Reggie sounded the alarm, and all the hens started taking cover. He was a good shepherd and counted out his flock as they fled to safety. I don't think he knows the exact number, but he won't come into the coop at night until every last hen is in before him. He is efficient and leaves no hen behind. When the hawk was spotted casually sitting on our gate, Reggie's sons, Michelangelo and Leonardo, raced to the scene. These two tiny roos took on a full-grown hawk. They puffed up their chest, raised their wings, and started trying to torpedo it with their spurs out. They were ready for a fight. The hawk was utterly shocked at these midget menaces and their audacity even to think to come at his lethal majesty, to which he promptly flew away. Reggie is not as pugnacious as his sons, but he was right behind them as they led the charge, ready to be their backup.

So, why did we just go in-depth about some silly chickens? Because I want to point out a few things. Roosters are designed to protect their flock. Yes, man has dabbled in their breeding and created more docile breeds, but overall, in their very makeup is the instinct to guard, protect, and provide, especially if there are babies. Now, the hens don't just sit around and watch while the roos are out fighting. They care for their babies and ensure they have what they need. They're with the other hens in their flock conversing, very loudly, I might add. They're not idle. They're tending to each other and their biddies. Before we had roosters, we had a couple of pugnacious hens, but they were not equipped to intimidate a hawk, especially not one six times their size.

God made men and women so perfectly. For what one inherently lacks in ways of gifts and talents, the other excels. Our world today will tell you that men and women are the same. We *are* the same in that we all have inherent dignity, in that we are all God's creatures, and in that Christ loved us all and died for us all. (See Galatians 3:28.) But, men and women are not the same, and how boring the world would be if we were! In a man's very makeup is the innate need to provide and protect. In a woman's very makeup is the innate need to care and nurture. These are not weaknesses. They are incredible gifts and monumental strengths.

Now, you might say, "Protect what? Nurture what? I don't need a man to protect me, and I don't currently have children to nurture." Have you ever looked at a tragic shooting and noticed how the victims reacted? In more than one tragic case, it is the men who run towards the shooter first. Why? Even if they don't have a wife or a child of their own with them, they run to take down the shooter. Why? Because engrained in their very being is the call to guard and protect. Does that mean that every man rises to the call, not just in a tragic situation? No. Some men are selfish cowards who never rise to that call. (*Please note here that I am not condemning any victim's reaction during a mass shooting. Lord only knows what we are capable of in such a horrific situation.*)

What are the women typically doing during an active shooting? They're working together to gather the children and other women around them to get them to a spot of safety. Why? Because engrained in their very being is the call to care and nurture. Does that mean that every woman rises to that call, not just in a tragic situation? No. Some women are selfish cowards who never rise to that call. In the case of tragic events, these innate natures more often than not take control, and men and women alike perform heroic acts that save lives.

Thankfully, I've never been involved in such a tragic event, but I was a selfish coward. I resisted the call engrained in every woman. My husband has never been a selfish coward, and it was partly through witnessing his bravery and his embrace of this natural calling that I wanted to do better.

Our husbands are the spiritual leaders of our family. It's a bold statement, I know. St. Paul tells us, "For the husband is the head of the wife as Christ is the head of the church, his body, and is himself its Savior." (Ephesians 5:23). We've already discussed how our husbands represent Christ in our marriages and what that ultimately means, his willingness to die and sacrifice his life for his family as Christ did for the Church. So, what does it mean for a husband to be a spiritual leader?

We've already touched on the fact that Jesus led not by tyranny or dictatorship but by love and invitation. We've also already established that though our husbands represent Christ in our marriage, he is not Christ. He is an imperfect human just like us, so how do we trust his leadership? What type of leader should he be? He's called to lead his family as Christ led the Church. He's called to be what's known as a servant-leader. The husband is tuned into his family's needs and spiritual welfare by imitating Christ. He leads by example and provides stability, support, encouragement, and, yes, protection if the need arises.

Would you be willing to follow such a leader? "But," you may say, "my boyfriend/fiancé/husband/future-husband-I-don't-know-yet can't and won't be this type of leader." I had that thought, too, many times. I set the bar unimaginably low for my husband regarding the spiritual and religious realm, and do you know what happened? I was wrong. He rose to the call, God's call for who he is supposed to be for our family's sake and for our family's good. Many men will rise to the call set before them. It's a challenge, and men, overall, enjoy challenges. Some men will not. They will choose to be selfish cowards unwilling to participate in the self-giving, sacrificial love that marriage requires. How do you avoid such men? By finding one in the beginning who is compatible with you and your faith. By discerning whether or not he is the man God is calling you to marry *before* you get married. Don't skip the leg work, and don't forget to ask for God's help. What happens if the man you marry doesn't rise to the call? Pray and seek help from a priest. He can help you navigate the bumpy road you may experience by trying to take on a role your husband should fulfill. A man must submit himself first to Christ and then to the service of his family. He is responsible for showing and practicing Christ's love for his family. This is what makes him a true leader. This is what makes him the head of his family. And, let me just be honest. There is nothing more attractive than a masculine man who loves the Lord.

Assuming our husbands are not selfish cowards and are men of integrity who love the Lord, what are we called to do as wives? First, let's remember that our submission to our husbands is to be under the mission of and that our shared mission is to bring each other and our children to heaven. How do we do that? By loving the Lord, following His divine will for us, and being His earthly vessels to distribute His love to others. Submitting to our husbands does NOT detract from our worth or dignity as a person. It enhances it. In the submission, we rise to God's call for us as women. God's call for us is ultimately good, true, and beautiful. A wife's call is to support her family, encourage them, nurture them, care for them, and guide them in virtue.

You may say, "But, that sounds like an old-fashioned housewife! I have so many more skills than that." I don't personally know you, but yes, I believe that you do. Providing love and support to my family does not diminish or take away from my gifts or talents or my dignity as a person. When I let this idea penetrate my soul, I suddenly yearned to rise to God's call for women. I didn't want to be a selfish coward any longer. I wanted to shed my self-centeredness and ego, look at those around me, tend to their needs, support them in the ways I could, and care for them. I wanted to love in a self-giving, sacrificial way, a way I had never understood before. I wanted to be Christ to them in this world. It's a daily walk with the Lord. Some days, it's such a struggle, and it feels as if I'm climbing a steep mountain with no end in sight. On other days, God's love flows through me like water, and I can see the flowers and fruits flourishing in their deliverance from thirst.

This kind of love in a marriage opens both the husband and wife up to a new way of living. It expands their love into something they couldn't possibly do by themselves. It invites Christ to dwell within their love, to be an active participant in their marriage, and to use it as a vessel for the ultimate good of others. What does it look like in practice? It's going to Mass and worshipping God together, both going to Confession (ideally monthly), praying (such as the rosary, novenas, daily intentions) together, reading Scripture or devotionals together, listening to Christ-focused podcasts together, discussing your faith within your family, and more. It looks like intentionally turning to God together.

Every five years, on our wedding anniversary, Arthur and I meet a priest at a church to renew our wedding vows. I was nine weeks pregnant with our first child the first time we did it. The second time, our second child was seven months old, sitting in her car seat in a pew watching on while our eldest stood under us as we said, "I do" to each other in front of Jesus in the Tabernacle for the third time. When I heard Father Barnabas read y'all those same vows out loud during our last talk, I was brought right back to those three moments: our wedding day, our 5th anniversary, and our 10th anniversary. A lot has changed since the first time we said them. We've grown and matured. We've become parents to two beautiful little girls. We've had so many joys and a handful of real trials. Renewing our vows in this way keeps us connected. It keeps us grounded. It keeps us focused. Your husband, as the spiritual leader, does not put him on an island or a pedestal. He doesn't fill the spiritual role for your family entirely by himself. It's through your support as a virtuous wife that he can lead at all. It's through your understanding of his and your role and living it out that you can both lean on, in complete trust and faith, the love of the Trinity.

I hope you've been able to follow our path as we journeyed from ballroom dancing to Adam and Eve to chickens and tragedies. Giving up control, giving in to trust, and surrendering your will to God will transfigure your relationship with your spouse. We walked through the Five Selves of Good a couple of chapters ago. There, they were just words on a page. Here is where we will dive deeper into applying those words on a daily level.

My husband and I have known each other since we were four years old. I'd say we knew each other fairly well, so it was shocking to find out that sometimes, we couldn't understand each other. When he graduated from college a year after I did, I had a full-time job. We bought his mother's home and intended to renovate it, but we were saving up for a wedding, had horses, dogs, and cats to care for, and were making ends meet on one income for about two months. Money was tight. It was stressful, and I had yet to learn how to properly handle high-stress situations at twenty-two years old. So, when I got to the house from work one day to tackle some little project, such as painting cabinets, it was somewhat unnerving to find the kitchen completely torn apart.

Electric wires were dangling from the ceiling. The cabinets were all in the living room. There was no sink. No countertop. There was dust and debris everywhere. Arthur hadn't started his full-time job yet, so he was at the house working all day. He had told me he was planning on tackling the kitchen that day, but he had failed to mention that there would no longer be a kitchen when he was done. I lost it. If I'm honest, I threw a chair. He still likes to bring that part up. It was in my way. Not one of my finer moments in life. He had said he was going to work on the kitchen. I didn't ask him to elaborate. I thought he knew the plan. We were going to paint the cabinets, get new pulls, replace the light fixture, etc. He saw a soffit, a useless space of about 6 inches above the cabinets that hid the wiring, and wanted to make the little galley kitchen feel bigger by removing it. Well, that entailed demo and mess. He had a great time that day while I was at work, so when I got there and was furious, he was so confused. He had said he was working on the kitchen, and he was, but all I saw was destruction. We had communicated, but we communicated differently. We didn't understand one another.

Millions of tiny opportunities for communication arise in a relationship. From what movie we will watch to what city we will live in, the need for communication is one of those things that never goes away. There are plenty of wrong ways to communicate with one another, but there's one crucial thing to keep in mind. What are we trying to do or should do when we communicate? Understand one another. It's as simple as that. We're trying to understand what the other is honestly saying. To understand one another, we can't be passive, aggressive, unclear, defensive, assuming, rude, unkind, indifferent, etc. These are all blockades to effective communication, with the common goal of understanding one another. It sounds too simple, doesn't it? How do we understand each other? We articulate our thoughts and feelings in a kind, respectful manner. Easy to say. Sometimes extremely hard to do.

Effective communication in a Catholic marriage brings us closer to God. How? Because it goes back to allowing Christ to live within our marriage. Jesus is the example of how we should live our entire lives. To which you may say,

"Well, He spoke in parables! Aren't those unclear?" We are intelligent beings, capable of free thinking, and though sometimes we forget that, we can follow rational lines of thought. Even in times of conflict, we can rationally talk through our differences.

When I was a teenager, my mother would call family meetings when things were out of whack in our family. They were super annoying. We'd all sit there staring at each other while she held up a communication chart, coaching us to talk. It said:

I feel... <u>angry</u>.
When... <u>the dishes aren't done when I ask.</u>
Going forward... <u>it would mean a lot to me if you obeyed the first time I ask.</u>

It was agonizing yet strangely effective. See what it does is this. It takes away placing the blame on someone else and forces you to accept your role in the matter. Our feelings shouldn't lead us, but they are wonderful tools God gave us to direct our attention to reality. Our emotions do not dictate reality but open us up to understanding reality if we let them. For instance, my mom felt angry. Why? Because I didn't do the dishes. Was she actually mad that the dishes weren't done? Well, yeah, but there was a much bigger issue than the dishes. I had disobeyed her. My mother was upset at my lack of respect for her in our home. How could this be remedied in the future so that the commandment to honor my mother was upheld? I could obey the first time she asked to do the dishes.

Now, I understand that this is a silly example and that in your past, present, and future, much more significant problems will arise. Believe it or not, this communication chart is effective even then. Trust me, I've tested it. Accepting that my feelings don't obscure reality but help me get to reality is against everything the world tells us nowadays. Culture tells us that if we feel something, then it must be true. God gave us feelings. Feelings are good. We just have to remember that they are tools. Tools for resolution. Tools for navigation. Tools for discernment. Tools for expression. Tools for the quest of truth.

I mentioned earlier that in our marriage, Arthur and I never say the d-word. It sparked some conversation, but the idea is this. We both come from divorced families. We knew coming into our marriage that we didn't want that to be our story. Many couples joke about divorce. They may have no intention to ever actually go through with it, but they'll say things like, "If he leaves his food on the counter one more time, I'm filing for divorce." Or "We tried to paint our bedroom together and almost got divorced." It's stupid, but it's hurtful. It might not be at that exact moment, but it sticks and festers. We devised a few "rules" for our marriage before we got married, and that was one of them.

Never say the d-word. Another one I encourage you to steal is to never yell at each other out of anger. Ever. Yelling accomplishes nothing except causing pain. In keeping with this is never to call each other names out of meanness. I call Arthur an idiot out of love and endearment while laughing when he's acting like a fool, but I'll never call him an idiot when he really messes something up or during an argument. If we're too angry about something to talk it out immediately, we'll pause and take a minute. That's hard for me, but we both need a minute to regroup to come back together to discuss rationally and respectfully. Having conversations like these and practicing them before you get married is essential.

We went a little into service earlier, but let's take a practical leap into it now. How can I serve my spouse? Well, what does service in marriage mean? And if you're thinking, "Hold up. I'm a queen, and he should serve me," please go back to chapter 1 of this book and begin again. Christ told us to serve one another. "Your light must shine before others, that they may see your good deeds and glorify your Heavenly Father." (Matthew 5:16). Serving one another is not a sign of weakness. It's quite the opposite. It's a sign of strength.

Why was Saint Mother Teresa of Calcutta so revered in the last century? Was it because she was a corporate genius who ran a global company? What do people know about Mother Teresa's life? She helped the poor, but it wasn't just the poor, was it? She helped the poorest of the poor in all of the world. She literally pulled sick and dying people out of gutters in Calcutta. One time, Mother Teresa was on her way to a meeting with the Pope. A driver picked her up to see Pope John Paul II and get her there on time. You are not supposed to be late for an appointment with the Pope, but on the way, Mother Teresa saw a person suffering from leprosy on the side of the road. She told the driver to stop and got out to care for and speak to the man. When she arrived at her appointment very late, a cardinal pointed out that she had kept the Vicar of Christ waiting. She replied, "Yes, I know, but I met Christ on the road." Do you think St. Pope John Paul II minded her tardiness? She stopped to give hope and love to another soul. I'd venture to say he wouldn't be a Saint if he did.

We are not above serving the people around us, especially our spouses and children. But, how? How do we serve? When I pushed aside my arrogance, the answer was right before my eyes. I was just too blind to see it. There are thousands of opportunities for service in every single day of our lives. When he gets home, I serve my husband with a warm smile and a hug. I'm not a very good cook, but some nights, I have dinner (mostly soup) ready and waiting for him, so it takes one less thing off his plate. I listen and support him as he goes through his day. I put my phone down and am present to him. I try to make sure I am in a good state mentally so that I can provide mental stability for him, and I pray unceasingly for him. I am available to serve his physical, emotional, mental, and spiritual needs. It's not perfect every day, but it is intentional. And, do you know what? He does the same for me. Through service, we take those words from the Five Selves of Good off the page and bring them to life. We rise to Christ's calling to glorify His Father with our very lives. It's not perfect, and there are times when one's needs are more than the other's, but when you enter into marriage, you're entering into a life of service. Not slavery. Not servitude. True, unconditional, self-giving, sacrificial love between each other and our Lord.

From here, we enter into gratitude. I've told you many times how my husband and I loved each other with a shallow love for many years. Though we did not know it then, it was a love in which we used one another. Part of this use was a lack of gratitude. In addition to not seeing one another as God sees us, we didn't appreciate one another for who we were. Because we made each other our idols, we couldn't truly appreciate one another. We were looking toward each other for fulfillment.

For years, when my husband would travel for work, I was riddled with anxiety that he would die on the journey. *What would I do without him? I'd never be able to go on. I'd never make it in a world where Arthur King did not exist.* I'd often drink the evenings away while he was gone to numb the fear and make time speed by. (This was before having our children.) As we began getting closer to the Lord, I put this fear at the foot of His cross. He is the almighty and ever-knowing God. He knows when we will die, not I, and worrying my days away about my healthy husband's future demise won't change a thing. No amount of fear or anxiety could control the outcome. I had to face the hard fact that my husband is not God. I obviously knew that on the surface, but deep down, I had made him out to be a god, an idol. Our relationship cannot be the foundation for our lives. Only God is up to that task. Only He is strong enough to withstand the burden. And, only He brings our ultimate fulfillment.

When your relationship with Him grows, all of your other relationships follow suit, especially those closest to you. Your life that once looked like a maze begins to straighten out because your gaze always remains the same. The road is still bumpy sometimes, but to look upon God is to look upon ourselves and to see ourselves the way He sees us. Once Arthur and I witnessed the Lord's infinite love for one another, we could channel that love to each other in a non-idol way. Together, we gazed upon our God and began to see our strengths and faults as He sees them.

Together, we could discuss and work on the areas where we needed improvement and healing. We still do.

As I mentioned, Arthur is incredibly thoughtful, so just as my blindness was cured to see opportunities for service, so was it cured to see opportunities for gratitude. For everything. Thank you for folding the clothes. Thank you for making dinner. Thank you for working so hard to provide for us. Thank you for saying "no" to something you may want for the good of the family. Thank you for showing up for your family day in and day out. Thank you for filling the car up with gas. Thank you for looking at me like that. Thank you for loving me. Thank you for being you. (He coined the last two. I have to pinch myself often that I ended up with someone so wonderful.) And, as I mentioned earlier, thank you for marrying me. Nothing is too big or too small to warrant a thank you. Sometimes, it doesn't take the words. We know the other is grateful, but there is so much power in those two little words. Thank you. Don't underestimate them. You don't have to be married to start overusing them, either. Watch the relationships around you transform when you start expressing gratitude and truly meaning it. We should shower God with our gratitude every day, and though our husbands are not God (we've established that much!), he deserves our thanks and praise, too.

Lastly, an indispensable ingredient to intimacy between spouses in a marriage is humility. We didn't get to touch on it last time, but it is crucial to a successful marriage. Why? Because we are to model our lives like Christ, who said, "Learn of me, because I am meek, and humble of heart: and you shall find rest to your souls." (Matthew 11:29). Meek is not weak, and humble is not becoming a doormat so what are they? Meek is often misunderstood and an adjective I use to describe my husband. It's enduring evil stoically.

If I'm slighted, my initial go-to is to get someone back, to return the infliction of pain. One time in high school, Arthur's friend had had too much to drink and was getting pushy with a girl. Arthur intervened and calmly told him to leave her alone. His friend, frustrated with his lack of progress and annoyed with the person in its way, proceeded to punch Arthur in the face. It's the only time he's ever been punched in the face, and it was by one of his best friends. Stunned, lying on the ground, and trying to gather his wits about him, he turned to look at the guy just as another friend tackled him and chastised him for hitting Arthur. When I heard the story, I was furious.

"What'd you do? Did you hit him back? We're never hanging out with him again!" Arthur, in his meekness, said, "No. I'm not going to "get back at him." What's done is done. It was stupid. I've forgiven him, and we're hanging out with him this weekend." That guy is still our friend, and we still hang out with him to this day. (Thankfully, he's matured! We all have.) Christ calls us to be meek, that is, to sometimes endure evil quietly through the strength of the Lord. It goes against most human inclination, but it once again guides us to avoid leaning on our own understanding of things and rely on the strength of God.

St. Peter said to, "clothe yourselves with humility in your dealings with one another, for: "God opposes the proud

but bestows favor on the humble." (1 Peter 5:5). Humility is one of those words you hear often but might have trouble putting into practice. From this scripture passage, humility looks to be the opposite of pride. Pride is a nasty thing. It leaves a wake of destruction in its path and decimates marriages where it takes root and is fed. When we talked about dying unto ourselves for the good of the other earlier, we were talking about shedding pride and embracing humility.

Humility comes into play in marriage on a daily basis. You might have heard before that you shouldn't go to bed angry at your spouse. It's a good tip, but let me expand on it. Don't go twenty minutes angry at your spouse. "What! Twenty minutes! I need to calm down." Take your time, even if it's a bit longer than twenty minutes, but here's the point. There will be times when you and your husband will hurt each other's feelings, offend one another, and do something to cause the other one to become angry. These are the times to look at yourself, the role you might have played in whatever happened, and say I'm sorry. Two words. Two simple words that have a monumental impact.

Sometimes, after a long day, you might not mean to, but it's easy to snap at the people we are closest to. We know we shouldn't take our frustrations out on them, but we're tired and grumpy. Say, "I'm sorry." Smooth it over, and even if you're still grumpy, show your spouse or whomever the respect they deserve. I'm not saying to apologize when it's unnecessary or when you're over-anxious, but often, an apology is necessary. It's nearly always appreciated. We just have to move past our pride to see that it is. Don't hesitate to genuinely apologize. It's meaningful, powerful, and another avenue to show your very real love for one another.

This whole chapter has been dedicated to emotional and spiritual intimacy between two loving spouses who have a Christ-centered marriage. We have been talking about the ideal situation for a married couple, all neat and tidy, but life is messy. People make mistakes. People hurt each other, even spouses. I shared a few stories from the past ten years of my marriage, but they aren't the whole story. We've had to overcome a lot of pain from past wounds and suffering from inflictions caused by the other, just like any couple. We've been to counseling. We've talked to priests. We've grown in our love of God individually and together by deepening our prayer life and leaning into the roles He designed for us.

Husbands and wives struggle every day to fulfill their vows to one another, but "I can do all things through Christ who strengthens me." (Philippians 4:13). We all have our baggage, but ugliness from our past does not have to determine our future. Give your pain to Jesus. Ask Him for healing. If the scab gets torn off of an old wound you thought you had worked through, give it to Him again. The reason Confession is such a gift is because we often make the same mistakes over and over again without meaning to. It's a Sacrament of healing. Always strive to grow in virtue, and don't forget to turn to our Lord. Being connected and intimate with your spouse deepens your friendship, your trust, and your love. Invite Christ into every inch of your marriage, and you will have a truly beautiful and good marriage, no matter the messiness.

"Love is never something ready made, something merely 'given' to man and woman, it is always at the same time a 'task' which they are set. Love should be seen as something which in a sense never 'is' but is always only 'becoming', and what it becomes depends upon the contribution of both persons and the depth of their commitment."

- Pope John Paul II, *Love and Responsibility*

Let Us Pray

In the name of the Father, the Son, and the Holy Spirit.
Amen.

> O God, who in creating the human race
> willed that man and wife should be one,
> keep, we pray, in a bond of inseparable love
> those who are united in the covenant of Marriage,
> so that, as you make their love fruitful,
> they may become, by your grace, witnesses to charity
> itself.
> Through Christ our Lord
> Amen.

In the name of the Father, the Son, and the Holy Spirit.
Amen.

(Source: Prayer for Married Couples, The United States Conference of Catholic Bishops)

Chapter 7

Physical Intimacy

Authentic married love is caught up into divine love and is governed and enriched by Christ's redeeming power and the saving activity of the Church. Thus this love can lead the spouses to God with powerful effect and can aid and strengthen them in the sublime office of being a father or a mother.
—Gaudium et spes

Deep breaths. This one is the icing on the cake. Talking to young women, growing up in this crazy culture, about our bodies and sex. It's going to be great. Gotta kiss my babies goodbye. "Bye Peanut, I love you. I'll see you shortly. Bye, Little Bug, I love you. Have a good rest." Kiss my husband goodbye, smile weakly, and ask for his prayers. Blessed Mother, I need your guidance. My hands are shaking. Please help these young women to see the

beauty of our bodies and how God designed them. St.
Ambrose, pray for me. Our Mother of Good Counsel, pray
for us.

Alright, y'all. Today, we're talking about physical
intimacy. It's a big one. You ready? Let's go.

We're going to start with a story. There was a young
woman who was a cradle Catholic. She graduated from this
very school. A couple of years after her high school
graduation, she met a guy who was wild but handsome and
very charming. Though she wasn't sure if he had good
intentions, she started dating him. Now, she had been a
virgin, but at some point, she let this guy she was dating
allure her. She was infatuated with him, thought it was real
love, and succumbed to his advances. Alcohol also played a
large factor that first time. Shortly thereafter, she got
pregnant. Not once, but twice. The first baby died. She lost
it in a miscarriage in the first trimester. The second baby
did not. The young woman went to her mother, a devout
Catholic woman, to tell her the news. Her mother told her
to get rid of it, or she'd disown her and never speak to her
again. So, in that moment of complete fear, what did she
do?

Student: "Do it."
Student 2: "Abort!"
Laughter.

Hmm. I wonder if they'll be laughing in a minute.

The young woman went to the abortion clinic. To the
guy's credit, abortion wasn't an option for him, but he

didn't have much say in the matter. She was waiting in the clinic lobby when the receptionist stopped her and said, "I don't know what it is about you, and I've only ever done this one other time, but God's telling me that you should have this baby." The woman completely broke down into tears, left the clinic, and chose life for her child.

I'm that baby.

Mic' drop. I'm out. Just kidding. There isn't much of a reaction, though. Did they hear me?

Student (*in a hushed tone*): "That was your mama?"

Yes, that was my mama.

All Students: "WHAT!"
Student: "I did not see that coming at all!"
Student 2: "Twist of events!"

Right! I've been gearing up that one for you. *There's the response I anticipated.*

Now, why did I share this rather serious story with you? For two reasons. Listen and listen good. One. IF you should ever find yourself in a similar situation, none of us ever think we will be in that situation, but if you ever do find yourself in that situation, I beg you to choose life for your child. If you are unable to keep your child for whatever reason, my husband and I will adopt him or her, no questions asked. Choose life for your child. I'm begging you. If we are unable to adopt for whatever reason, we will help you find an adoption agency that can place your child with a wonderful, loving family. Please, dear God, choose life for your child. You may be thinking, "What's one more person mean to the world?" I don't know what it means to the world, but to me and my children, it means our very existence.

Reason number two. My mother was a cradle Catholic. She knew what God said and the Church's teachings on sex before marriage. She loved God. Did it prevent her from having sex before marriage? No. My mother told me that story when I was 16 years old. It altered how I viewed abortion, but do you think it prevented me from choosing to have sex before I got married? No. Why? Because the "Sex bad before marriage. Sex good after marriage" narrative doesn't work. When I was little, my mom put a mousetrap in the kitchen and told me not to touch it. Well, what'd I do? I touched it, and it slammed on my little hand. It's part of our brokenness as humans to want to test the boundaries and push the limits, especially when it comes to God. Additionally, the "Don't have sex before marriage because you'll get pregnant" narrative rarely works.

Student: "Was that first miscarriage an accident?"

Yes, it happened naturally. She was only twenty years old. She didn't know what was happening but found out later that's what it was, so I have a full sibling in heaven. I have many half-siblings here, but I'm excited to hopefully meet my full-sibling one day, too. Let me also say that when my mother went back to my grandmother to tell her she was keeping me, my uncle stepped in and told my grandmother that he and his wife and children would never see her again if she disowned my mother. It was all very dramatic, but it worked. My grandmother loved me fiercely. Our first child's middle name comes from my great-great-grandfather, who picked up his cross and returned to work to provide for his daughter and grandchildren. Our second child's middle name is my grandmother's name. I never asked her about any of it, but I know deep down that she regretted it and intensely repented. I loved my grandmother dearly. Also, my mother wanted me to make sure I let you know that after that first time, when alcohol had dramatically affected her fortitude and her virginity was taken from her, not freely given, she went to the closest Catholic church the next day, sat in the back of the church, cried and prayed for hours. She felt helpless.

In my opinion, the narrative of sex is bad before marriage, but good in marriage doesn't work, so I'm not going to preach that narrative to you. Instead, what we need to understand is how to have an ordered life with God. This is what we've been talking about the whole time. God is like a magnet. He made us and is a magnet for us because throughout our entire lives, He's pulling us towards Him. We have free will, so we don't have to choose to go near Him. We don't have to choose to strive for an ordered life centered on Him the way He designed it, but He asks and invites us to. We feel the magnet's pull whether we recognize it as God or not. When we don't accept his invitation, that's when it's disordered. Does that make sense? You've heard me say ordered and disordered a few times before now. When we're in order with God's design, we're with Him. That doesn't mean everything is perfect and peachy, but it's ordered. It's how it's supposed to be within God's design. That being said. What is sex for?

Student: "Babies."

Sex is procreative. What else is sex for?

Student: "Some people use it for pleasure."
Laughter.

Girl, you're right! I thought y'all would be shy about this. I'm glad you're not. Some people do misuse sex solely for pleasure. Pleasure is not what it is for but is a fruit of it. Sex is not supposed to be used solely for pleasure, but sex is pleasurable.

Student: "Is it to like finalize your marriage?"

Yes, to renew your wedding vows.
Confused look.

Oh! You're talking about consummating your marriage. Yes, that, too.

Sex is for two things: 1. Procreation 2. Unification. Physical intimacy is not just sex, is it? Some of you have boyfriends. Do you hold his hand?

Students: "Kissing."

Yeah, kissing. Why do you express love through physical intimacy?

Student: "I don't know why. Like really. I wonder why."

Why do people express love through touch? Those of you who have really loving parents, hopefully, all of you, do they ever just give you a hug or a squeeze?

Students: "Yeah...."

Sometimes, as you get older, you can get uncomfortable and be like, "Mom... come on." My mom insists on giving like 5,000 hugs whenever we leave, and I'm always like, "Mom... come on, I'm going to see you tomorrow." Or at least I hope I will. What is physical intimacy? What is physical touch?

Student: "It's love."

It's love. It's an expression of love, so why do we express it through physical touch? Why don't we just say, "I love you?"

Student: "It's more intimate."
Student 2: "It like shows it."
Student 3: "It's more real."
Student 4: "Actions speak louder than words."

Exactly. Yes, all correct. So what you're doing through physical intimacy is you're full of love, and it spills over onto the other person. When it comes to a parent/child relationship, it's something simple like a hug or a kiss on the forehead. Sometimes, my daughter comes and snuggles next to me, and I'll brush my hand through her rose gold hair or gently rub her back. From a parent/child perspective, it's a simple, meaningful touch to say, "I love you." There are no strings attached. No conditions. When it comes to dating though, it may be hand-holding or kissing. How many of you get tingly when your boyfriend holds your hand or you kiss? *Lots of chatter.* You get butterflies, right? It's pleasurable, but it's not just not. That touch signifies something, or it should. It signifies, "I love you," or at the very least am starting to. Before we move on, there was a question about how far is too far. Probably half of you are wondering that right now. It's the age-old question. There is no definitive answer. The answer is, does it lead to sexual arousal? If it does, then it's too far before marriage. So, procreative and unitive. Why is sex procreative?

Student: "Because it makes babies!"

Because it makes babies. How amazing is that! It brings us back to the word fruitful from our wedding vows. Remember earlier, when I said we'll touch on this later? Here we are, back to fruitful. What did God say?

Students: "Be fruitful and multiply."

Thank you! Yes, go forth and multiply. Does that mean we go and procreate like rabbits?

All Students: "No!"

No, why?

Student: "You should say like cats. Cats have a lot of babies.

Cats? Yeah, they sometimes have a lot in a litter, but rabbits have a shorter gestation period.

Student: "Wait! Can animals like get married?"
Student 2: "Maybe they can, and we like just don't know."

Yeah, not touching that one. Procreative. Be fruitful and multiply. Does that mean you have to have twenty kids?

Students: "No."

It means that in order to have a marriage based in Christ, based in the love of the Trinity, you vow to be fruitful. You might one day find that you are infertile and unable to have biological children, but you vowed to be fruitful, which means that you are ordered towards an openness to life.

When I was in high school, I would get really bad cramps during my period, and if I got one while playing soccer, I'd throw up on the field. My mother took me to the gynecologist who prescribed me, you guessed it, birth control to "fix" my cramps. You know what it did? It "fixed" my extreme cramps, but it also made me gain weight and become lethargic. The irony in it, too, was that I actually lost my starting job on the soccer team because of how out of shape I got, so that didn't work out. I stayed on birth control for 12 years. I told you that my husband and I have always had a good relationship. Even when we were codependent, we've always loved each other, even if it was with an immature love, but we used each other. It's because we removed fruitful. Even when we were married, we used each other for the pleasure of sex but said to one another, "Not your fertility. I don't want that." Do you see how that could be a problem?

Here's the problem. It's in our vows. We vowed in the covenant, the pact, that we made with God that we would be fruitful and open to life because why? Because in Genesis, He said, "Go forth and multiply." It was God's first commandment to man. A life in which we are in keeping with God, an ordered life when we enter into our marriage, requires that when we say our vows, we mean them. Now, I didn't mean it when I said, "I do," when it came to fruitfully in our vows. I stripped the fertility away from our marriage by being on birth control for the sole purpose of avoiding having children. Why did we do that? For material reasons. We have five properties that we've renovated; four are rentals, and for years, we were grinding and working hard. I had my own business. Arthur was working his way up through his company. I had little siblings. We wanted more funds for comfort and ease. We had all these reasons, but how we went about it was all wrong. It was disordered. When I was on birth control, I removed my fertility.

When I had sex before marriage, I was saying, "Here's my body. Here's my soul. I'm giving it to you," but without the vows that were designed to go along with that gift of my entire being. Every time you have sex in marriage, you are renewing your marriage vows. **Every single time.** It doesn't mean every single time is the best sex of your life. *Gasps and laughter.*

I thought they'd like that line, but it's true. This isn't some romantic comedy. It's real life. Sheesh, sometimes you even have to schedule times to be intimate because otherwise, you wouldn't find the time to connect with one another.

Every single time you have sex with your husband, you're renewing your wedding vows. Did you know that? That's how serious it is. It doesn't mean it can't be joyful. It doesn't mean it can't be pleasurable. Those are fruits of a good relationship and marriage and the sexual embrace within it. It does mean that you need to be open to life.

Now, if we're not supposed to have twenty babies, then how does this work? You might have heard of Natural Family Planning. It gets a bad rap because it used to be based on set cycle times and didn't have the wiggle room to accommodate women's unique bodies and cycles all being a little different. They didn't know enough back then to fully understand the female body. For those of you who are not on birth control, I want you to think about your month. You have your period. You go through a cycle; we're going to get a little technical, so bear with me, a cycle of dryness. Then it progresses, and you get a little cervical mucus. And, then, in the times when your body is most fertile, that's when it looks like you cracked an egg in your underwear, minus the yoke. *Laughter.* I know. I know, but you know what? These are our bodies that God gave us. It's actually really, really cool. When I got off birth control and started tracking my cycle...

Student: "I'm going to throw up."

Haha, you can start tracking your cycle right now. You don't have to wait until you're tracking just for signs of fertility. When you start tracking, you begin to learn your body's patterns, like when your period is going to start, when you may be a little tired, or when you might have tons of energy. It's all hormones. Birth control pumps your body with synthetic hormones to make your body think that it's pregnant. I didn't realize that.

Students: "Wait, what?"

Birth control, through synthetic hormones, tricks your body into thinking it's pregnant. Our bodies are not designed to have forty children. We typically ovulate every month, so if we got pregnant every time, that'd be a problem. That'd be ridiculous. So, what do you do?

Sometimes, you need to space out children. I had a c-section last year, for example, and have to wait until at least a year from my daughter's birth until I get pregnant again for medical reasons. Spacing out children for a just cause, not for a purely selfish reason, is totally acceptable. Sometimes, spacing out children or accepting that you should avoid having more children in the future for medical, economic, or societal reasons is the right path. In my and Arthur's case, in our first four years of marriage, it was for purely selfish reasons that we didn't want to have children. Well, and to be fair to Arthur, he has always been open to having children when I was ready, but I wanted to make sure we had enough money and not *just* enough. We had enough. I wanted to make sure our children were completely comfortable. My mother had me when she was twenty-one. We were on food stamps for a little while when I was a child. I was avoiding having children because I was scared. I was operating out of fear, the type of fear that is never in keeping with God and His will. Operating out of fear often happens when we aren't in a close relationship with Him and are unable to hear His voice or trust Him.

When you're tracking your natural cycle and you're married, what should happen is that your husband enters into that conversation. He should know almost as much about what's going on with your body as you do. You should be having that conversation together. What happens when this is the case? When a husband and wife converse about and understand this together? Good things, right? Good fruits because it's in keeping with the "I do" they said to fruitfully in their vows with God. My husband and I have grown even closer together since we entered into this conversation about our fertility together.

Do you remember that Fulton Sheen quote I shared with you a few of chapters ago? The one I shouted out while y'all were leaving. The part that I really wanted you to get was when Sheen says that the man and the woman are fused together in God's fire. I like to think of it like a forge. Do you know what a forge is? When metal or iron is forged together to become something new and stronger. That's how strong the marital bond is. That's what God designed for marriage, so when you say, "yes freely, yes totally, yes faithfully, and yes fruitfully" and include the fruitfully, you're saying "yes" to God fusing the two of you together in that fire. It's a different fire than the fires of hell. It's a good fire like the Holy Spirit's fire.

Student: "I was just wondering, is sex like, not illegal..., (*Laughter*), is it like, even when you are married, do you only have it when you're trying to have a baby?"

No. Good question. What happens in a month when you're trying to avoid for just cause? Like in my case right now, I shouldn't get pregnant until it is medically deemed okay to do so, and even with that, I'd like to get my body back in shape. That sounds selfish, but to prepare for the next baby, you should prepare your body to get ready for the next baby, to make sure it's healthy enough to provide what a future baby may need. During your cycle, when you're not trying to get pregnant, you have sex in the infertile window of your cycle.

Our bodies are incredible, y'all. I know you might be thinking, "Yay, we're talking about sex. I'm not even thinking about that right now." You might not be in a situation to think about it for another ten years, but even now, even today, just go look into our bodies. God made them remarkable, and learning about them now gives us so much understanding. I was really tired this week, and now I know it's because ovulation is coming up next week. Sometimes, you get acne, and you're like, "What?! How'd that happen?" Well, it's your hormones. They're telling you something is happening in your body. There are many mechanics that I'm not going to go into, but it's super cool just to know your body. So, yes, you can have sex when you're not trying to have a baby. The second part of what sex is for is unity.

When you are connected with your spouse, how do you express physical intimacy? Through touch. Arthur and I still hold hands. I remember the first time we held hands in the cafeteria at school. He reached over and gently cupped my hand while I melted, blushed, and ate my peanut butter and jelly sandwich. And now, twenty years later, we still hold hands. Holding hands and kissing are good. They help us express our love, but please remember to avoid anything that leads to sexual arousal before marriage. The sexual embrace was made solely for marriage. What's the problem with sex outside of marriage? I'm not going to stand here and tell you that sex is bad. Sex is not bad. Sex is designed by God. St. Pope John Paul II did a series of talks over four to five years that are now known as *Theology of the Body*. His talks were all about the goodness and beauty of the sexual embrace. Not good as in a solely pleasurable way. Good in a way that points us to God.

When you express your love physically, whether it be for something as simple as a handhold or something as complex as sex, you're connecting with your spouse in a way that you do not connect with other people. I'll say that again. Entering the sexual embrace with your spouse is entering into a connection that you do not and should not have with other people. If we take sex outside of marriage, it becomes disordered. If we have multiple partners, we're shattering what sex it meant to be. If we show up to a marriage and have had multiple partners, we're coming in with heavy baggage. We all have our own baggage and our own wounds. We don't need that baggage too, I assure you. That mutual trust and vulnerability are a lot harder to reach when you come in with that type of baggage. Why?

Because there's comparison. There's always a comparison. There's also a lot of shame, whether hidden or out in the open. You have to work through all of that and heal.

Sex with multiple partners is definitely something I do not recommend. I also don't recommend the route I took with having sex before marriage for this reason. It wasn't until the past few years that my husband and I realized that we were still living in mortal, sexual sin *in* our marriage. Even when I got off birth control, we were doing things in a way that was not in keeping with God's design for sex. I won't go into details, but it's called the sin of Onan. That's what it's called. If you want to look that up, then go for it. What did that do? What did it do when, even in marriage, my husband and I were using each other by removing our fertility from the sexual embrace? It put a wedge between us that we did not know existed until it was gone, and we saw it for what it was.

I've been on all sides of all of this. I've been in a state of mortal sin for having sex before marriage, in marriage while still in a state of mortal sexual sin, and living out my marriage in a state of grace. You may be thinking, "So? You had sex with your boyfriend, but look at you. It all worked out. You married him." To which I say, yeah, you're right. It did end up working out. I thank God for that every single day of my life, but do you know how much ugliness we had to wade through to get to where we are now? It took five to ten years of our marriage to work through the mess we had created for ourselves by removing God from our physical intimacy. I am telling you, when we finally opened ourselves to being fruitful and going about sex in the way God designed it, it broadened our love and understanding of one another and God. At this time, while we are trying to avoid pregnancy for a just cause, we often have to practice self-control and self-denial. We finally truly will the good of the other and don't operate in a relationship of use. We die unto ourselves all the time, and what does that do? It brings us closer to God.

I have this analogy I want to tell you. I ran it past my husband last night, and he laughed and said, "Well, at least they'll remember it." How many of you like canned tuna?

Students: "Ewwwww."
Students: "I love canned tuna!"

I like it too. How many of you like sushi?

Students: "Yes! Love sushi!"

Is the tuna in sushi the same as canned tuna?

Students: "NO!"

But it's the same fish!

Student: "Ughhh. No, it's not."

It's not the same, is it? My husband overnighted tuna caught the day before in Hawaii for my birthday one year. That fresh, delectable tuna was not the same as canned tuna! I know it's a fish analogy, and that's funny, but you might just remember it.

Student: "But, I really do like canned tuna."

I do, too, but it's not the same. So, you might think, "Well, it's just sex, and I love my partner. We're going to be together forever anyway." Both sex before marriage and within marriage might be known as sex, but sex before marriage is not the same as sex within marriage that is open to life and a part of God's will. And that's the point.

To make it very clear, sex outside of marriage is a grave sin. Sex inside of marriage but outside of God's design is a grave sin and, though it may not appear so on the surface, is a form of use. Marital sex that is in keeping with God's design for marriage and the sexual embrace is divinely blessed. The point is the first two are mortal sins, and the latter is an extraordinary gift from God.

I gave in to the temptation to have sex with my boyfriend in high school. I think about how young we were when we first decided to dive headfirst into mortal sin, and I cringe. We knew fornication was a sin, but we wanted to. We didn't care if it offended God. Remember how Father Mike Schmitz describes sin? "God, I know what you want, but I want what I want." We grew up with the narrative, "Sex before marriage is bad." It felt like it was constantly being forced on us, so like any good rebel teenager who likes to buck authority, I did what I wanted. I often wonder if a different approach had been taken, if we had understood why God designed sex for marriage and marriage alone, if we would have made the same decision. I wonder if willingly walking into the devil's snare would have been so easy.

Let's get back to our bodies for a second. During our cycles, the times when we might feel unattractive are times when we might be infertile. Isn't that incredible? To get into the nitty gritty a bit, it's the time when there isn't cervical mucus and the cervix itself is low, hard, and not fully open. Is it possible to get pregnant during this time? It depends on the person and the length of the phases within their cycle. Each woman is unique, and though there is a general cycle we all typically abide by, we all have a bit of variation. The times when we might feel super attractive are when we might be most fertile. There is ample cervical mucus, and the cervix is high, soft, and open. If there are no underlying issues with fertility, this is the prime time for a woman to get pregnant. When you are living day to day with your spouse one day, you'll be astonished that he can actually pick up on your fertility. He may not realize that's what he's doing at first, but he can sense that you are fertile by your physical appearance, smell, and actions. You might even be more flirty or more open to cuddling. Y'all, God is astonishing. I really do encourage you to learn more about your body and to one day find a certified NFP instructor who can help you understand your unique cycle.

I am ashamed that I was on birth control. When I finally got off it and saw how my body was supposed to act, I was utterly perplexed and impressed. Here I was, pumping synthetic who knows what into my body when our Lord knew way better than me how a woman's body should work. I started tracking my cycle and seeing patterns emerge. I was able to know when we should have sex if we were trying to conceive or when to have sex if we were in a time when we were trying to avoid pregnancy (for a just cause). There are tried and true methods of Natural Family Planning, and I'm here to tell you they do work. The main components of NFP while trying to avoid pregnancy are self-control and self-denial. Remember those two little words from our "5 Selves of Good" chart? When you are trying to conceive a child, those times when you're feeling really pretty, have a high desire to be with your husband in the sexual embrace, and have all the biomarkers that you're in your fertility window are the times to give of yourself to each other fully physically. When you're trying to avoid, your fertile window is the time to abstain from sex with your spouse. In that situation, you simply have sex in the non-fertile windows of your cycle. God gave women periods of fertility and infertility during their cycles. People say that Catholics don't believe sex should be pleasurable. That's not true at all. Pleasure is a fruit of the sexual embrace, but it is not the overall goal. Our culture places pleasure as the number one goal and reason for sex, but they're wrong.

Sex is procreative and unitive. Sex can and does lead to babies. Sex can and should be unitive. It physically, emotionally, spiritually, and mentally brings you closer to your significant other. It's the literal application of the man and woman becoming one flesh. So, why is that "bad" before marriage? Well, let's remember why God designed sex for marriage at all. Every single time a husband and wife enter into the sexual embrace, it's as if they are standing before God, reciting their "I do" all over again. That's kind of hard to do if you haven't said "I do" to begin with. The sexual embrace within your marriage is renewing the covenant that you and your husband will vow to enter freely, totally, faithfully, and fruitfully on your wedding day. It's incredible. There it is again, the word fruitfully. Let's go over it one more time. What does it mean to be fruitful in your marriage? It means you and your husband agree to and must be open to the possibility of children. It doesn't mean that you are required to have fifteen children. It means what it says: that you are open to participating in the creation of life, even if that creation is on hold until the future or is no longer physically possible.

You may be thinking, "But didn't you just say we could avoid pregnancy if we needed to? Isn't that the same as birth control?" No, and I'll tell you why. The ends of birth control do not justify the means. Birth control and other hormonal contraception methods (IUD, shots, patches, etc.) work in three ways: by preventing ovulation, inhibiting sperm mobility, and interfering with implantation if the first two methods fail and fertilization does occur. If an egg is released and a sperm is able to fertilize it, then a zygote, a new human life, is formed. Hormonal contraception then makes the woman's body inhospitable so that the blastocyst is unable to implant and live on. In other words, it aborts the baby. I don't think enough Catholics know this reality. I didn't fully, and I pray that God has mercy on me. I sometimes wonder, if I do make it to heaven one day, how many of my children who were killed in this way will be waiting for me there, and it's crushing to think about. Absolutely crushing...

Our bodies are not mistakes. They were designed by the almighty and everliving God. He does not make mistakes. He designed a man and a woman's body to enter into the sexual embrace to bring life into the world, which we'll get more into next time, to bring them closer in their union, and to connect them with Him. As spouses, we share in the eternal exchange of love of the Trinity. The Catechism of the Catholic Church says that in the joys of their love, God gives spouses here on earth a foretaste of heaven. Physical intimacy in marriage is a gift exchanged between a husband and a wife. This gift is given with their minds, their hearts, their bodies, and their souls. It's given with everything that they are and all that they have to give. It's true. It's good. And, it's beautiful.

Whew. Action-packed talk. I've been anticipating that one for months. Our culture makes sex out to be some thoughtless pastime with zero consequences or just something you do when you feel you love somebody, like it's the next logical step in any good relationship. The fulfillment of God's love through physical expression with your spouse, aka the sexual embrace in marriage, can't even be compared to something so distorted. It's in an entirely different realm, a spiritual realm. I hope they gathered that much. Ultimately, I think it comes down to worth. How much do you value yourself? Do you see yourself and love yourself the way God sees you? Do you trust Him to know what's best for you? I hope they do. Ah, well. Lord, please give these young women the fortitude they need. Please help them to see that fornication is canned tuna and... haha, I'm done. I'm done, but really, please open their hearts to you and help them to understand your love. And, Lord, I know I've said it a thousand times before, but thank you for giving my mother the strength to choose life for me. Thank you for the woman whose name I will never know, who had the courage to share your message amid an atmosphere of death and suffering.

Blessed Mother, thank you for your help today. I give it all to you for your son. Amen.

What Did You Learn?

Class One
- I loved your talk today! I feel like there is so much shame around that topic as teenage girls, and I love how you said it's not a bad thing. Obviously, Jesus wants us to wait for marriage, and that's what we are supposed to do, but I like how you related that to your life too, and how you didn't but should've, you know, because we related a lot.
- Sexual intercourse with your spouse.
- That we should truly wait until marriage if we are going to have sex. It is supposed to be something special, and it's where the soul and body unite in one.
- I learned today that waiting for marriage is the right and most sacred thing to do.
- I learned that having physical intimacy is for after being married and mostly for making children. *Note here: Please don't miss the significance of the unification of sex between spouses. Sex is a beautiful gift from God to join in His love even when a couple is infertile or too old to physically have babies.*
- Marriage is built on more than physical.

Class Two
- About sex and what it values.
- I learned that sex is good and is not evil. *Yes, sex within marriage can and should be a transcendent good, a foretaste of heaven here on earth. When sex is a form of use, whether inside or outside of a marriage, it is not.*

Class Three
- Nobody is perfect.
- Physical Intimacy and how to balance it with desire.
- Marriage lessons have been good!

Class Four

- When you start feeling sexual tension in your relationship, you are going too far.

You will find the questions and answers for Chapter 7 on page 338.

Let Us Pray

(If you have a rosary, please use it to pray the Divine Mercy Chaplet. If not, God gave us ten fingers to pray with!)

In the name of Father, and of the Son, and of the Holy Spirit, Amen.

1. "O Blood and Water, which gushed forth from the Heart of Jesus as a fount of mercy for us, I trust in You!" (Repeat three times)

2. Our Father...

3. Hail Mary...

4. The Apostles' Creed
   I believe in God, the Father almighty, Creator of heaven and earth, and in Jesus Christ, His only Son, our Lord, who was conceived by the Holy Spirit, born of the Virgin Mary, suffered under Pontius Pilate, was crucified, died and was buried; He descended into hell; on the third day He rose again from the dead; He ascended into heaven, and is seated at the right hand of God the Father almighty; from there He will come to judge the living and the dead. I believe in the Holy Spirit, the holy catholic Church, the communion of saints, the forgiveness of sins, the resurrection of the body, and life everlasting. Amen.

5. Eternal Father, I offer you the Body and Blood, Soul and Divinity of Your Dearly Beloved Son, Our Lord, Jesus Christ, in atonement for our sins and those of the whole world.

6. On the 10 Small Beads of Each Decade. (5 decades in total)

"For the sake of His sorrowful Passion, have mercy on us and on the whole world." Repeat for the remaining decades.
Saying the "Eternal Father" on the "Our Father" bead and then 10 "For the sake of His sorrowful Passion" on the following "Hail Mary" beads.

7. Conclude with Holy God. (Repeat three times)
"Holy God, Holy Mighty One, Holy Immortal One, have mercy on us and on the whole world."

In the name of Father, and of the Son, and of the Holy Spirit, Amen.

(Source: www.divinemercy.org)

Chapter 8

Motherhood

"The loveliest masterpiece of the heart of God is the heart of a mother."
- St. Therese of Lisieux

What a beautiful day! It's the perfect spring day to talk about motherhood. Spring is such a time of new life and renewal. Lord, thank you for the seasons. I have come to appreciate each of them, even Winter. Holy Spirit, please use me to share your message on motherhood with these young women. Help them to see it as the magnificent blessing that it is and not the ugly misfortune that our culture makes it out to be. Blessed Mother, you are the perfect example of what it means to be "mother." Please give me the gentleness I need to speak about motherhood. O Mary, conceived without sin, pray for us who have recourse to thee. Amen. St. Gianna Molla, pray for us.

Today, we're talking about motherhood, but first, we have to start with something else.

Student: "A prayer?"

A prayer? You can pray if you'd like. *Laughter.*
We're going to start with what it means to be a homemaker. I know that's a fun word. It has about the same reputation as the word "submission." Alright, for this next part, take a minute to close your eyes if you're comfortable. Think about what makes a home. What makes a home? What kind of smells?

Student: "Wood."
Student 2: "Food."

What does it feel like?

Student: "Comfortable."

Does it have an overall atmosphere? Envision your home one day, or if that's too abstract, think of your home right now. What makes it a home? Is it the four walls?

Student: "The people in it."
Student 2: "Yeah, I was going to say the structure."

Like the actual structure?

Student 2: "No, like the people who live there."

The people structure, okay. We've been envisioning your future this whole time, your possible future in your possible vocation. How many of y'all have ever really thought about what home means to you? What in your home now do you really love and would love to carry on in your home one day? What in your home do you not really like and don't want to carry on? You know the smell of Christmas, that Christmas tree smell, and how it gives you all those warm, cozy feelings inside? Maybe you envision your home to have a certain smell, like bread in the oven or soup on the stove, something that brings that idea of home to real life for you.

The word "homemaker" may make you go, "Wait! Hold on. I'm educated. I want a career. I'm not a 50s housewife with her vacuum." But, it's so much more than that. In your family, one day, with your husband, you will help create a home. We've talked about the husband's role and the wife's role as God designed it. We've spoken of order and disorder and how there will be times when the roles will flip-flop or something tragic happens where the wife will have to take on more of the husband's role or vice versa, but in an ideal situation, you and your husband are a true team. You make your home together, and you can start doing that before you have children. You create what is known as your family culture, your family atmosphere, your domestic church.

Take a minute to think through this. Maybe there's a casserole that you absolutely love, and you want to make sure, not every day obviously, that when your children get home one day and smell that smell, they know they are home. Or it could be something as simple as the smell of clean clothes, the tidiness of the house, or a vibrantly colored bouquet that brings the wonders of nature in. Little touches that say, "This is home." What changes a house into a home is that comfort, that safety, and that place of refuge. What makes a house a home is love.

As you get older, and you have a home, even when you live in your apartment or dorm in college, you can make it homey and a comfortable space to be in. Part of making a home is, of course, the decorations and the aesthetics. It's the physical atmosphere and creation of what you envision your home to look like. I don't know how many of y'all have done DIY home projects, but they're super fun, especially when you're doing an entire house. They can be stressful, but it's fun to make a house feel like your own. When you and your husband bring a child into your future home, whether you live in a rental that you're unable to drastically change or whether it be a home that you and your husband have designed, they're home. As they grow up in that atmosphere and that family culture, it's not the four walls that make the home. It's you. It's you and your spouse who make the home what it is.

We talked about our souls and how they're eternal. When you're handed your baby after birth, you're handed an eternal soul. Does anybody know why they're an eternal soul? It's a broad question, I know, but why did God make us eternal souls? Because He made us in His image and likeness, <u>for our own sakes</u>. We had a priest out to dinner last night, and he told us that. He said he used to do talks here at the school and that he shared this message in one of his talks. A few years later, he was sitting in a restaurant, and a young woman who had since graduated came up to him to tell him that she would never forget him telling her class that they were made in God's image and likeness, for their own sakes. I heard this story and just knew I had to share it with you, too. If we're made in God's image and likeness, for our own sakes, then it's safe to say that your children one day will be too, whether they're biological or adopted. Whether or not you have children, we're all called to be a mother in some sense. Edith Stein, also known as St. Teresa Benedicta of the Cross, said, "The destiny of every woman is to be a bride and mother." We're women. Being a mother to all is part of our superpower. We can nurture and care for everyone, though for our purposes here, we are going to stay in the context of children.

When we realize that a child is an eternal soul, we realize that a child is not just an accessory, a clone, or an idol. Remember when we talked about how even good things could be idols? Things like your relationship, your career, and your school can all be idols if they're put before God. Oftentimes, people put their children ahead of God, and they make them idols. What happens when that is done? It results in what's known by some as a Zamboni parent now. They pave the way and make the path perfectly smooth so their child never has any issues. They never have to face hardship. That's not realistic, is it? That's not how it should be. We all have our trials and tribulations we have to overcome, even as children.

Our daughter fell last night. The priest we had over brought his new puppy, and she was playing with it when she tripped and landed hard on the tile floor. She got up, and I could tell she was embarrassed. She didn't want to cry in front of him. I had the baby with me on the floor, and I told her, "You can come over here, and I'll give you a hug, or you can go outside to your father. He's out there getting the food off the grill." She went outside and wailed.

Wailed, but her father was out there. She went to him as a place of refuge. He comforted her, and when she came back in, she wasn't embarrassed. When the priest asked her if she was okay, she said with a big smile, "I'm fine!" We all have our hardships to overcome. At four years old, that's a big deal to her. She ate it and wanted to be brave in front of him, so she pulled herself together where she couldn't be seen or heard and where she felt safe. We were there as a support, but didn't overact with a, "Oh my gosh!! We'll fix this!" Because we can't. My point is even small children face things they have to overcome that we as parents can't physically prevent from happening.

Why did God give us the gift and ability to have children? So the human race can go on, right? That's kind of important. Secondly, our God is an amazing god. He's our creator. Through His love, He created us. It's the only reason we exist. We were born forth out of His love. When we enter into the sexual embrace within marriage and we are open to life, we get to participate in His creation. How cool is that? I've been pregnant to term twice so far. I have no idea how to build a baby. I obviously know how a baby is initially made, but I have no idea how to construct a human being inside my belly. It's the most transcendent thing that could ever happen, and I was terrified of it. I was terrified of it, y'all. When I was pregnant the first time, I'd see a woman walking down the street with her newborn, and I'd say to myself, "If she can do it, I can do it." I was so scared to be pregnant and to give birth. I was scared of all of it. It sounds so ridiculous now, but how many of y'all are scared? Like truly scared? *Most raise their hands.* Exactly. I think it's a natural fear, but we have to realize that our bodies were designed to do this. It's phenomenal.

When you're pregnant one day, you'll go to your regular doctor's appointments to check on you and the baby, and you'll look at the pregnancy apps that tell you your baby is the size of a mango this week and a banana next week or what have you. They're really fun to track, especially the first time. You'll try to eat what you're supposed to to give your baby the nutrition they need, and you'll make sure to get enough rest. You'll avoid alcohol and raw fish. You provide what you can while a human is growing inside of you and strive to follow all the guidelines, but you quickly realize that you have zero control. This is where surrendering to God is ultimately what takes away that fear.

We've talked about surrendering a bit before now and how we can and should give our lives to God, offer our days to Him, and endeavor to do His will. When you open your life to be fruitful, open your body to His design, and He grows a human being inside of you, there aren't many more things to surrender after that. You've surrendered your entire mind and body to His will of bringing this child into the world, whether you realize it or not. A lot of people have shallow fears such as being scared to lose their figure or their me-time. I was so nervous about gaining weight during my first pregnancy and worked out constantly. Keeping healthy and fit while pregnant is a wonderful thing, but I did it mostly out of selfishness and vanity. My second pregnancy was more challenging, and I was told I couldn't work out. I did gain a little weight. I still have a little weight, but it doesn't matter. The things I fretted over, like my body changing or losing my independence, don't matter now because I trust in God's plan. I know He has this, regardless of what happens, good or bad. When I can, I'll get my body back into the shape it's made to be in at my age to be healthy, and I still find time to read, pray, be creative, and be me. I look back at how much time I wasted before I had children, and it makes me treasure every moment even more now.

Some women come up against complications and hardships. There's genetic testing you can get in your first trimester of pregnancy, and if they find something quote-unquote wrong with your child, oftentimes, they'll offer you a medical abortion. Are you going to take it?

Trusting in God and His plan for you and your family is a very real surrender. It's a very real surrender.

Surrendering and trusting in God is the hardest thing for me to do. I imagine it's extremely hard for you to do too, but it's such a beautiful gift because, through motherhood, you fully understand that self-giving, sacrificial love, the same love that we've been talking about between the spouses and God. When your love with your spouse is literally shown in the form of another human being, I can't tell you how cool it is. It's the coolest thing ever, and it's not because they look like you. Our baby has my husband's eyes and eyebrows and looks at me sometimes exactly like he does. It's hysterical. I'm destined to be stared at by those piercing blue eyes. That is super cool, but it's not about all that. It's about participation in God's creation. It's about our love with God, bringing forth an eternal soul.

Let's go back to creating your atmosphere. What do you think should be in your atmosphere, your family culture?

Student: "Religion."
Student 2: "Show our faith."

How are you going to do that?

Student: "Go to Church every Sunday and by building up the faith so they understand it. We prayed every night as I was growing up. When I started to absorb it and think about it, I want to pray every night and go to Church every single Sunday."

That was a part of your family culture. Did you appreciate or do you appreciate that?

Student: "Yeah, and I want to continue that with my kids."

That's great. You can look at your family's life now and see what you like and don't like. We're all going to look at our parents and see what they've done wrong. I guarantee you that our girls will look at us one day and say, "Y'all could have done this or that better," to which I'll reply, "We tried real hard." Going forward, when you're trying to create your own family atmosphere, it's easy to get stuck into thinking that it has to be exactly like how your parents did it, and it doesn't. Like I said before, my husband and I both came from divorced backgrounds. We knew we didn't want that to be a part of our family's story. We made a point to make sure it's not. There are so many other things, too, like where to spend Christmas as a family, with what spouse's family, or what traditions are important for us to keep and what new ones we can make.

You can ask each other these types of questions before you get married. What do we want our family culture to look like? What do we want it to say? When someone walks into our home, what do we want them to feel? Do you want them to feel welcomed? Do you want them to feel loved? Do you want them to know that you're Catholic? I looked around our house a few years ago, shortly after we decided we were going to homeschool our children one day, and I noticed we had like one crucifix. Our kids will not be in a Catholic school with prayers on the wall and statues of Mary in the halls, so I panicked. We went to Church, but in our home, our domestic church, at the time, there was nothing that said, "I'm a Catholic. I love the Lord." Now, our cross/crucifix gallery wall has grown, and I went to a thrift store and got some Marian statues and a Sacred Heart of Jesus statue. What do they do? They just remind us that they're here and that we can talk to them, not the statues themselves obviously, but the people they represent. The physical image brings our attention to their spiritual presence.

I have never been closer to the Blessed Mother than I am now as a mother. I don't know how many of y'all talk to her or reach out to her, but she's a treasure. As a mother, I lean on her tremendously. Have any of you ever heard of SIDS? Sudden Infant Death Syndrome. It's terrifying. When you lay your child down, everything is fine, and then in the morning, they're no longer there. They die. They stop breathing for seemingly no reason during the night. They don't know exactly why this happens, but they suggest laying your baby on their back to sleep to help prevent it. The anxiety of a new mother, especially the first time, is extremely high. When our first daughter was born, I had her bassinet literally right beside my bed so that I could constantly check on her. I was terrified she was going to die. I was terrified she was going to stop breathing for no reason. I woke up constantly to look at her to make sure she was still breathing. When our second baby came along, I wasn't as obsessive, and it's not because I care less about our second daughter than I do our first daughter. I had more trust in God the second time around.

Now, when I lay my girls down every night, I say a little prayer. I say, "Blessed Mother, hold my children tight. Keep them warm and safe tonight." I hold their little faces while I say it and kiss their foreheads when it's finished. If, for whatever reason, I forget to say it or haven't said it in a timely manner, our oldest will stick her chin out at me for me to put my hand on her sweet little cheeks and say, "Mama, you forgot the Blessed Mother!" Now, she even says it back to me and asks Mary to watch over me at night. This simple prayer just gives me hope and a sense of peace, and do you know what? SIDS is still a possibility, though it is rare and less common after eight months. I want my children to live, obviously, but now, I trust in God. I'm not saying that He guarantees that they will outlive me, but I know that whatever happens, He has them, and He loves them.

One of the common questions of being a Catholic in this post-Christianity world is how do I keep my kids Catholic? We've been talking about y'all this whole time. We've been talking about your growth in virtue. We touched on what you should look for in a future spouse and what he might look like, but we've mostly been talking about you this whole time. Your prayer, your relationship with God, your growth in virtue, and your understanding of our faith are the cornerstone for your parenting, or they're not. It's a choice. How are you going to teach your child our faith if you don't know it? If you don't know what it means to pray, what it means to be in a relationship with God, and what it means to be Catholic, how will they? I quickly realized when we were going to homeschool that it was up to me and my husband to pass down the faith. There weren't going to be religion teachers. It is entirely up to us. That's when things got real. That's when I really started diving down and learning more about our faith. Not everyone is going to choose to homeschool, but it's not the school's job to educate a child in religion. It's the parents' job. A Catholic school education is a supplement, and it's why parents pay money to send their children to Catholic schools, but it's ultimately the parents' job. Now, as you're getting older, it's not your parents' job anymore; it's your job and responsibility to learn and understand not just religion but faith and what it means to have a relationship with God.

When you're going forward with your future husband, you can talk about these things. My husband and I do the parenting talk at our parish's Pre-Cana marriage prep retreat for engaged couples. During our talk, we have discussion questions for the couples. I'm going to share a few with y'all for you to think about. One is, what are your top three parenting ideals? Take a minute and think on it. I'll give you a couple of examples of ours. We never want to yell, out of anger, at our children. That's a practical example and one that we have to work hard at.

Another one is that we agreed that we never wanted to put our children on a pedestal above our relationship or above God. When things are ordered, God always comes first, then my spouse, and then my children. God should always be above my spouse. When you have those cute, innocent, tiny children, it can be real easy to put them above your spouse, even if you don't mean to. Lots of people do that. You can probably think of the couples you know that put their children above their spouses. Maybe some of your parents even do that. Idolizing the children destroys the foundation because it's disordered. Once again, let's visualize the table analogy. Two sides of the table are sitting on the three legs of the Blessed Trinity, which makes the table itself sturdy enough to hold the children up. When we have that strong foundation, our children can rest nicely on the top of the table because it's stable enough to hold them.

Student: "In a hypothetical situation, where you've done the best that you can to teach the faith, what would you do if they were to be atheist?"

I mentioned St. Monica for a lot of reasons a few talks ago. I would pray, pray, pray, pray, pray. [St. Augustine said about St. Monica, "And now thou didst 'stretch forth thy hand from above' and didst draw up my soul out of that profound darkness [of Manicheism] because my mother, thy faithful one, wept to thee on my behalf more than mothers are accustomed to weep for the bodily deaths of their children....And thou didst hear her, O Lord." (*Confessions, Chapter XI*).]

There are so many parents asking that same question right now because y'all are growing up in a world where Jesus is not known. He's not, and if He is, He's some mythical creature that has all these stories that people think are fake. They're not pretend stories. Jesus actually lived, and thousands witnessed his miracles. If your child turns their back on God one day, you pray. You pray. You lay the strong foundation of God, and then you give it over to Him. I mean, think about it. At your age, say one of you is an atheist, is your parent going to force you to change your mind?

Students: "No."

No. It comes back to that invitation that we've talked about incessantly. God is inviting us to participate in love with Him, and then we're asking and inviting our spouse to participate in that love with Him and vice versa. It's the same thing with our kids. There are times when our four-year-old says she wants to be a nun. I was alarmed the first time she said it. "What! I would like grandbabies one day." I selfishly wrestled with this idea at first, and then I thought, no. This is beautiful. If that's her vocation, then she'll figure that out. She's four. It might change, but if that's what God is calling her to, then what a beautiful life she will have. The are other days when she angrily exclaims, "I don't like Mass!" I say, "What'd you say?! Do you want to go tell the Sisters you love to sit with at Mass that you don't like it?" She looks aghast, "No, Mama!" There's the sweet spot. I reply, "Right, because that's not true. You love Mass, and you love talking with the Sisters afterward." She really does. You're going to have things like that come up. Your kids are going to want to be lazy about their faith one day, just as I was, and you probably have been at different times growing up. It's our job as parents to help them through those moments. It also helps to provide them with good books that help explain the Mass. I, a cradle Catholic, learned a lot from children's books about our faith while I was reading them to our daughter.

There are other times when the child takes the lead. Our daughter asked to go to Stations of the Cross last week because she had never been. I had told her about them and we've read books about the Stations so she wanted to experience it. It was the first time I'd been to the Stations of the Cross in over ten years. When I started praying the rosary again, it was because she asked me to pray it with her, and when I started praying it daily, it was because she wanted to. Does that mean she prays it every day with me? No, but maybe one day she will. You, as a mother, will get the privilege of seeing God through their eyes. It's all so innocent and pure. They have a lot more understanding of God than we do in reality. Not of the stories or teachings, but "God is love. He loves you. He's our father." They accept it. They understand it, and they love Him back. Their world is so small that they understand love, and they understand the parent relationship to its core because it's all they really know. It's all they've got.

Student: "What made you decide to homeschool your children, and how does that work?"

Honestly? I went to Catholic schools for most of my education, and I didn't know what it meant to be a Catholic, and the same for my husband. It seems to be much better now in most schools, but I didn't know how to be a Catholic. The goal of our marriage is to get each other to heaven and to get our children to heaven, so our faith is of the utmost importance for us to pass on to our children. I also live on a little farm. If our daughters want to ride their horses at lunchtime after they've finished their schoolwork in the morning, then go for it. It'd be so sad to send them off to school 8-9 hours a day and deny them that.

Students: "That is so cool."
Student: "Besides the religion aspect, are they still learning the same things as us? Like Math and English?"

Of course, but in a different way. We're not replicating school at home. It's more of an atmosphere of education. From the Marian statues and crucifixes to classical art on the walls and listening to classical music to language charts strewn about and historical letters, pictures, and artifacts hanging in frames, we try to surround them with visual education as well as education through books and nature and math through experiences. There are a lot of literary books in our present and future. They're learning the same things, just in a different way.

About six months before we had our first child, I started searching for a nanny. I had my own business and was helping my stepfather run his business, too. I just knew that I would need "me-time" and a break from my baby when she got here. My husband, in his wisdom, implored, "Don't hire a nanny just yet. Let's wait until the baby gets here." I think our daughter was out in the world all of ten minutes before I scrapped the nanny plan. You see, in addition to being selfish, I was once again letting fear operate my decisions. I wasn't just scared of being pregnant and giving birth. I was terrified to actually be a mother. I wasn't afraid of the actual caretaking part. As I said, I babysat a lot and had much younger siblings, so I knew how to take care of a baby's natural needs. No. I was petrified that I would fail. I would fail my daughter. I would fail my husband. I would fail my clients. I would fail myself, and I would fail life. I think we all have that fear of failure implanted deep somewhere inside of us. We know we're called to something higher, but we are quick to discard that calling when the going gets tough. It's easier sometimes to invite the failure and make it seem like it was our idea to begin with than it is to work really hard and then fail.

I was scared of motherhood because I was afraid I was going to mess it up. I was scared I wouldn't have the maternal instinct, the care, or the grit to be a good mother. My husband used to assure me, "You'll be fine. Look at how much you love and nurture your dog and horse and all our other animals." I did and still do adore both my dog and horse (both are up there in years now). I remember thinking that the love I had for Shay, my blue merle Australian Shepherd, and Willow, my chestnut draft cross mare, would never be topped. "I'd die for them," I would often say to get the point across to how much I loved them. When our first daughter arrived, I finally had an understanding of what people used to say that would annoy me to no end, "You'll see one day. You're not a parent yet." It used to drive me crazy. "I won't! I know already what it means to be a parent. It looks like a whole lot of work and hardship with some fun lightly sprinkled on top." I was under no illusion of how hard being a parent would be. However, I was gravely mistaken, and my fears of failure were senseless.

Why? Because women are programmed by God to be mothers. Does that mean that every single woman will embrace this natural gift? Unfortunately, no, but it does mean that if we allow Him to, God will shape us into beautiful mothers for our children. He gives us the children that we can handle, that we can nurture, and that we can love, all through His love. They are not clay for us to mold in our likeness. They are made in His image and likeness. They are their own person outside of us completely. Knowing this lessens the burdens on our shoulders, especially from the fear of failure. Does this mean that I can neglect to care for my children's physical, emotional, and spiritual needs? Absolutely not, but I will never be "enough" for my children. If I put the weight of the universe on myself to make them perfect people, and their ultimate foundation is me and my husband, then I've attempted to take control away from God. Things would quickly spin into disorder. It is through God that I am able to meet their needs. It is through His love that I am able to mother as He designed.

And for those of you wondering, my love for my animals didn't change, but my heart was opened to a new kind of love with my children. One love did not replace the other as many people told me it would. It's just a different type of love, much like my love for my husband differs from the love I have for our children. I probably wouldn't choose to die for Shay, Willow, and all the rest of our animals now because that'd be irresponsible for my role as a parent, but I want to reassure you that you can and will still love your pet one day when you have children.

After our first child was born, I would take her to the office and work part-time. When Covid hit, I started working full-time from home. I know not every woman can stay home with their children for several reasons, but I strongly encourage you to discern being a stay-at-home mom with your husband one day before you have children. I used to think my worth was in the salary I brought home and in the career that defined me. When I found my worth as a child of God and realized that the ideal situation for a child in their early life is to be with their mother, I altered that outlook and never looked back. I know not every woman is able to be a stay-at-home mom, but there is immeasurable value in being present to our children, especially in their early years.

Here's a practical tip that might help you discern one day. My husband and I do what we call a "recalibration" sometimes. When we feel things becoming unbalanced in our lives, we sit down to talk them out and figure out how to go forward. One question we always come back to when talking about careers or time obligations is, where are you replaceable? It can seem harsh when you're in a career that you've worked hard for years to get to or when you finally reached a pedestal in your company or what have you, but it's true. Are you replaceable at your job? Are you replaceable in your extracurricular obligations? Probably. Are you replaceable at home? The answer is 100% no, every single time.

Another good tip I want to share with you is to alter your perspective. When you're tired, it's easy to blame the baby or the toddler or the rambunctious little kid for making you uncomfortable or angry. Instead of saying, "You never let me sleep," when your infant wakes you up at night, try looking at it from a different perspective. "Oh, you're awake! You must be hungry. I'm so happy to see you." Even if you're exhausted, even if it's the 10th time you've gotten up that night, come at every challenge as an opportunity for love. When your small child spills the entire carton of milk while they're trying to make their own cereal bowl the first time, how are you going to react? Are you going to scream and yell that they wasted all the milk and made a mess? Or are you going to calmly praise them for trying so hard, help them clean it up, and teach them tricks to be successful next time? Children don't purposely make your life hard or inconvenient. They just need you, and you can look at this need as a burden or a blessing. It's up to you. Your reactions are a choice. Choose peace and calm, even in the tough moments. Try replacing "I have to do xyz" with "I *get* to do xyz," and see how it changes your life. Altering your perspective is difficult, but it radically changed how Arthur and I parent our children. It radically altered how we approach life and our faith.

Let's pause here for a second. I'd like to go off on an important tangent. If you struggle with Mass, I encourage you to try to view it in a new light. Look at it with a renewed perspective. The altar is not a stage. The priest is not up there for our entertainment, and we are not casual onlookers. I used to feel bored to tears at Mass. When I finally was able to grasp an understanding of the highest form of worship there is on the planet Earth, my boredom was replaced with wonder and awe. We are not fans in the bleachers. We are participants in the sacrifice of Jesus Christ at Calvary. God does not operate in time and space. When we celebrate the Mass, it's as if we are literally at the foot of Jesus dying on the cross to save us from our sins, every single time, every single Mass, no matter if the homily is dry that day, your kids are misbehaving, or the church's AC is broken. You don't *have* to go to Mass. You *get* to go to Mass. It is not a burden. It is an unbelievable gift.

If you're a visual thinker, gaze at the crucifix above the altar during Mass and envision Christ's chest slowly rising in extreme agony as he heaves each dying breath. Visualize the blood slowly dripping from every wound and the dark bruises already coming to the light on his innocent shoulder from the heavy burden of the cross. It was revealed to St. Bridget of Sweden that Jesus received 5,480 blows upon his body during his passion. Our Lord was struck 5,480 times. Let that extraordinary number sink in.

If you're more of an auditory thinker, listen as the priest acknowledges all of the angels and saints who have gathered with you to share in this heavenly worship. Let the words, "This is my body, which will be given up for you," enter into the depths of your heart while the bells ring. If you're a feeling thinker, allow the words of the Psalms to wash over your mind and soul. Feel the weight of Christ's sacrifice for you in the mystery of the Eucharist. It's not a symbol. It's our Lord and Savior's flesh and blood.

If you're more of a rational thinker, think of the gruesome torture that the man who lived and walked the earth, named Jesus of Nazareth, experienced on that Friday on Golgotha 2,000 years ago. Think of the millions of people since who have sat before His sacrifice just as you do now. Think of the martyrs, of the past and the present, who lay down their very lives for this, for His body sacrificed out of a love we will only know and understand if we one day see the beatific vision. Find the perspective that allows you the grace to see. There is nothing more transcendent, more breathtakingly magnificent in our world than the Catholic Mass.

Alright, back to motherhood. God gives parents authority over their children. Authority is another word people squirm at today in our culture, and for good reason sometimes, but in this case, it is the responsibility of the parents to provide for and protect their children. It's a responsibility given to parents by God. I think we can all agree that this is a common sense understanding of a parent's authority. Through God's given authority, it is the duty of the parents to train the will and the reason of their children.

Have you ever heard of a child being described as strong-willed? It's often a term of exasperation mixed with endearment used to label a stubborn child. It's incorrect, and I'll tell you why. If a child is stubborn and only has the goal of getting his or her own way, they don't have a strong will. They have a weak will, a will that is unable to practice self-control and self-denial. They want what they want when they want it, no matter if it's a cookie on the counter and it's not the right time or good for them or the shiny ring they know they shouldn't take from the nightstand. I can definitely think of times in my life when I manipulated people or situations to get what I wanted. I'm sure you can, too.

Children with quote-unquote strong wills are unable to surrender themselves to another's requests or suggestions, even if it is for their greater good or the good of another. In fact, one could argue that they are self-indulged, self-absorbed, and only seeking what they believe to be in their own self-interest. If these all sound familiar, you are remembering our "Selves" chart from earlier. It is the parent's obligation to help their children strengthen their will. They do so by training their reason. Y'all, this is an area where parenting gets tough, and many people mentally jump ship. It's so much easier to give your child what they want when they want it to "keep the peace." When in reality, neglecting to train your children's reason creates little selfish monsters. You can probably think of some little monsters who have never been told no and always get what they want, can't you? Selfish children who are slaves to their wants grow up into selfish teens and then selfish adults. Are you one of them? I know I have been.

Children must have rules and guidelines not only to help them grow into the person God intended them to be but to also keep them safe. Imagine letting your kid have full access to the kitchen with all its sharp knives and hot burners without any rules or without letting them know that the burner isn't just hot; it can actually do real harm to their little hand. Or telling them they could play wherever they wanted, even in the middle of the road during rush hour. Those cars probably wouldn't hit a small child, would they? Rules and guidelines can help keep them safe, and they can also help them begin to reason.

Reason can be used for evil, as we've seen in many wars throughout history, slavery, and all things that corrupt humans reason to be justified. Many people have used reason to justify hurting others or solely benefit themselves, but when used in the order God intended it to be, reason is a tool. It's not used to mold children to be just like you, as we stated before, but it's a tool used to bring them closer to God, to help them grow in virtue, and to give them a moral foundation. We can be gentle, peaceful parents while we give our children the stability and the structure they need to thrive. We should aim to lovingly steer them for their better good and the good of others, but it's essentially up to them to reason through what you teach them.

Reason doesn't mean justification. Rather, it means thinking, problem-solving, and acting. If we're going to teach our children to reason, they need help on how to do that. That's where rules and boundaries come in. I need my child to understand and adopt the idea that the stovetop burner is hot, but if she doesn't eventually reason through that idea herself and just blindly listens, then she isn't learning the bigger lesson of thinking through something and seeing that actions have natural reactions and consequences. Before she is mentally able to reason through that, I obviously need her to blindly obey and trust what I've told her so that she stays safe. Obedience is very important, especially during early childhood.

Starting around age 3, kids start asking, "Why," to everything. Why do we feed the dog? Why do we need an umbrella? Why do we have to take a bath? Why are the leaves falling from the tree? Why are you making supper? Why, why, why? They question everything. It's how they process and learn, especially in the beginning. When you answer them, they either accept your answer as truth, they may be skeptical and try to find the truth themselves, or they reject your answer. The "why" stage lasts for a long time. In the case of the stovetop example, when I say, "Don't touch that. It's hot and can burn you," my daughter responds with, "Why?" She doesn't know what being burned means. She, thankfully, has never experienced the word 'burn' for herself, but she's trying to reason through the idea. That's what the "why" stage is. The child is trying to figure out, "If this action has a reaction, then maybe I should avoid the action to begin with." And vice versa. This applies to good actions, too. Our 4-year-old loves to bring in fresh flowers from the garden to put in vases. We started doing it when she was younger, but she does it often on her own initiative now. She knows that if she puts beautiful flowers around the house, then the reaction is mom gets excited, she gets to look at the flower itself more closely, and the house looks prettier. She uses her thinking skills to project a hopeful and good outcome.

We've used the word invitation a lot so far. As a parent, you invite your child to learn, but it's up to them whether or not they do so. You can't digest the knowledge for them. Have you ever had a teacher who was simply a fantastic teacher? Why were they amazing?

Students: "Because they showed us respect."

Okay, did that respect help you to learn what they were trying to teach you? *Many shake heads "yes".* Of course it did. Why? Because they respectfully invited you to participate in their class and in learning the material they were sharing with you. They didn't try to force it down your throat. They respected your personhood and had hope that you would, in turn, accept the knowledge, reason through it, and then somehow use it for good in the future, assuming they had good intentions. The same goes for parenting.

We invite our children to learn and join us as we walk through the lessons of life. This applies to their spiritual and moral lives, too. It will be up to you as parents and as a mother to train your child's will, through reason, to love, honor, and glorify God in their thoughts, words, and actions, but how do you do that? Everything thus far in this chapter has been somewhat abstract, so how do you go about it practically? How do you help them reason, learn, and go about life as they grow? Where do you even begin? Do you know of the Spiritual & Corporeal Works of Mercy? Here they are.

Spiritual Works of Mercy	Corporal Works of Mercy
Admonish the sinner.	To feed the hungry.
Instruct the ignorant.	To give water to the thirsty.
Counsel the doubtful.	To clothe the naked.
Comfort the sorrowful.	To shelter the homeless.
Bear wrongs patiently.	To visit the sick.
Forgive all injuries.	To visit the imprisoned, or ransom the captive.
Pray for the living and the dead.	To bury the dead.

Jesus gave us the Corporal Works of Mercy in Chapter 25 of the Gospel of Matthew. The Spiritual Works of Mercy are a longstanding tradition of Christianity. When anyone ever refers to the practical applications of Catholicism, this is it. Here are our guidelines as Catholics and parents to help us raise our children to be loving children of God. You will live a handful of these works of mercy out every single day when you become a mother.

I remember the first time I heard that said. It was in one of Father Mike's homilies. I agreed with most of what he shared. Of course, we feed our hungry babies, give water to our thirsty children, clothe their naked bodies, and shelter them, but visit the imprisoned? Bury the dead? Those were the two I didn't even want to think about. I've never visited a prison. I've never physically buried the dead, but as I came to a better understanding, I realized that I have visited people who are imprisoned in their own minds or imprisoned in a nursing home. I have attended wakes, funerals, and burials. I've heard it said that visiting the imprisoned in motherhood happens when you approach your child during a time-out to discuss how they ended up in time-out to begin with. Seems a stretch, but I suppose it applies.

I've never buried a child. I can't even begin to fathom that amount of pain and hope that I never have to. When I finally got off of birth control and became open to life as God intended us to be in our marriage, it was a shock for me to find that it can actually be hard to get pregnant. Not everyone struggles to. Some people get pregnant the first time and on the first try. Everything works out, but that's not always the case. One of the first indications that you are pregnant is a lack of a period. When I finally missed my period and we thought that we were pregnant, we were so excited. We were just waiting on that little faint line on the pregnancy test to confirm it. There were other signs that I was pregnant happening too such as a heightened sense of smell and exhaustion. We were so excited.

I started planning. I mapped out their due date and started a registry. I started designing their nursery and more. This is all in the span of two to three weeks. And then, I experienced a very early miscarriage, I think. It was never officially diagnosed, but the way it all played out, it was indicative of something called a chemical pregnancy.

So, I didn't have to bury my child, but I didn't have him or her anymore. It was devastating. It was devastating...

Whew, I hadn't anticipated sharing that story. Holy Spirit, you must have had other plans, and now I'm crying, and my voice is cracking. Please help me to get through the rest of our talk.

Burying the dead as a mother is awful. It's awful, but it is sometimes what happens. Miscarriage is not something people talk a lot about. They think they deserve a child. "God will give me a child. I'm a good person." When it took us eight months to get pregnant with our second child, and I saw other women getting pregnant around me, some who weren't excited or didn't even want their child, I thought, "Wait! We have what it takes to have a child. We can provide for a child. We want a child." Month after month, there was no child. If infertility is a part of your story one day, you have to wrestle with this pain. You have to understand that God might have a bigger plan even if you don't understand it and even if you're suffering. We do not have a right to have children. Nothing we do ever makes us worthy or deserving to be given a child. They are a gift, an incredible gift, and are not ours to keep. They'll always be your child, but God-willing, they will grow into adulthood and live their own lives. So to bring it around, burying the dead may mean your child has left this world and you've had to say goodbye or it may just mean that you take your child with you to a funeral to honor another person's life and pray for their eternal life during your nightly prayers together.

When you're trying to train your child to be a good person, turn to the Spiritual and Corporeal Works of Mercy. They help us answer the question that we discussed earlier: does this bring me closer or further away from God? Sometimes, you'll have to admonish the sinner, and it's not very fun. That's discipline and training of the will and reason, and it's far easier to give your child what they want when they want it so they're quiet and leave you alone. But, we can't do that, can we? That's not the call God has for us as mothers.

When teaching your children, you're instructing the ignorant, right? Today, our 1-year-old discovered her belly button, and I gave her the word for it. "Belly button." Ignorance is not always in a negative connotation. I'm instructing you in your ignorance of being a wife and mother right now, or at least I hope I am, and my instruction is prayerfully giving you hope. That's my goal in all of this. The point is you will do every work of mercy as a mother.

How do you teach your children the works of mercy? It's going to be through what you do in your life. It's the reason we've talked about you so much and about your relationship with God. It's why we're ending with you and your relationship with God. Walking in your life with God and Christ, you will be an example for your children. You are your child's entire world until they grow and their understanding of life expands. They are sponges that watch you constantly, even when they're older, and act like they aren't paying attention. How you live your life will teach your children what it means to be a child of God, or it won't. You are your child's entire world until they grow and their understanding of life and faith expands. Your relationship with God will be yours and their strong foundation.

This part is up to you and your spouse. It's your responsibility to invite your child to be closer to God through your family culture, your actions, your words, and your love. Kids learn immeasurable lessons at the dinner table over nightly family dinners. They learn from family read-alouds such as scripture, Saint stories, and wholesome novels. They learn from projects done as a family, whether they are around the house or volunteering to help someone else. They learn through every casserole made to give to someone who's sick or grieving, every outward sign of beauty you bring into your home like a freshly cut rose in a vase or a new paint color on the wall, and every dollar tithed or time willingly given to help the Church and the poor. They learn from each lesson in discipline and every hug and gentle, "I love you." They learn from every single thing that you say and every single thing that you do. Don't dumb the faith down for them. Live it with them. Grow in virtue together. Does this mean they will grow up to be the perfect little Christians who never do anything wrong? No, but your walk and what you do is the invitation to them for holiness, or it isn't. Start now. Intentionally practice the Spiritual and Corporeal Works of Mercy in your daily life.

The goal of parenthood is to create saints. A saint, with a little 's', is anyone in paradise with God in heaven. There is no secret key to being the perfect parent. My husband and I are bumbling along, trying to figure it all out as we go and do our best, just like any other good parent. As I mentioned, I am not enough for my children and never will be, but just as Jesus multiplied the fishes and the loaves to feed the 5,000, Christ will take my meager offering of being the best parent I can be and make it infinitely better. St. Ignatius of Loyola said, "Act as if everything depended on you; trust as if everything depended on God."

I mentioned a discussion question from our Pre-Cana parenting presentation earlier. Here are a few more for you to think about. What makes you nervous about becoming a parent? What areas do you think you'll struggle in? How can you work on these before becoming a parent? It's really fun, y'all. Parenting is hard and humbling, but it's a lot of fun. The culture tells you it's ugly and unworthy of your time, but there isn't much in the world that's more beautiful than the face of a mother the first time she lays eyes on her child or the dedication of a couple to provide and protect for their child(ren) every single day, no matter the circumstances. Before we married, I told my husband that I would commit to having two children, tops. He wanted at least four but agreed to compromise. To be honest, I wasn't sure I wanted any, but I knew he wouldn't marry me if I wasn't open to children. I also knew that you have to have at least two so the only child isn't a brat. I was ridiculous, y'all. I thought I could control everything and tried to. When we struggled to get pregnant the first time and then again the second time, God gave me the grace to see. Arthur and I can plan and dream of our family and its future, but it's ultimately up to God. I don't know how many children we'll have now. I'm leaving it up to the one who knows best, and I'm excited to see how things turn out for this little King family.

You probably won't get a trophy or world-renowned recognition for being a mother. You won't, but every single moment, whether monotonous or grand, that you say,

"Yes," is a moment to be a vessel for Christ's love to your child. Every "yes" to burping your baby after they've spit up on you for the 100th time. Every "yes" to potty-training your toddler when you just don't understand how tee-teeing in that white ceramic basin could be so scary. Every "yes" to teaching your child how to bake cookies while you watch flour poof into the air and all over the floor. Every "yes" to consoling your preteen when in the next hour you know they may resist your love yet again. Every "yes" to helping your teenager learn to fly by giving them the wings needed for independence, knowing that that means they'll fly away from you. And, with every "yes" to being the nest, they can always come back home for unconditional love and rest. Your "yes" in your child's lifetime will number more than the stars in the sky. It isn't just a sign or a symbol of love. You're not just showing love to your child by providing and protecting them. You're not kind of like love or an expression of love to them. You're not a symbol or a sign of love. You *are* love to them. The choices you make in every single moment of every single day will be Christ to another eternal soul that God put here on this earth, or they won't. It's your choice.

Motherhood is such a sacred calling. I pray all of you who desire it experience its beauty and goodness one day.

This talk was broken up into two parts in person.

Part 1: I was surprised there weren't more questions, even just practical ones. Maybe they'll come later. The main point is to understand that we were all intentionally created by our Creator and designed to create. Tongue twister, but life-altering. A student has stayed behind to talk. "Mrs. King, I've always wanted to be a mother. What is your favorite part of being a mom?" Wow, good for her! It took me years to embrace the yearning to be a mom. "Your desire to be a mother is beautiful. My favorite part is participating in creation with God. I get chills just thinking about it." She looks puzzled. "I was the one who messaged you on social media." Ohhh, I recall. She doesn't believe in God. "I see, so my first answer doesn't hit home with you too much, does it?"

Shakes her head no. "Well, the second best thing about being a mom is how challenging it is while being so beautiful simultaneously. It's hard work every day, but it's noble." She goes a bit into her career calling, foster care work, a noble one indeed, and I say to her, "You will see the pits of hell." She shoots back, "Someone has to do it." I smile. "You're right. Someone does. You will have many opportunities to give love to many people, and you can be a ray of hope and love to the children you'll come across. It will help you shape your own motherhood. And I will pray for you. I've tried life with and without God. It's a lot harder without Him." Lord, please watch over this sweet young woman as she strives to bring love to some of the most broken areas in our world. Holy Spirit, thank you for giving me the words today. Blessed Mother, please be with these women when they become mothers. Show them what it means to be "mother." Amen.

Part 2. Aw, one of them hugged me on the way out. I cannot believe I just got so choked up in front of everyone. Honestly, I'm bound to pull it together and get better at this speaking thing at some point.

The same student from last time has stayed behind. "Mrs. King, I have something to tell you." She looks pretty serious. Worried, I ask, "Is everything okay?" She smiles, "Oh yes, I just want to tell you something that's happened to me. I don't know how to describe it, but I got this feeling of being very overwhelmed this past weekend. I can only describe it as wanting more. I called my boyfriend's mom and asked if I could go to Mass with them. She said I was welcome anytime, and Mrs. King, it was the first time I've ever felt God's presence at Mass." Whelp. Here I am crying again, and I have chills from head to toe. "Ohhhh, that's incredible! I'm so happy for you! You've opened your heart to His love! That's amazing!" We talked a bit more, but I couldn't believe it. I've been praying for this sweet young woman, all of them but especially this one, since the moment she told me a few months ago that she was an atheist. God, you're so good. You gave her the grace she needed to see you. Thank you! I called my stepmom as soon as I got to my car to tell her the story. She hooted and hollered so loudly you would have thought I told her she had won a million dollars. Bad example. She wouldn't care if she won the lottery. You would have thought I told her she was having another grandchild! We celebrated, not for us, but for this young woman and for God. Young lady, you know who you are. Welcome home. We're so glad you're here.

Lord, thank you.

What Did You Learn?

All Classes

- I learned that with raising kids comes with a lot of responsibilities.
- You have to talk with your husband before marrying him about life.
- That not only do we have to be moms and nurture our children, but it is also our job to teach them. It is not guaranteed that they will learn religion at school or learn everything at school. It is also our job to teach our children and make sure they get to heaven.
- Motherhood is scary.
- Marriage is great.
- The things you learn as your child grows up and what techniques are best.
- Thank you so much for coming to talk to us! I have thoroughly enjoyed your talks and have learned so much. We never have anyone talk to us about marriage or children and I feel like we really needed that, especially me, because for some of us marriage and children are only years away. Thank you for sharing your life experiences with us as well.

You will find the questions and answers for chapter 8 on page 341.

Let Us Pray

In the name of Father, and of the Son, and of the Holy Spirit, Amen.

> "O Jesus, I surrender myself to You, take care of everything." (Repeat 10x)

In the name of Father, and of the Son, and of the Holy Spirit, Amen.

(Source: Fr. Dolindo Ruotolo's Surrender Novena)

Chapter 9

What Does It All Mean?

"Be one of the small number who find the way to life, and enter by the narrow gate into Heaven. Take care not to follow the majority and the common herd, so many of whom are lost. Do not be deceived; there are only two roads: one that leads to life and is narrow; the other that leads to death and is wide. There is no middle way."
–St. Louis de Montfort

We started this journey with your present and are closing it with your hopeful future. This brings us to the end of our time together. So, did we get to the answers to the three big questions we started with? What does it mean to be a Catholic woman? What does it look like to be a Catholic wife? What is a Catholic mother?

I believe we did. The answer to all three is simple yet incredibly complex and unique to each person. Here it is.

Seek. Love. Trust. Surrender. Repeat.

Seek God. We truly do live in a golden age for discovering knowledge. The world's database of information is quite literally within our grasp. With the touch of a few fingers, we can find any and everything there is to know about our Catholic faith. There are searchable free apps with the entire Catholic Bible and Catechism. There are reliable sources for all Catholic doctrines. You can even access Vatican archives. There are books galore and podcasts featuring men and women who are just like you, hungry for more understanding and trying to wade through that understanding to apply it to their own lives. Learn more.

Talk to Him who loves you. Start by saying, "Hello," and end by saying, "Thank you for my life." It's so simple and yet so powerful. Be intentional. Remember from way back in the beginning when we went through the analogy of imagining if you had some wonderful or terrible news to share with your boyfriend, parents, or best friend, and when you shared it, they had nothing to give you? No reaction at all to show you they care about you, and then we imagined that you were the one doing the ignoring, but the one you were ignoring was God. God wants to share with you. He's love. He wants to share that with you, and that's the invitation He gives us all. We have so many beautiful prayers in the Catholic Church. I used to think the rosary was monotonous and boring. As I learned more about it, I came to appreciate it for the powerful spiritual weapon that it is. Every bead can be an intention. I've prayed at least one bead for each one of you. For those who have asked deep questions that have come from a place of hurt, pain, or love, I've offered the whole rosary for you. There are ways to do intentional prayer where you don't have to make it all up yourself. That's why we talked about the Liturgy of the Hours, but at its simplicity, prayer is just talking to God. It's asking and inviting His help and His love into your life. And, then we have the tremendous gift of the intercession of the Blessed Mother and the saints on top of that.

If you have questions, that's a good thing. Keep asking why. Your search for "why" will send you into the very depths of the richness of Catholicism. Learn more about the human element of it and its messy history. Don't shy away or condemn it without knowledge, as many people do. Try to understand it by diving deeper into it. What went wrong? Why did it go wrong? Who were the people on the "good" side championing Christ? Look for the helpers, the ones who stood up for the innocent and the weak. There were lots of those, too. They just don't always get all of the attention. From the smallness of our daily lives to the largeness of the life of the Church, past and present, when we try to take control from God and give in to temptations by the evil one, it never ends well. If there are doctrines or dogmas you don't understand, find the answers. Find their sources in scripture or from the Magisterium. I assure you, there are answers. You just have to ask the question and seek.

Seek our Lord's physical presence in the Eucharist. We are blessed beyond measure that we, as Catholics, have the ability to not only adore Him but also to receive God the Son in the Blessed Sacrament. Your questions are good. Seek truth. The Catholic Church is so intricate, so interwoven, and so beautiful. After all, Christ started it. How could it not be?

Love God. To know God is to love God. Love is the next step. God is love (1 John 4:16), so to experience true, unconditional love in any type of relationship is to know God whether you know Him by name or not. To receive the grace to learn and understand more about Him, His Son, the Spirit, His Church, and His creation can only result in love and awe for the Trinity. Through your prayer life, a love for God will develop. Maybe you already have it. We all have the yearning for God's love. We just have to open our hearts to it. We talked about how, as a mother, you're not just showing love. You are love to your child. That's what God is to us. My husband and I started understanding God on another level after becoming parents. You don't just mold this person and say, "You're a little me, and you'll do exactly what I want. Just stay right there." No. You invite them to live life with you even though sometimes they make things slower or more difficult by "helping" or being with you. It's the invitation that we've been talking about. God invites us to do the same thing. How marvelous is that! In turn, we do the same to our spouses and our children. Love is the next step.

When given this grace of understanding, we take on the responsibility of applying God's principles, Christ's teachings, and the Spirit's love to our lives. Remember when we zoomed in and out of our lives? Every minute is an opportunity to love God. Every day we offer Him is a sacrifice and form of worship. Every year that we do His will praises Him, and every life in communion with the Father, Son, and Holy Spirit glorifies our almighty and everliving Creator. It's a choice to accept this call. It's a choice to make changes to our daily life that make up the pages that make up the chapters that make up the book of our whole, entire life. How do we accept His will for us?

Trust God. You can't have love without trust. Why is it called true love? There are many different definitions of love. I love my favorite pair of leather boots. I think they're super cute. That's a completely different love than the love I have for my husband and my children, isn't it? Today, the culture tells us there are many definitions for love, but what does true love mean? It means self-sacrificing, self-giving, fully trusting, and vulnerable. Father Barnabas came to our last Farm to Jesus and said that holiness is love. So, when we've been talking about attaining holiness and helping our spouses, our children, and those around us reach holiness, what we've really been saying is we're helping them reach divine love, the ultimate love, God's love, eternal love. That's something we can trust. That's something we can be vulnerable with. Trust is the next step in love. It's called true love because it's rooted in the truth of and trust in God's love. There are times in life when life can be really, really hard, but we can let things go because we trust.

Trusting in God is part one of the most challenging aspects of being a Catholic. "Ask and it will be given to you; seek and you will find; knock and the door will be opened to you. For everyone who asks, receives; and the one who seeks, finds; and to the one who knocks, the door will be opened. (Matthew 7:7-8) I remember reading this scripture at the bottom of a page of the Stations of Cross booklet in middle school. Every Friday during Lent, I dwelt on this scripture. As a child, I thought it meant that God could and would give me everything I wanted if I just had the faith to ask. It wasn't until I dove deeper into my faith that I understood that though He could give us anything and everything we ever ask for, He doesn't. Why? Because He knows what is best for us, and what is best for us might not necessarily mean that our time on Earth will be without suffering. It's easy to trust God when our lives are going just as we plan, when every puzzle piece seems to fit perfectly in place. It's a whole lot harder to trust in God when the wheels are falling off the car, and your world is crashing around you.

When we struggled with infertility for eight long months (And please, I beg you, pray for women who struggle to conceive and/or never receive that positive pregnancy test. They understand the meaning of the word agony.), I asked, "Why? Why God? Why won't you give us a baby right now? We're ready. We're a loving family who can provide for a child. Why did you give a child to that woman who didn't want one when we want one so badly?" What did my "why" show? It displayed my extreme lack of trust in a God whom I know and love. I have faith that He knows what's best for me, no matter how awful it may look to me. My lack of trust was me saying to Him, "You know what, God? I think I have this all figured out. Just give me what I want, or at least let me understand it, and I'll take it from here." Trust doesn't work like that, as I hope you'll come to understand more in your marriage one day.

By trusting in God, we say, "Lord, you know what is best for me. You know my heart. You know every hair on my head. Help me to choose you even when things become difficult. Jesus, I trust in you." I struggled with anxiety, as many do, but especially about possible future scenarios.

"Everything in my life is too good right now. The bottom is bound to drop out soon. I have to harden my heart and prepare. I have to control." The irony is that no amount of worrying or anxiety will change what happens in the future. Anxiety doesn't do anything but ruin today. I can't control the future any more than I can control the weather. It's stupid and futile. Trust in the God who made the sun, moon, and stars. Trust in the God who made the oceans with all its many creatures. Trust in the God who made the sky and mountains, the grasslands, and the animals. Trust in the God that made you.

Surrender to God's will. Part two of the most challenging aspect of being a Catholic, at least in my opinion, is surrender. We can know. We can love. We can trust, but if we don't surrender, then we don't understand what it means to love. Surrendering goes against all of our desires to control. To be clear, surrender does not mean quitting.

On the contrary, it means to try harder by giving it to God. What do I mean? If I woke up this morning and said, "God, you wanted me to talk to these young women, so you do it. I'll sit here while you type it up and package it nicely for them. I know you've got this," that'd be ridiculous. Rather, I can approach Him in this way. "Lord, I am yours to use as you will. I give you my life. I give you my day. I give you this book. Please give me the words you want these young women to hear." Mind you, I'm the one typing this now. I'm the one who has searched out the necessary educational material and organized it all physically. Spiritually, I've done nothing but surrender it all over to Him.

There have been times when I completely black out while typing or talking to you about all of this. Well, not really lose consciousness, that'd be unfortunate, but I literally finish and can't remember what I've written or said. I look back over it or listen to the recording and think, "Wow. That came out of my mouth? Deep." I in no way take credit for any profound statement I ever utter because I know I've surrendered even my words to Him. This is a small example but a big principle that can and does apply to every single moment of our lives if we are intentional.

Surrendering is letting go. Again, does it mean not caring? Absolutely not. It means letting God's light shine through us and our surrender. It means every opportunity of every single day of our lives, right now, in five minutes, tomorrow is an opportunity to do God's will. One of you asked, "What is God's will? How do I do that?" You discern and pray that He shows you the way. People tend to think that God's will is this lifelong thing, which your vocation is a lifelong path, but on a daily basis, God's will is showing His love. It's being a vessel for His love, and you can't do that unless you surrender yourself to Him.

Father Barnabas said something at Farm to Jesus I asked him to repeat. He said, "Fasting without love is meaningless." When I asked him to repeat it, he said, "Anything without love is meaningless." I thought that was profound. When my husband and I took those two breaks from one another while dating, it was because our love was shallow and we used one another. The priest who came to dinner shared this quote by Edith Stein when I asked him about love. Stein, also known as St. Teresa Benedicta of the Cross, said, "Do not accept anything as love which lacks truth." Arthur and I struggled with the trust and the vulnerability of true love, and our relationship during that period in our lives had become meaningless.

I didn't know our day could be a sacrifice to God. I was unaware that it would have any significance at all. Why would God care if I surrendered something as silly as that? He does care more than we could ever imagine. Why? Because He loves us. He made us and desires us to be in communion with Him. Do I mess up? Every single day. We all do. I land myself in the confessional often. It's a daily walk, really a daily climb, to actually undertake what God asks us to do, but it's one that we willingly do when we understand and love Him. He desires us to be close to Him, but it's up to us to accept His invitation to holiness. When you feel desolation creeping in and a crack starting to form in the foundation, repeat. Seek. Love. Trust. Surrender.

So many people say they haven't "heard" God. That's fake news. Did you wake up today? You heard Him when the light hit your face from your window, letting you know that the sun was out to greet you. Did you eat today? You heard Him when your hunger was satisfied as you enjoyed your meal. Did you experience love today through another human's kind word, gentle smile, or loving embrace? You've heard Him every minute of every day for your entire life. You just haven't been paying attention or refuse to see the miracle that is your life, your entire existence, as a gift from a God who loves you. Or maybe you have been paying attention and are still unsure how to love, trust, and surrender, or better yet, maybe you're lightyears ahead of me in my understanding of love, trust, and surrender. I look forward to reading your book or listening to your podcast one day, and I mean that sincerely.

Regardless, Jesus said, "I am the way and the truth and the life. No one comes to the Father except through me." (John 14:6). Was he lying? Do we honestly think that the man who affected the moral compass of the entire world was not telling the truth? Are we so vain that we know of a better way than to do what God, the Son, our Savior, told us to do? I'll let you answer that question. The point is, let go. Surrender your will to His. Note that surrender does not promise you a perfect life with little to no hardships. However, it does promise true inner peace and joy, and it does promise you eternal life with Him in heaven. It promises you salvation.

So, what does it mean to be a Catholic? It means willingly giving your life over to our Lord out of love. It means detaching from worldliness and remembering that you are in this world but not of this world. You are a member of Christ's mystical body, the one, holy, apostolic Catholic Church. As a Catholic who receives the Eucharist, the Body of Christ, you are a walking tabernacle. Every second in your day is an opportunity to be Christ to another human being, an opportunity to be a vessel of the Spirit to pour forth God's love into the world, and an opportunity to do God's divine will. This starts right now. This starts in your marriage, and this starts in your family. Open yourself up to this transcendent love, consecrate your life, and watch the abundance of good fruits surge forth.

When you're driving down the road, heading to your home, how do you know you're going the right way? You've learned, right? But what if you saw cars coming at you in your lane going the opposite way? What would you do besides trying to avoid them? Would you second guess which way you were going? Maybe there's a wreck ahead or a tornado forcing people to go the wrong way in your lane. Perhaps some people are parking their cars in the middle of the street, getting out, and conversing with each other. You think to yourself, there must be some unforeseen obstacle that I'm not prepared to handle. Do you keep trying to get home? Or do you turn around and follow the other people or stop and lollygag? You know for certain that you're going the right way. You've learned and know the directions. All the road signs are facing you correctly, but you second guess yourself when you see others choosing to go back or the opposite way, don't you?

I know you're living in a culture that condemns Christianity, especially Catholicism, and it's hard to be a faithful Catholic. It is. It's hard to be thought of as a radical religious when, in reality, you're just living in and walking by your faith. It's sometimes difficult to relate to others when your love for God is seen as fanatical. Do it anyway. Love God anyway. Try to be faithful anyway. Glorify Him with your very life, your future marriage, and your motherhood, anyway. Ask Him to give you the strength you need to love Him, to praise Him, to worship Him, and to serve Him with everything that you have and everything that you are.

Marriage is often painted out to be a fairytale. It has fairytale moments, but it's not a storybook of "once upon a times." With its ups and downs, joys and hardships, marriage is more of a novel filled with many different chapters. Some are joyful. Some are sad. Some are downright hard. All are true, good, and beautiful in their own way. How do you write a novel? One word at a time. One gift of a moment at a time.

Everything we've talked about, from submission to humility, from trust to vulnerability, God's design for marriage, I know is attainable. How? Because I'm living it. It's the only thing that qualifies me to give you these talks and write this book. I know you can have a wonderful marriage. We focused on an ideal marriage based on the love of the Trinity. Every marriage is unique and different, but every beautiful and good marriage is the same in this aspect or should be.

Once, Arthur's uncle told me how proud he was of me and Arthur for having such a wonderful marriage. He asked what our secret was. At the time, I hadn't dove too far into our faith, so it wasn't my initial answer, but I responded with, "We like each other, Uncle Billy. It's as simple as that." It's true. Our marriage was founded on romantic love, of course, but also on a deep friendship. I pray yours is too. When we gave our marriage to God, it took that love and friendship to a completely new level, a level that we didn't know was even possible. It transcended our marriage, and it's been incredible to witness and to be a part of.

I'll end with this. I recently saw a video of Corrie Ten Boom. If you don't know much about her, I encourage you to read her book, *The Hiding Place,* about her life hiding Jewish refugees during Nazi occupation and eventually of life within a German concentration camp. After she was released from the camp and recovered, she spent the rest of her days traveling and speaking about God's love and mercy. In the video, she held up a glove and asked what it was capable of. Could it write? Could it cook? Could it do anything by itself? No, of course not, but once a hand was placed in it, it could do all kinds of marvelous things.

We're the glove. God is the hand. Let Him direct your life. Let Him be your foundation. He will take you to places and heights you've never imagined. He will welcome you home, to Him.

Let Us Pray

In the name of the Father, the Son, and the Holy Spirit. Amen.

> Eternal Father,
> I offer You the most precious blood
> of thy Divine Son, Jesus,
> in union with the Masses said
> throughout the world today,
> for all the Holy Souls in Purgatory,
> for sinners everywhere,
> for sinners in the universal Church,
> for those in my own home,
> and in my family. Amen.

In the name of the Father, the Son, and the Holy Spirit. Amen.

(Source: The Prayer of St. Gertrude the Great for the Souls in Purgatory)

Epilogue

"O Holy Mary! My Mother; into thy blessed trust and special custody, and into the bosom of thy mercy, I this day, and every day, and in the hour of my death, commend my soul and body. To thee I commit all my anxieties and sorrows, my life and the end of my life, that by thy most holy intercession, and by thy merits, all my actions may be directed and governed by thy will and that of thy Son."
—St. Aloysius Gonzaga

Dear Sister in Christ,

Thank you for joining in the conversation. I pray that this book has and will be helpful to you as you go forward into your adult life. I hope you have been able to think through some of the wisdom shared, have found snippets of helpful tips you'll be able to implement and adapt to fit into your relationships, and have ultimately discovered hope through these talks. So many of us suffer from past wounds that we think will determine our futures, but they don't have to. If you do have pain or hurt, I pray for your healing so that you may see yourself the way God sees you, love yourself the way He loves you, and live more than the half-life that the culture guarantees you. We were made for so much more.

Many of you asked why I decided to give these talks. If you would have told me this time last year that I would 1. Be talking to 17-18-year-old young women about marriage and motherhood 2. Be writing it all down in a book, I would have laughed out loud in disbelief, hard. The short answer is that God told me to do it. The long answer is that God rarely shouts at you. His voice is a quiet whisper over a period of time. Last Spring, without fully understanding what it meant, I went through the Consecration to St. Joseph on the Hallow Prayer App. Then, my stepmother told me how she had done St. Louis de Montfort's Consecration to Jesus through Mary when she was pregnant with her two children. When Hallow also released this consecration, I prayed it too for the 33 days. During all of this, my sister, Yzzy, came to stay with us for three weeks over the summer. We talked extensively about all of the topics you and I have just been through. As I listened to her lament about being her age in the craziness that is happening around us, I thought to myself, "Wow, that would suck to be a teenage girl right now. How do you even begin to date in a world where a guy might be a girl and a girl might be a guy? Yikes, dating and marriage are confusing enough without all of that. There's so much anxiety and fear. I'm glad I'm not growing up in this mess of a culture."

Those were my intelligent inner thoughts, but I heard God whisper somewhere inside, "If your sister, who loves Me, is struggling to find hope, what about the others?"

What others? I have another sister this age, but we tend to struggle to understand each other.

"The others who don't know Me," He responded.

Listen, Lord. I feel like we just met for the first time. I've known you all my life. You were right in front of me the entire time, but I am just now understanding your love. I am just now feeling your presence. I am not equipped to do what you're asking me to. I don't have a theology degree, and no amount of podcasts or books will give me the education I need to share your message.

I ignored His nudges. God does not force us to do anything, and I was not about to be forced to step out of my comfort zone to do this. But, within a span of two weeks, as I mentioned in my first talk, three women I grew up with and I were talking about how crazy the world our children are growing up in is, how we weren't prepared for being a Catholic wife, let alone a mother, and how is that even possibly an issue when we all attended Catholic schools our entire lives? Shouldn't we have touched on this vocation, even if just a little bit? When we agreed something should be done about that, they all three, separately, pointed to me. Why? Why me? There are countless other women, older and wiser, with more children, more experience, more understanding, and more love for God than me, but,

264

Message received, Lord. I'll call the school.

When we ask why, we lack trust, but if we surrender and put our trust in God, our lives are full of joy, peace, and freedom no matter the circumstances. The president of St. Vincent's Academy, my alma mater, is a friend of my mom's, so I called her up one day last summer to pitch the idea. "You know, y'all do a great job of preparing us for college, and you might already be doing this. I mean, I did graduate 15 years ago, but why weren't we prepared to be Catholic wives and moms? It's the vocation that most of us are called to. It feels like something that should be covered in an all-girls Catholic school." I expected some pushback. I had kind of just insulted her school, but to my surprise, she wholeheartedly agreed. She said she'd talk to the principal and get back to me. I made sure to mention that this was just an idea and that I wasn't the one to do it, but surely there's a perfect woman out there who would volunteer.

Alright, God. Are you happy? I planted the seed. Now let someone else water it.

The current principal is a wonderful woman who was there when I was a student, so she knows me pretty well. When she and I talked, I went through the main hot topics that my sister and I had talked about on that blue couch in my sunroom while I cradled my baby in the afternoon sunlight. I made sure the principal knew that I didn't want to be the one to do it, but I had some ideas for whoever did. "Here's where I think the girls could really use some guidance. There are many great women out there who could lead these talks." She looked at me and said matter of factly, "No, you are going to." I replied, "Hold on now. I'm not a teacher. I don't have a theology degree. I have a degree in journalism. I've been consuming a lot of information about our faith, but that's just for me and my family and now Farm to Jesus. I have a pretty cushy life. I'm not looking for a career change." She looked at me with the face she used to use sometimes when I was a teenager and would try to get out of conditioning training in volleyball practice (She coached my volleyball team too.), the kind of look that says, "You're full of it." Alright, fine. I'll do it.

Really, God? Do you really want me to do this? Why? How? My husband reminded me that I didn't like 17-year-old girls when I was one. It's such a hard age. Why would they listen to me? I don't even know any of these girls.

I heard Him gently push back, "You were one of these girls."

Yes, sir.

I know it sounds unbelievable when I say God talked to me. I don't mean it in a mystical way or a mentally challenged way, but when you lean into His love for you and actively pursue His will, you begin to see what He has laid out for you and to hear His voice through the happenings of your day. I read a made-up story recently about a man whose house was flooding. Rescuers came by three times, and each time, he said, "I don't need your help. God will save me." When he finally drowned and got in front of St. Peter, he spat out, "Where was God? He was supposed to save me." St. Peter exclaimed, "We sent you three boats!" God's voice comes through opportunities, through others' words, through the small, still inner voice of your heart, through scripture, and through good. It's never accusing. It never pulls you away from Him. It always helps you to grow in your love for Him. That's how I came to recognize God speaking to me. A few years ago, I wouldn't have heard Him if He had stood before me shouting.

I studied and studied the material I was going to speak about. I watched videos on how to be a public speaker. In college, when Fox News flew Arthur and me up to New York City to be on their morning show, I literally ran when the cameras started rolling. I hid in their break room. They ended up finding me and forcing me onto the after-show, but regardless, I was not excited to be a "speaker." And, then it dawned on me that I didn't have to be. Yzzy and I sat in my sunroom every afternoon and just talked. These talks to the students didn't have to be some spectacular performance. It was just a conversation between me and seventy-nine young women who were all looking for the same thing: purpose and hope.

I felt the Holy Spirit working through me immediately. Some of their responses after that first talk were incredible. They were hungry for real meaning, purpose, and objective truth. Some had hardened hearts, but overall, they wanted to join in on this conversation. After all, it's about them, their past, present, and future, and God's infinite love for them. We didn't have much time together, but I prayed that the Holy Spirit would plant the seeds they needed to want more. More knowledge. More love. More trust in God. More surrender to His divine will for them.

Somewhere in all of this, I heard God whisper "more" to me too. "You can do more."

More? I'm already leaving my children to do this. Peyton Lillis doesn't take a bottle and doesn't like anyone but Arthur and me, so he has to leave work to be with them for me to come here because she won't stay with my mom. It's a sacrifice for all involved. There is no more.

"You can write," He said.

Write what? They're already sitting there in front of me. Why would they read what I wrote, too? But I mean, I guess it's true it's not enough time, and these are huge topics to cover and digest. Alright, Lord. I'll write it all down, but just for the girls! I'm not looking to become an author or anything. I can barely keep up my homestead blog.

I told one of the classes once that these are my qualifications for giving these talks. 1. I'm Catholic. 2. I'm a wife. 3. I'm a mother. 4. I'm falling more in love with our Lord every single day of my life. That's it. It doesn't seem like much, does it? And yet, it's all that I am and all that I have to give. It's my entire life.

I don't know God's plan for any of this, but I do know He has one. I trust that He is touching the lives who need Him most through a story shared, an idea brainstormed, or His word on marriage and motherhood, and I am confident that the Holy Spirit guided these talks. I started embroidering during my second pregnancy as a way to feel productive. It's like painting with thread. One side is being threaded with an array of colors into something that is clearly going to be beautiful. The other side looks like a jumble of colors all knotted up. It's a disaster. There's a famous poem about this and how things look like a mess from our perspective, but from God's, He sees the beauty of His creation. I feel like I can understand that more now.

When my plan for our talks was derailed and some of the students were so angry and hurt, I tried to hold on to control. I had a plan. It was a good plan, and we were sticking to it. The next morning, I relented. I emailed the principal, "The plan has changed. We have to help them. We have to meet them where they are in their anger and pain. I'm bringing a priest in." Leading up to that talk, my stomach was in knots. I couldn't sleep. I talked through it over and over again, prayed for it all to work out, and begged God to open the girls' hearts. I told my husband that I felt like God was stretching me like taffy. I was at the part of the stretch where the middle starts cracking, and it's all about to fall apart. Surely, God was going to fold me to strengthen me soon, right? This had to be God pushing me to level up, and it hurt.

If you've ever played sports, you know what it's like leading up to a huge game. You've pushed through all the pain and mistakes in practice and conditioned your body to get you ready, but you still get the jitters when it comes time for the game. I wasn't intimidated by their anger or the material. After all, God designed marriage. It's perfect in its design and certainly doesn't need anything extra from me in the way of truth. I'm rarely intimidated by other people, but do you know who does intimidate me? Me. When and if I reflect on my own shortcomings, I'm brought to my knees, figuratively and literally. I was scared I was going to mess it all up. I was scared I was going to ruin the plan. I was scared I would fail the girls and those who put their faith in me to rise to the occasion. I used to feel the exact same way before a big game. It all came down to me, and what if I wasn't up for the task? What if I failed?

About an hour before that talk, I heard a quiet voice inside say, "You're trying to control this. You're not placing your trust in me. I have them, and I have you. Surrender." I have stepped foot into my high school a total of three times since I graduated before all of this, once for a reunion, once for an honor society speech, and once for a career talk. During the career talk, I asked the girls, "What is Public Relations?" A student answered, "It's when you control what other people think about you or your business." Puh-lease, don't I wish. You can't control what other people think. Not really. You can spin things to seem attractive or unattractive, but ultimately, if an idea takes root in someone's mind, it's through their acceptance of the idea based on, hopefully, their own experience or understanding or the experience or understanding of someone they trust. That's what separates us from robots, right? We are capable of reasoning through thoughts and ideas. No, I couldn't control this outcome despite how much I wanted to. All I could do was prepare and surrender.

Yes, sir. I give it all to you.

I prayed a few prayers from Father Ripperger's Deliverance Prayers book and turned on some Gregorian chants as I got ready. Instantly, my stomach was fine. No more knots. I don't typically listen to Gregorian chants for fun, but I've heard that demons hate those chants. I knew they weren't too keen on what I was doing, so I figured it could only help the situation. I kissed my family goodbye, blared Brother Isaiah's happy and upbeat music in my red mom bus, and got excited. It felt like a soccer game on steroids, and I wasn't alone. I had God. I had Father Barnabas, who had said "yes" to my call for help immediately without question when I had called him. I had the principal, the vice principal, and all the teachers. I had my husband who encouraged and supported me the entire way, and I had my two little girls who would one day be in these young women's shoes. No, I wasn't alone. I consecrated my life last year, and I don't recognize it anymore because it's not mine. It's His.

I encourage you to take a leap of faith and offer your life to our Lord. You'll be amazed, I promise. Have you ever seen the little black and white rectangle dominoes standing up in an intricate design? In a spiral pattern or some other complex pattern. All it takes is one tiny push on the front domino, and all the rest follow suit. They all fall seamlessly unless one of the pieces isn't lined up correctly. It somehow shifted, and the shift messes up the whole pattern. I think of sin like this. God has a beautiful plan and pattern for our lives. He gently nudges, and if we say "yes" to His will, the pieces begin to fall into place.

When we say "no", one of the pieces gets out of position, and the whole thing comes to a standstill. When this happens, none of the pieces going forward are able to fall as they were designed. When we say "no" to God, we're saying that we know better than He does. We're putting ourselves and our needs before Him. Are we really that arrogant? Yes, we are, but we don't have to be. We have free will, and love is a choice. Love is a commitment. Love is freely, totally, faithfully, and fruitfully saying, "I do." I choose love. Our love for God trickles into every other aspect of our lives. We are His vessels, made to spread His love to those around us. Whatever that may mean for you, dear sister, I pray you always keep your gaze focused on our almighty Creator. You matter to the one who created the entire universe, and He loves you.

To the young women who sat through these talks, this book was written for you. I apologize it's not directed at you the whole time, and I couldn't articulate everything I intended to in person. I'm much better in writing than I am in talking, but nevertheless, if you are the only ones who ever see or hear any of this, know this. You are important to me. Not because I know you because I don't, but because God loves you. He wanted you to hear all of this. He made my life rather uncomfortable to do so. As I type this, my 1-year-old is yelling at me for not feeding her for the fifth time in ten minutes (the girls are empty!) and my 4-year-old is off collecting flowers from the garden to put in the 15th vase she's pulled down off the shelf to strategically place around our home. It smells like a florist shop in here. We open for business next week. No, this hasn't been the easiest journey, for me or for you, but I would and will do it all again for you to hear that you matter. You're a child of God, and He loves you.

I asked a handful of women, Catholic and non, to read this as I wrote it to check my theology and grammar and to determine whether or not it was compelling. All but one said that it would change your life. (The one that didn't say that said I was too blunt. That word has been a blessing and a curse my entire life.) I don't know how it will affect your life, but I know it's changed mine. The moves God pulled off to orchestrate all of this. There were too many coincidences, countless signs, and a crystal clear path to follow. Once the ball got rolling, it never stopped. It never even hit a bump, well maybe a small one. :)

I've always pushed back against authority. It didn't matter who it was. I'd find an argument, reason, and justification not to listen to them. When it came to God and the Catholic Church, I've always believed in God. I was proud to be Catholic. It's in my makeup. It's a part of who I am. Still, I didn't appreciate either of them telling me what to do with my life. They don't know me. "I don't need your help. I can figure it all out for myself, thanks." I was wrong. Humility is a virtue I struggle with, but I am humble enough to admit when I'm wrong. I was wrong, and I made a mess of my life. Don't get me wrong. I've had a wonderful life. It could have been much worse, it's true, but ignoring God caused a lot of heartache, fear, and anxiety that could have easily been avoided. A simple change of perspective altered how I view the Church.

Christ and the Catholic Church go hand in hand. Just as God designed marriage to work in an orderly fashion, He designed the Church to hold our hands on our quest for heaven. I tend to turn things into transactions without meaning to. If I do this, then I won't feel pain. If I do that, then everything will work out as planned. If I learn enough about God and do what He says, then He'll love me, and I'll see those pearly gates when I die. God isn't transactional.

He doesn't need our love to exist or to create. He yearns for our love because He is love. He's not kind of like love or an expression of love. He is not a symbol or a sign of love. He is love. God=Love. Love=God. By loving another, we are participating in His divine love because He is the very definition of love.

I hope this story has been relatable and helpful. At heart, my only desire for this book is for it to bring you hope. Hope for a wonderful life full of love, joy, peace, and freedom, a life devoid of bitterness, cynicism, and resentment, and a marriage and motherhood full of truth, goodness, and beauty. I titled the book *Veiled in Goodness* because I think that in our culture, the realities of a Christ-centered marriage are hidden behind a thick curtain. When God grants you the grace to pull back the heavy fabric, even just a little bit, your life will never be the same. You realize that the curtain isn't so heavy after all. It's as light, as delicate, and as translucent as a veil.

Thank you for opening your hearts up to God's love for you. It will alter your entire life, including the love you have for your future husband and, God willing, your future children, in ways that you could have never imagined yourself. Trust in our Lord, sweet young woman. He's got you.

Will you please say a prayer with me?

In the name of the Father, the Son, and the Holy Spirit.

Come, Holy Spirit.
Come, Holy Spirit.
Come, Holy Spirit.

Lord, we ask you to bless these young women's lives. Help them to see your goodness in all things, especially their relationships. Show them your divine will for their lives, and be with them, Lord, as they place their trust in you. Watch over their future husbands, and help them turn to you. We pray for their future children. Be with these women as they embark on their vocational calling. Jesus, we trust in you. We surrender to you. Amen.

Mary, mother of God, pray for us.

In the name of the Father, the Son, and the Holy Spirt.

With all my love,

Kira

Questions & Answers
Chapter One

Class One

- How do you know when you have found the person that you want to marry and spend the rest of your life with?
    - *Great question! Stay tuned for more ways to discern.*
- I want to learn more about how to find a Godly man and how my relationships can fully embody Jesus. Past trauma haunts my current relationships with boys, on minor and major scales. It is something I would like to work on, and I often worry about finding the "right" man for me.
    - *I love your fervor for wanting a relationship that embodies Jesus. I am sorry you have suffered, but wounds from your past do not have to determine the outcome of your future. We'll cover the rest soon. I'll be praying for you.*
- What is my purpose? Why did God put me on this Earth?
    - *When I got your questions, I asked our 4-year-old the same questions. She said, "To love God, to serve God, and to glorify God so that we can be in heaven with Him one day." Out of the mouth of babes, but she's right.*
- In your opinion, what is a good age to start seriously thinking about having kids?
    - *In my honest opinion, this is the wrong question to ask. "But wait! You said there were no wrong questions." You're correct, but this is the wrong way to approach it. Why? Because there is no magical age to think about having children or to get married or to do anything really. You go through school according to your age. You go through life according to God's will for you and whether or not you choose to listen to Him. To answer your question, though, **now** is the time to*

start seriously praying for your future children. I'm in no way saying have children while in high school, but I am saying that you can add your future children to your list of prayers every day and in that way, think of them.

- How did you know that you found your husband? When did you know you wanted a family and wanted to have kids?

    - *Me, personally? If I had listened to God, I would have known much much earlier than if I hadn't tried to take control and make a mess of things. My husband knew he wanted to marry me when we first started dating when we were 14 years old. It took me much longer to discern. He adores children and always told me what a wonderful mother I would be, so in some way, we agreed that we wanted children were we to get married. It was just the number of children that was up in the air. It still is, but now we're putting it in God's hands.*

- Did you have to help your husband learn to love God like you said or was he already deep in faith?

    - *Yes, I did have to help him in the ways that I was able. I tried to never nag, but I did invite him to join me in the praying the rosary or one of the Hallow prayer challenges on their app. I shared things that I had learned and asked his thoughts. Eventually, he started seeking more understanding himself and started deepening his relationship with the Lord.*

- How do I get my prayer life more fulfilling?

    - *It's easy for us to look at God or the Mass and say, "I'm not getting anything out of this." We are, of course. We have many blessings to be grateful for, but we're a feeling people, and we want to feel like we're accomplishing something like fulfillment. The answer is to love Him more. The how is to talk to Him more. To see Him in the Blessed Sacrament, more. To receive Him into your body and soul, more. Open your heart to God. Ask Him* to reveal Himself to you, and give more of yourself to Him. Instead of asking what you're getting out of it, ask what are you putting into it. Are you intentionally praying every day? Are you attending Mass and receiving the Eucharist? Are you loving others? Are you growing in virtue? Are you trying to become more like Jesus in your daily life? This is every human being's path to fulfillment.

- How to know if you're not in the right steps toward God?
  - *I mentioned St. Ignatius of Loyola's Discernment of Spirits, which he included in the Spiritual Exercises. According to ignatianspirituality.com, "the rules deal with ways to interpret the states of consolation (joy, peace, gratitude, and the like) and desolation (depression, anxiety, fear) that people typically experience in the course of cultivating a spiritual life." I encourage you to look into his guidance for our spiritual lives to help you discern. In the meantime, remember to ask the simple question, "Does this bring me closer or further away from God?" When the answer is further away, even if it's uncomfortable to do so, choose to reject whatever it is that would harm your relationship with Jesus. It will work wonders in your life.*
- Is there any advice you would give to someone who is dating someone from a different Christian denomination? What if you fall in love with someone of a different faith?
  - *Oh yes, we will absolutely be covering this soon. Remember that other Christian denominations stem from Catholicism, so there are many commonalities. However, they differ in extremely important areas of our faith, and these differences affect specific areas our of daily life and walk with God. These areas include how we worship, how we pray, how we approach family life, and how we ultimately view eternity. The most important*

*aspects of a couple of two different Christian faiths
are communication and respect. You must respect
each other's faith while also being able to
communicate your differences and what those
might mean for you and your future family if you
end up getting married.*

- I liked everything you said but I just didn't exactly understand your main point, so I guess my question would be what exactly that was. I just thought your talk was slightly all over the place. I really liked how you talked about the center of every relationship being God. I learned that I should be prioritizing God in everything between friendships and romantic relationships.

  - *Thank you for your honesty. I do jump around. I am glad to see that you did, in fact, receive the point, though.*

- Should you move in with your boyfriend even when y'all have been dating for a while and thinking about an engagement? Are you supposed to wait till you're married to live together?

  - *Cohabitating. In short, no to your first question, and yes to your second. Why? Because you are a witness of God's love to everyone around you whether you recognize it or not. This means that when you sin or appear to be sinning, such as living together even if you're not explicitly in sexual sin, it has a negative ripple effect on those around you. It could affect people you don't even know, such as your neighbor or the utility office who sees both your names on the bill. It may sound unfair, but when you think about it, it makes sense. Every action has a reaction, somehow somewhere. Sin does not only affect the individual choosing to sin. It negatively affects the souls of others whether you realize it or not. Another thing to think about is the bond that is formed through cohabitation before there is true commitment. It's really hard to depart from a relationship with*

279

someone that you may be in a sexual relationship with or even just living intimately with if the need arises. There's a lot to consider because it affects your freedom. Cohabitating constrains the relationship. Even in a super committed relationship, cohabitation clouds the intellect and will. It emphasizes the idea of habituation of living as married without actually being married. There's no distinction between the two, no significant change, which ultimately skews the order of your relationship. In the back of your mind, there's always the perceived ability to walk away.

- What made you decide to come talk to us?
  - *All I can say is that the Holy Spirit's promptings were not subtle, and I listened to them.*
- Was it planned for you to have kids? When you had your first kid, how did it change your life and daily routines? What are the joys and scares of pregnancy? Like how scary is childbirth?
  - *Yes. Overly planned, you might say. It changed everything in a way I wasn't anticipating. We'll get more into that in our motherhood talk. In terms of daily routine, it changed it for the better in more ways than I can count. I can't wait to talk to y'all about pregnancy and childbirth. I was terrified of both before I went through it!*

Class Two

- Are we supposed to pray 3 times a day? like 369?
  - *Haha yes and no. I did have to run through the Liturgy of Hours with your class, so I think you mean 3:00, 6:00, and 9:00. No, you do not have to pray at those exact times every day. Yes, you should be praying even more than 3x a day! Not every prayer has to be a formal prayer though. It can be as simple as a quiet moment with God.*
- How did you know he was the one?

- *I knew he was the one for many reasons. He loved me for who I was. He loved my family and was so good with my younger siblings. He envisioned the same future with me and wanted to be a loving father to our future children. He helped me work through my past wounds, and he was my best friend. At some point, I couldn't imagine a life without him.*
- How to pray better?
  - *Remember that you are in a relationship with God. He is our loving father. Praying "better" may mean just beginning to participate in that relationship with him.*
- How have you found time to prioritize God in your everyday life when having so many other things to deal with such as kids?
  - *By beginning and ending with Him, every single day. I talk to Him in the morning before my head leaves the pillow. I pray the Morning Offering prayer and offer Him my entire day. I read daily devotionals and a scripture out loud to my children during breakfast time. I pray a rosary and talk to Him at night before I go to sleep. I say formal prayers like the Liturgy of Hours, the Act of Contrition, and the prayer to St. Michael the Archangel, and I talk freely to Him about my cares and worries. I give them all to Him so that I can sleep freely. Throughout my day, I try to remember to intentionally be grateful for every little thing- like the light breeze that rustles the leaves in the trees on our 4-acre homestead or the sunlight that dances on the flowers and berry bushes in our garden. I thank Him for the rainy day that forces me to rest. I thank Him when the goats break down the perimeter fence and escape to newfound freedom, as I chase them with my two-month-old baby on my shoulder, only to run into a few kind neighbors who drag them back*

*home to me (true story). I thanked Him when we
had to put one of our beloved horses down because
of cancer. I thanked Him every time our malamute
somehow got out and killed yet another of our
chickens. I thanked Him for the spilled milk that
our 4-year-old accidentally dropped while proudly
trying to show me how she could make her own
bowl of cereal. I thank Him for the radiant smile
on my husband's face and the glimmer in his eyes
when he hears the loud squeals from our children
as he opens the front door after a day away from
us at work. I thank Him for the smell and warmth
of our baby's skin and the joy in our daughter's
heart. I thank Him for the pain He allows me to
sometimes feel because without it, I wouldn't feel
the love. We find time for Him in every waking
moment that we have because every single
moment of our lives is a gift from Him.*

Class Three

- Was your husband always as faithful as you?
    - *Yes and no. We have helped each other grow in
    different ways.*
- How did you balance societal expectations and overall fun
with your faith?
    - *Not well. My faith suffered.*
- I am so scared that I do not want the same thing that God
wants for me. I want to be married and be a mother and
what if God does not want that for me. How do I know what
God wants from me??
    - *I feel you. So much. But, fear (aside from natural
    fear) and anxiety are never of God, so try to place
    them at the foot of His cross to help you carry it.
    Literally, visualize yourself putting these cares and
    worries at the bottom of His cross while He is
    crucified and dying above you. He can and will
    shoulder all our fears. The Bible says, "Do not be
    afraid" in various ways 365 times, one for every*

day of the year. God knows your heart. He knows your vocation. When you open your heart to hear His will for you, your vocation will slowly reveal itself. Remember too that you have free will. Though God knows His will for us, we are still free to do what we want though it should be according to His will. What does that mean? In short, it means our choices should bring us closer to Him. God desires our ultimate good. His presence brings us happiness in all our trials. He gives us a deeper grace because God is a good father who wants our good.

- Is it hard being a mom?
  - *Cliche answer- the hardest, most beautifully challenging thing I've ever done.*
- How did you continue with your faith after high school and after living under your parents' roof? How do you plan to grow your children's faith? How do you personally try and lead others to Christ?
  - *1. I didn't try very hard. I always prayed and was "proud" to be Catholic, but I let most other aspects of our faith go when I was on my own in the early years. 2. With solid faith formation, service to others, and lots of prayers, especially to St. Monica. 3. By trying to walk with God in a way that spreads love to others and by talking to you. :)*
- How would you recommend still leading a life with God if you don't agree with some of the Catholic church's teachings?
  - *First, I would say that disagreement with Church teachings does not change the truth of them. Secondly, I would say, have you attempted to study and learn why the teachings you may disagree with are teachings in the first place? It may surprise you. It certainly did me. The Catholic Church is incredibly rich and deep in history and knowledge. It's easier now than ever to access this*

knowledge. Utilize technology to learn more. Find trusted, Catholic sources. Then, if you still disagree, I would ask you to pray about it. Ask God to help you understand. The Catholic Church is like a deep well filled to the brim with beauty, but at its heart, its message is very simple. Love God. Serve God. Love others as He does. "There are not one hundred people in the United States who hate The Catholic Church, but there are millions who hate what they wrongly perceive the Catholic Church to be." — Ven. Fulton J. Sheen

- How do you live with current social standards without falling into temptation?
  - *Tough one for sure. Rooting yourself in a close relationship with God is the only way. He will make you strong enough to withstand the cultural storm around you. What does this look like? Prayer, worship, and finding a faith-filled community.*
- How should I tell my friends what I know about God without making them uncomfortable?
  - *By living your life with Him at your center. You don't have to "tell" your friends about Him. Your joy and peace will radiate when you are in a close relationship with Him, and they will take notice. If He comes up in your conversations, hopefully, you have the kind of friends who will love you enough to understand that your faith is a part of who you are and won't get uncomfortable. I have one such friend. She is a treasure. Do be careful to not be condescending towards others who may not know God. Remember, He would never do that to us.*
- If I go in and out of time when I pray a lot, and times when I just don't talk to him at all (except when I ask him to give me grace for something like once a week) how can I stay in a period of prayer?

- *It's easy to let the busyness of life get in the way of a lot of things, but somehow, it's extra easy to let it get in the way of our relationship with God. Pray to Him to help you get rid of your distraction and forgetfulness. On a practical level, write yourself little notes or set reminders to say a short hello and thank you to Him or dedicate a specific time a day for formal prayers and to talk to Him. Do an examination of conscience every night before bed. Thank Him for your blessings and ask for forgiveness for the ways you may have offended Him.*
- How to balance marriage and faith and your devotion to both?
    - *Balancing both separately would appear from the outside to be the thing worth striving towards. In reality, they are one and the same. They are interwoven in such a way that my devotion to both is more of a way of life rather than a balancing act, if that makes sense. In an ordered life, God always comes first. From there, all other things fall into place, including my relationship with my husband.*
- What were you like in high school? What experience did you have before marriage?
    - *This is a loaded question. One I'm not quite ready to devolve an answer to yet. It will reveal itself as we go along. In the meantime, I imagine I was very much like you, trying my very best to make it through. In terms of experience before marriage, we'll get to that.*
- How do you get close to God when you are not a believer whatsoever? (not for me but for a friend) How do you get your relationship with your partner closer to God?
    - *1. Well, I suppose the answer is that you can't. God's existence does not rely on our beliefs, thankfully! But, we do need to believe in Him in order to be close to Him. I would (and will) pray*

for your friend. I have similar friends. I love them despite their lack of faith that God exists. I pray the St. Anthony prayer for miracles every day for this group of friends. It truly has worked miracles in at least one of their lives thus far. Pray that their hearts are opened to hear God's voice. They may just not understand His language. 2. For your relationship, it's important to offer everything we are, everything we have, and everything we do to God. Offer your relationship to Him. Pray for your relationship. Talk with your partner about your faith. Ask him to walk with you in it. He may choose not to, but He may. I know it can be scary, but He may be prompting you to talk with your partner about Him in order to help him open his heart to Him. You never know what God has planned.

- What was your transition as parents like with your husband?
    - *This is a dramatic answer, but it's true. It was like watching a flower that was a small, delicate bud open its enormous petals to reveal its true beauty, like a camellia. Our relationship transformed into what God designed it to be, and while it was beautiful before, it became simply stunning. Just having the children didn't create this transformation, but having the children opened our hearts to yearning for a loving relationship with God.*
- How to get into having a good prayer life?
    - *Ask Him for a good prayer life. Ask Him to help you get closer to Him. Talk to Him. Eventually, your conversations with God will put you in a loving relationship with Him and give you a "good" prayer life.*
- How did your sister start her spiritual journey after the rough period?
    - *One day at a time. She struggled with anger for months. She sought help in counseling and*

guidance from her spiritual director. She prayed and asked God to release her from the anger and hurt, and He did. He helped her overcome rejection, fear, and anxiety at that moment and will probably have to help her (and me and everyone else in the world) again and again in the future. She rose out of that dark place, on fire for the Lord because in her time of need, she sought Him, and He comforted her. He loved her with a fatherly love, and she grew and thrived in His love.

- What about partying? What is motherhood like? How to not get peer pressured into backing out of your faith?
    - *1. Partying… Sometimes, being faithful can look like zero fun from an outsider's perspective. The happiness and excitement one may get from "partying," which I assume means binge drinking or other such things to help numb us and feel elation, is fleeting. Sure, it can make for a 'good story' sometimes (and even bad or traumatic ones), but once it's all said and done, what do you have to show for it? Not lasting happiness. Not lasting excitement. True joy. True peace. Those are real, tangible, and lasting. They are lifelong pursuits that are attainable through God and our relationship with Him. 2. Motherhood is a wonderful, messy vocation. Some days, it feels like heaven on earth. Others, it feels like your heart has been cracked open. We'll get more into that soon. 3. By building your faith foundation now and by finding peers who will journey with you in your faith or, at the very least, those who respect you for it.*
- Keep giving real-life examples, and PLS BRING A BABY GOAT. *:)*
- Can you tell us more about the devil and how to not be tempted?

287

- *I don't really have time to go too much into the devil, definitely not as much as I'd like to. Not because he's all that interesting but because God's power and magnificence are earth-shaking. The reality is whether or not we realize it, Satan is trying to get us to turn away from God every moment of our day. He relishes in any choice we make in his favor. Working on our prayer life will help keep him at bay. It's kind of like how you get stronger when you exercise. Working on our prayer life and striving to be in communion with God will strengthen our abilities to resist temptation.*
- How to balance my religious and everyday life?
    - *Put your faith in everything that you do. Don't focus on the balance. Focus on God and giving everything to Him. Everyday life will fall into place within your faith life.*
- How to get stronger in your faith, maybe not much of a Catholic way, more like for anyone?
    - *For Catholics and anyone else of another Christian denomination, it's as simple as loving God, listening to what He has revealed to us, discerning what He's asked of us, and letting Him guide our lives by those revelations. He told us to love Him, so start there. He told us to worship Him, so worship Him. He told us to love others, so love them.*

Class Four
- In your discussion, did you mean our only obligation as women/wives is to bring our husbands to heaven?
    - *The goal, spiritually, of marriage is to get ourselves, our spouse, and our children to heaven. We will face countless obligations to prayerfully*

attain that goal, not by our own merit, but by God's grace through us.

- Why must the woman lead her husband to heaven?
  - *We'll get more into the details of this in the marriage talk. Until then, remember that it is a mutual calling for both spouses. Also, in the meantime, contemplate the true meaning of the Sacrament of Marriage. You may answer your own question before we cover it.*
- How to determine real love?
  - *What a beautiful, raw, and real question. Real love is unconditional. Real love is totally self-giving. God is our example for real, perfect love. However, we are all broken humans, so to expect perfect love from another human being can and will lead to disappointment and discouragement, but we can and should aspire for real love in all of our relationships. Real love is truly willing the good of the other.*
- I would like to know a little more about your journey to getting closer to God and how you decided to grow your relationship with him. Did you go through an experience that made you turn to God more?
  - *My journey with getting close to God started with wanting to understand Him more. I became a mother and knew it was our job as parents to pass the faith to our children. We vowed to do so on our wedding day. How would I do that in good conscious if I didn't know all that I could learn about our faith? Through educating myself more on the Bible, Church teaching, Our Lady, the saints, the devil, and more, my love for God expanded in ways that I never foresaw happening. God grants us the grace to want to know Him more, but we are responsible for saying "yes" to the Holy Spirit's promptings. To know Him is to love Him, and it has been abundantly true in my life.*

- How do you know if he's the one?
  - *Do you love him? Are you ready to commit to him freely, faithfully, totally, and fruitfully? Does he reciprocate self-giving, sacrificial love? Will he help get you to heaven? Are you able to help him get to heaven? Then he could be the one.*
- Where do I begin if I want to create a stronger relationship with God?
  - *Begin by talking to Him. Talk to Him throughout your day. Thank Him for the birds' song that wakes you up in the morning and for the stars that glimmer as you sleep. Thank Him for your life, for your parents, for your many blessings, and even for your hardships. Praise Him for this day and all of its immense beauty. It's easy to become so indifferent to the beauty of the world. Be intentional. Learn more about Him. Lastly, ask Him to help you have a stronger relationship with Him.*
- How do you begin to talk to God?
  - *One word at a time. An idea to perhaps start with, "Hello. Thank you for my life."*
- What does a faith-based marriage look like? What should a relationship look like with two different religions?
  - *1. A faith-based marriage is one where a husband and wife "fight the good fight to the end, run the race to the finish, and keep the faith" (2 Timothy 4:7) together. 2. We'll talk a bit about interfaith marriages in the marriage talk, but the same answer from your first question applies.*
- What can I do to help my husband get to heaven?
  - *Wonderful question! I enjoy helpful directions too. Firstly, you can pray for him, even now. From there, progress in your spiritual journey by growing in virtue and shedding attachments to sin. Virtues are good habits that help us attain holiness. Strive to be a virtuous wife to your husband one day.*

- How do I pray without saying already made prayers?
  - *The prayers given to us by Jesus (the Our Father) and His Church (Hail Mary, Hail Holy Queen, Apostles Creed, etc.) are beautiful gifts that help give us the words when we fumble on how to approach the almighty and ever-living God. That being said, God is our loving father. Approach Him as His daughter. You can talk to Him about everything. Praise Him. Worship Him by participating in the Mass and receiving His Body and Blood. Ask the Lord for His mediation. Give Him gratitude for the blessings in your life.*
- How do you keep God in the center of your relationship?
  - *Great question! Very intentionally. It's easy to get caught up in the busyness of life and forget to pray or lose focus on God. Both the man and a woman in a relationship have to intentionally make time to keep God the center of the relationship. Praying and worshipping together is a wonderful way to do this.*
- How would you deal with a relationship when your boyfriend is not your religion or any religion?
  - *There are many people in the world who make interfaith marriages work. There are others who do not. The obstacles prove too great for some to overcome. Does your boyfriend believe in God? The answer to that question is very important for the future of the relationship.*
- How do you keep a healthy relationship and keep the spark?
  - *Thankfully, the spark rarely fades when you have a healthy relationship! When your relationship is totally oriented towards how God designed it, it's healthy and often very fun.*
- What challenges have you gone through like with your relationship with God and your marriage? If any.
  - *The main challenge I can think of is accepting that my husband's spiritual journey is his own. I can't force him to be on the exact same page as me*

spiritually. When I started binge-learning, I wanted him to obsessively learn more about God alongside me, but that's not how my husband learns. He learns at his own pace, more by doing than by reading or watching lectures. I also share my findings, and we discuss them, which is really nice. The challenge for me is respecting how my husband acquires knowledge and loves others and trusting that God is reaching his heart just as He is reaching mine, even if His approach doesn't always look the same for us both.

- What has been the impact of motherhood on your life?
  - *I would not be in front of you speaking about God or writing it down for you and others if I had not become a mother. It has impacted everything in my life, the biggest one being that it forced me to look outside myself completely, and I will be forever grateful.*
- What if you can't tell if you actually like someone?
  - *This is tough. Pray about it. Ask God to help you in your discernment.*
- How to stay involved in my relationship with God going into college?
  - *Find a community that helps you stay involved. We'll talk more about this next time.*
- How to keep God in your relationship or how to find a good guy who believes in God?
  - *Be purposeful. Bring God into your relationship and into your everyday life.*
- How to know you are ready for marriage?
  - *When you are ready to truly love another person with the same love that the Church loves her bridegroom, Jesus, you are ready.*
- What is ok to do before marriage?
  - *Ohhhhh. I knew this question would come at some point. It's coming from the wrong angle, though. The real question is, how do I love this man and show my attraction to him in a way that respects*

292

*his everlasting soul and mine? The actual answer to your question is to stick to the firm guideline of saving sexual arousal for marriage. Kissing and hugging can be done in a way that is not sexually arousing. Many other things toe the line, so it's best to avoid them. You can **use** another person even if you quote-unquote love them. My husband and I used each other in many different ways for years while still loving each other. It wasn't until we learned more about our faith and God's design for marriage and relationships that our love truly blossomed. We'll also dive more into this in the sexual embrace and intimacy in marriage talk.*

- How can we ensure that things will work out for us according to God's plan?
    - *We can't ensure it. God never promised that following His plan would be simple or easy. However, He loves us so His plan for us is always inherently good in the long run even in the times when it may not seem so to us in the short run.*
- What are some basic prayer techniques you find most helpful to incorporate into your daily routine, rather than morning or night?
    - *I enjoy listening to podcasts, Catholic sermons/ lectures, and reading. I especially enjoy daily devotionals or podcasts that keep me on track and make me ponder. I love learning more about our faith, and a podcast is something I can easily listen to while driving or walking the neighborhood. Other than that, I try to remember to thank Him for all the little things throughout my day- for the way my baby's face lights up when she sees her bigger sister dancing silly or for the sunlight trickling through the windows on a winter's afternoon. I give Him any anxiety or worry I feel myself carrying and ask Him to help me through it. I beg Him to teach me how to trust and surrender to Him and His divine will for me. I may*

not speak to Him every minute or every day, but I offer each day to Him in the morning, knowing that He will accept my meager offering.

- I would like you to back up what you are saying with scripture.

  - *I believe you may be referring to the bold claim that husbands and wives are responsible for getting each other and their children to heaven. Ephesians Chapter 5. Many of the other big topics we are covering, apart from my own experiences and ideas, are gleaned from St. Pope John Paul II/ Karol Wojtyła's books, "Love and Responsibility" and "Theology of the Body." I encourage you to research the areas that you'd like to further. I assure you that I have not fabricated any of the material we're covering, though I am human and do sometimes make mistakes. The website www.catholic.com is an incredible resource to search for answers and Biblical truths to "back up" Church teaching.*

Questions & Answers
Chapter Two

Class One

- How has your faith affected motherhood? Did your faith bring comfort and strength to becoming a mother?
    - *Truth be told, my motherhood affected my faith. To be a mother is to be forced to learn the meaning of self-sacrifice. Growing in my faith and love of God has brought tremendous comfort and strength. In fact, I cringe to think of the mother I would be if I had not started leaning on God. Also, I talk to Our Lady way more now as a mother than I used to. She's become a wonderful friend and mentor to me.*
- Do you think that a person can be truly "good" if they do not believe in God?
    - *100%. I mentioned my friend who doesn't know God. She's a fabulous person!*
- Why is it a mortal sin/why can't you receive communion at Church if you get married (a priest marries you), not in an actual church?
    - *I don't think I understand the question, but I think you're asking about getting married outside of the Church. A Catholic marriage is a sacred Sacrament. The Sacrament of Marriage is a covenant between a man and woman and God. We'll get more into marriage next time. A Catholic priest will not marry you outside of the Church. You cannot receive communion if you are not in a state of grace aka without the stain of mortal sin unless the person is in a grave circumstance such as dying in which case they would receive Apostolic Pardon before receiving Viaticum, so they'd no longer be in a state of mortal sin at the time. What makes a sin mortal? 1. It's grave*

matter. 2. Committed with full knowledge. 3. Done with deliberate consent. For more information on mortal sins, visit www.catholic.com and type 'mortal sin' in the search bar. In fact, Catholic Answers has the answers to so many questions Catholics may have. It's a wonderful resource!

- How do you keep yourself grounded in your religion (like reminding yourself to pray every day and motivating yourself to go to Mass)?
    - *At some point, after I started to talk to God and then started to learn more about God and then started to walk with God and then started to really love God, I didn't have to motivate myself to get to Mass. I want desperately to go to Mass to receive the Eucharist and worship Him. I want to be cleansed by confession. I want to hear His word. I yearn to read it or listen to an explanation of it. Learning more about my faith has taken the place of idle nothingness. You know how you get when you're super excited about something that's coming up soon, like prom or a vacation? You can't forget it because it's front and center in your brain. It's like that.*
- The qualities of a man who walks with Christ and how to properly discern if he is?
    - *We're going to dive deeper into this next time. In the meantime, please read Corinthians 13:4-8.*
- Is it a sin not to get married?
    - *Absolutely not. There is a vocation to single life as well as a vocation to religious life. Both are beautiful vocations that glorify God in this world.*
- I have no questions, you explained everything very well! :)
- Does God have a way of telling us if we are or are not with the right person?
    - *He does. We just have to listen to Him. Does the relationship bear good or bad fruits? Is it healthy and complementary? Does it bring you closer to God?*

296

- How can I balance a relationship with God and a romantic relationship?
    - *Romantic love is being spiritually, mentally, emotionally, and physically attracted to another person. When you love God, He will be in the very makeup of your relationship. You won't have to find a balance.*
- Do you have any tips for keeping a stable relationship with God if we are busy in college and can't find the time to go to church even when we try?
    - *My first tip would be to tell you that I know you can find the time. You have large pockets of time in college that you don't anticipate. Yes, you'll be busy. Yes, college is hard. But, you'll have time to give God one hour of your week. When you love Him, one hour doesn't feel like enough time. Mass can become a part of the rhythm of your college life. Besides Mass, talk to Him. Ask for His guidance and help. You'll need it. We all do. Also, try setting reminders for yourself on your phone or planner to remind yourself to pray. Get a Catholic liturgical planner that will keep you on track with holy days of obligation, Saints' feast days, and what's happening within the Church.*
- How can I hear God and what He is telling me?
    - *In the quiet of your heart, you will hear Him. What does that mean? It means that when you have a loving relationship with Him, you get to know Him. You can hear the Holy Spirit prompting you or giving you ideas that you otherwise would not have had. These gentle nudges always bear good fruits. That's where the discernment of spirits comes in. Look up some of Fr. Timothy Gallagher's interviews. He explains it beautifully.*
- How did you know what people to cut out of your life (the bad fruits), and how do you do it in a "nice" way?
    - *This is tough. Sometimes gently and sometimes abruptly, depending on the situation. As you orient*

your life towards God, most of the people who do not bring you closer to Him start to fade from your life on their own. Typically, if a relationship bears bad fruits, as you get closer to God, the other person wants to get further away from you. If, for whatever reason, they do not, God might be trying to teach you virtue or allowing you to be a witness to the faith of that other person in order that they may know Him.

- How did you gain the confidence to present yourself in the communities you want to immerse yourself in?
  - *I often toed the line between arrogance and confidence. I think the best way is to practice, though. Practice small talk at the grocery store or coffee shop. Smile at a stranger and compliment something about them. Strike up a conversation with the person in the waiting room with you at the doctor's office. Practice putting yourself out there to gain social skills. It will do wonders to boost your confidence.*

- How can you date someone non-religious but still make it work fine?
  - *If they respect your faith and love of God, dating can work out just fine. Marriage, if it comes to that, will have its challenges. I suggest you look up 'disparity of cult" from a reliable Catholic source to learn more.*

- Is it a mortal sin to date without upholding a completely God-centered relationship?
  - *No, not if by dating you mean remaining chaste and in a state of grace.*

- How do you differentiate between a friendship that isn't good for you and a friendship where you are meant to help the other person?
  - *This is a great question! Sometimes, God does put people in our lives to help us grow in virtue and to help bring others to Him. Just think of someone who really annoys you but is stuck in your life*

(often a family member!). You may need to grow in the virtue of fortitude. I would say: 1. Pray and ask for God's help to discern this. 2. Ask yourself if it is a healthy relationship. Are boundaries respected? Are you codependent on one another? Can you communicate respectfully? Is there trust? Kindness? Start there.

- Is it ok to not have a completely Christ-centered relationship as a teen?
    - *Great question! I think you may be referring to a boyfriend-type relationship. A Christ-centered relationship would be one where you treat one another as Christ would treat you and one where you mutually love and worship God. Though it may be 'okay' to not have this type of relationship, I would say that it is not ideal. In any relationship, a friendship or romantic one, loving one another as God calls us to love others is imperative.*
- HOW to create a relationship with God and build a foundation in Christ. Also, what is blocking someone from building their identity in Christ, and how it plays out in someone's head?
    - *Oh, good but tough one. Building that foundation starts with you. It starts with your "yes" to God. Yes to getting to know Him. Yes, to loving Him. Yes, to surrendering your life to Him. Remember, even our typical every day can be surrendered to Him. He doesn't always ask us to climb the highest peaks or do something impossible. He asks us to love Him. The easiest way to enter into this relationship is to think of what any relationship requires- love, respect, trust, and communication. He asks us to remember our Creator and why we were created- to be in communion with Him. When we begin to understand this and begin to participate in this love, the foundation in Christ takes root. In my opinion, many people get caught up in religion versus faith versus relationship*

without realizing it's all the same thing. I can't say how it plays out in someone's head, but I can take a guess that it's separate. People tend to compartmentalize things, including religion/faith/ relationship with God. When you talk to God, love God, and love your neighbors as yourself, you walk with Him. It's extremely simple and incredibly complex at the same time, but it comes down to offering yourself and your life to God. It comes down to trust in God. Do you trust Him with your life?

- How to know if your current boyfriend is the one you should marry?
    - *What are the fruits of your relationship? Is there kindness, patience, love, respect, healthy communication, mutual commitment, forgiveness, honesty, mutual support, healthy boundaries, God? Are you spiritually, emotionally, and physically attracted to him? Does he share in this attraction? Take stock of your relationship and its fruits. Be honest. You both most likely have areas listed above that you can grow and mature in. Are you both willing to do so? Start now.*
- How do you balance work and school and a social life plus a relationship with God?
    - *God created us. As our Creator, He honestly doesn't ask much. He asks us to love Him, to worship Him, and to love others. We can do all three within the framework of every other aspect of our lives.*
- What are ways to implement God in your marriage?
    - *Practically, we pray together every night. We worship together every week. We talk about God at the dinner table or while riding in the car. We ask Him to reveal Himself to us and His divine will for us. And, we try to listen to the Holy Spirit when a path is laid out for us that seems too perfectly coincidental to ignore. We seek His forgiveness.*

We beg for His help in raising our children. We implore Him to bless our marriage and to heal us of our past wounds. We ask Him to help us grow in virtue and to help us shed our attachments to sin. We do all of this separately and together. We pray for each other. We pray for sanctifying grace so that we can be with Him and each other in heaven one day. We pray for our children's future spouses. We pray for our children to know and love God. We offer our marriage and our entire lives to Him. Overall, treat your spouse as Jesus calls us to treat others. As a wife, you represent the body of Christ, His Church, in your relationship. Your husband represents Christ in your relationship. We'll get more into this next time.

Class Two

- What would your advice be for someone who is dating someone of another Christian denomination in terms of helping each other become better in our faiths?
    - *Love one another as Christ loves you. If you start there, you're bound to both grow in your faith, and it's something that you both have in common even if you're from different denominations.*
- How do you become sure that the man you are with is sent from God and is worthy of being the father of your children?
    - *Great question! Are you worthy of being the mother to your children? Are you sent from God to your future partner? Begin by looking inward. Are you walking with God as you would like your future spouse to be walking with Him? Are there areas where you can grow and mature before you get married? I'll answer that for you. Yes, there are always opportunities to grow in virtue. Do not let fear of commitment or anxiety for the future paralyze you, and pray. Pray, pray, pray. Ask God to send you a man worthy to be your children's*

father and your husband. Ask God to make you worthy of such a man.

- How to continue to grow your faith in God in college? What struggles did you go through? How to stay away from bad things in college?
  - *1. I failed in growing closer to God in college, but looking back, I would say: A. Befriend other practicing Catholics. B. Learn more about your faith. Read books. Listen to podcasts on your walk to classes or your long drive home for weekends and holidays. There's a treasury of Catholic podcasts and YouTube channels, and they're so interesting! Utilize them. I wish I had taken responsibility for learning more about our faith long before I became a mother. 2. I struggled with so many things, and at the time, I didn't recognize them all as struggles. I struggled to find my identity outside of a Catholic student in Savannah, Georgia. I struggled to find my way after years of idolizing my boyfriend, sports, and what university I wanted to attend. I struggled to find my purpose or meaning when it came time to graduate into the unknown. 3. Surround yourself with good people and talk to God. Remember: Will this bring me closer or further away from God? Apply it to everything. It'll keep you out of some of those sticky situations.*
- Is it ok that my boyfriend is Methodist and I am Catholic?
  - *Yes. There are challenges in interfaith marriages, but that doesn't mean that they can't work beautifully. It just means if you were to ever marry one another, you'd have to make a commitment to overcome those challenges.*
- Did you ever receive criticism in college for being Catholic?
  - *Not in college, that I remember. The first time I remember experiencing prejudice against Catholics was when I was on a cemetery tour of an old Catholic cemetery in New Orleans as an adult.*

302

Another tourist made some nasty comments about Catholics, and I was totally shocked. It doesn't happen often in my circles, so I wasn't prepared for it in the slightest. Thankfully, the tour guide seemed to be a Catholic, too, so I stuck close to him. My husband was at a conference, and I was touring the city by myself, so it was nice to have an unspoken friend at that moment.

- My boyfriend is Methodist, and I am Catholic. We both go to church together, and we worship God together. We are very strong in our relationship with Christ and center everything around him. We try to bring each other to Christ in every way that we can. We inspire each other to be better people and stronger believers. Would you say our situation is a good situation for being believers but different denominations?

  - *How wonderful! I would say, how wonderful. I'm so happy for you. Yes. It sounds like a beautiful relationship, one built on mutual respect for the other and on a true love of Christ.*

- What kinds of temptations did you face when you were in college? What was the hardest thing to do in college when it came to your faith? Is it a sin to indulge in college parties?

  - *1. All the typical temptations one might think of minus drugs and porn. Gross. 2. The hardest thing was to walk in it. I struggled to. 3. No, it is not a sin to have fun. Drinking alcohol is not a sin. Purposely becoming intoxicated (binge drinking) is sinful. Why? A few reasons but here are two. One is that it deprives the drinker of the use of reason. Secondly, its impact on the body. Excessive alcohol consumption can devastate your body even over short periods of time. Both our bodies and the ability to reason are gifts given to us by God. We are stewards of these gifts.*

- What if I am not Catholic and do not regularly go to church, and the same for my boyfriend? Do these rules still apply to me but without Mass and church?

- *I'm not sure what rules you're referring to, but I'm going to say yes. We're all called to love God and be in communion with Him, and that means abiding by His 'rules' for us. But remember, they aren't really rules. They're instructions for how to get to heaven.*
- How do you know you're on the right path that God wants you on?
    - *Ask Him. Go to adoration. Kneel before the Eucharist, and ask Him. If your church doesn't have an adoration chapel, pray in the church before the Eucharist in the Tabernacle. Be still. Be quiet. Listen. You probably won't hear His voice booming from the altar, but you might hear His spirit whispering in your heart.*
- How do you know the will of God?
    - *By asking Him. Seeking and doing His will for our lives is ultimately what will lead to our salvation. Spend time with Him. Pray. Discern. Follow the path He points you to.*
- How can we be Godly wives to our husbands when we get married and how can we prep ourselves for that with our boyfriends that we have today?
    - *Love this! I can't wait to get into your first question in our next talk. Prepping now for marriage will be a beautiful gift to yourself and your future spouse. Ask God and your Guardian Angel to show you your defects in virtue. Think about the places where you know you need to grow. Maybe it's in selflessness or in communication skills. Maybe it's in treating the other person with respect and dignity. Say 'hello' to God. Offer your day to Him. Offer your life. You'll be amazed where He will take you.*
- How to know if you are ready for marriage (in the future)?
    - *Great question! You will never be fully 'ready.' There isn't a magical moment where all of a sudden you're all set for marriage or for kids or*

for fill-in-the-blank. You can long for marriage or children. You can want it, but there's no way to be 100% prepped and ready. It's like a test in that way. You can prepare and prepare, and when you get to the test, you just do your very best. One day, if you are in a mutually loving, Christ-centered relationship, you may be ready for marriage.

- How do you get to the point where you no longer question your faith?
    - *By learning more about it. So many people have convictions about what the Catholic Church says or does. They're often missing the main point. We're on this earth to know and love God so that we can be with Him forever in heaven. How do we know how to do that? The Church teaches us how. Catholicism is truth and beauty. Take responsibility for your faith. Learn more about it while you begin your relationship with God. You may still question it in the future. That's the devil at work. Tell him, in the name of Jesus Christ, to leave you alone, and ask God to help you with your questioning. If you ask the questions, you'll find the answers. The 'Bible in a Year' and 'Catechism in a Year' podcasts are wonderful ways to learn more about our faith.*
- Can you talk more about things teenage girls struggle with and basic things to help them get through it?
    - *I wish I could. I came here to focus on the vocation of being a wife and mother. I'll pray for God to grant you the strength to endure your struggles. Being a teenage girl is tough!*
- How do you recognize when the devil is trying to make you sin?
    - *By getting closer to God, it's easier to see the devil's handiwork.*
- How to encourage your children to want to learn more about Catholicism or be more interested in it?

305

- *Great question! By walking in it. Our daughter loves everything Catholic- Jesus, Mary, the saints and their stories, her guardian angel, the rosary, the Bible, daily devotionals, prayers even in Latin, and more. Her child's innocence understands God even more than we do. It's amazing. She even proclaims that she wants to be a nun one day so that she can spend her entire life glorifying God. She's four, so we'll see if that is her calling, but because we walk in our faith, she has her own relationship with God and Catholicism.*

Class Three

- Why is marriage the gateway to heaven?
  - *God gave us the gift of marriage to help those whose vocation it is to attain holiness. The ultimate goal for all individuals, married or not, is to reach heaven. Marriage is not the sole path to heaven. However, in the covenant of marriage, two individuals agree to will the good of the other for their entire lives, no matter the circumstances, trials, or tribulations they may face. In this way, it is a sanctifying path to heaven.*
- How did you know that your husband was your lifelong partner? How do you find a good, virtuous husband?
  - *1. At some point in my husband and I's relationship, our young, somewhat shallow love transformed into real, self-giving love. We did not fully enter into this until a few years into our marriage, and we will always be maturing into the love God designed for us, but once the initial transformation started taking place and our love became unconditional and not codependent, I knew he was the one. 2. Pray for him. Pray that God helps you find a virtuous man. Pray that He helps you discern whether or not the man that you*

306

are dating is virtuous or can grow alongside you in virtue. God works in incredible ways. Ask Him to provide a man worthy of your love and to make you a woman worthy of his.

- What were you like at our age?
  - *Very much like you, I would guess. I enjoyed my friends, my family, playing sports and training, going to dances and games, doing well in school, and having fun. I had friend and family struggles, some that were universal things we all go through, some that were unique to my situation. There's a poem on my blog (www.thehomesteadkings.com) that I wrote in 2016 about being a big sister to a child with Autistic Spectrum Disorder. It goes a bit into the deeper side of my teenage years. Life was not perfect or always easy, but thankfully, God has always given me the gift of trying to handle situations as best as I can amidst a reality that isn't always perfect.*
- How to actually live and balance your faith realistically?
  - *Realistically, it isn't a balance. Your faith is who you are. When you realize that, your life and faith are the same. Logistically balancing, be intentional. Set calendar alarms to pray or attend Mass if you tend to forget things. Treat prayer as importantly as you do your other responsibilities. Eventually, you will find that prayer becomes second nature and that your conversations with God will flow as naturally as your conversation with others.*
- How do I know I'm being used?
  - *Great question! What are the fruits of the relationship in question? How does it make you feel? Recognize your own value. Does the other person see it, too? Are you the only one making sacrifices in the relationship? Are you the only one showing appreciation? Are you the only one showing real interest or willing the good of the*

other? Think deeply on the matter and seek
professional guidance from a faithful counselor if
you need help setting healthy boundaries or help
discerning whether or not to end a relationship.
Good counselors give us the tools to cope with less-
than-ideal relationships or situations. Also, pray
about it.

- How do you not make someone uncomfortable talking about
religion if they aren't used to it?
  - *You can't make them comfortable. If the person in
  question loves you and your faith is a part of who
  you are, they shouldn't mind as long as you're not
  obsessive or condescending about it. However, if
  they still struggle, maybe have a conversation with
  them. Check in with them to see why it makes them
  uncomfortable and how you can respect their
  discomfort while also being yourself in the future.*

- How do I go into relationships looking for a good husband
when most guys do not have that mindset right now? How to
find the right guy, and how to create a good relationship?
  - *That is hard. The key, I think, is to not go looking
  for the "good husband." It's kind of like putting the
  cart before the horse. Instead, look for a man with
  a virtuous character. Look for friendship and
  mutual attraction. A "good husband" may grow
  from those. Also, give it time. Let God work.
  Putting yourself in the "right" atmosphere,
  communities, and situations will help you find the
  right man. What does that mean? Does your
  church have a youth group? Are there communal
  opportunities for service? Can you attend a retreat
  or a church event? These are just some ideas for
  the "right" kind of places to find your community,
  among others. Creating a good relationship starts
  with you. Are you confident and assured in who
  you are and know the areas in which you can
  work on growth? A good relationship is one with*

mutual love and respect, one that will help get both parties to heaven.

- What problems did you and your husband have before marriage, and how did you work through them?
  - *We have thankfully always had a loving relationship. We just didn't know what true self-giving love looked like. It was a challenge to mature into a sacrificial relationship built on God rather than relying entirely on ourselves. We both went to counseling to help us let go of the codependent habits we had formed. We slowly but surely welcomed God into our relationship, and He gives us the strength to work through everything and anything.*
- What can I do to help my husband get into heaven?
  - *Love this question! Strive to be a woman of virtue. Pray for him, even now. Read about St. Monica and how she helped her pagan husband (and also her son, St. Augustine, a doctor of the Church) turn to God. Grow in your love of Jesus, and ask him to be with you in that growth.*
- What if your future husband shows all good signs in the beginning but becomes a person you no longer want to spend your life with?
  - *Ephesians 5:33. St. Paul says, "the wife should respect her husband." He does not add conditions to the respect. He does not say they should respect their husbands IF he deserves it. A Sacramental marriage is a covenant. It is not a contract. A covenant cannot be broken. The Catechism of the Catholic Church lays out the specifics for abuse situations, but whether or not a person becomes someone you're no longer attracted to physically or emotionally is not a form of spousal abuse. When I asked my husband for help in weighing in on this question, he said, "Planning for the exit makes the journeying a lot easier." People usually are looking for the easy route. A marriage*

covenant does not have an exit strategy, nor should you want one. Imagine how empty vows are with an exit plan already in mind. There is no promise that marriage will be easy. It will be edifying. Father Mike says, "A contract is an agreement for an exchange of goods and services. A covenant is an exchange of persons. It's saying, 'I'm yours and you're mine.' It's unconditional."

- How Catholicism can work with science instead of against it?
    - Interesting question! The Catholic Church has been at the forefront of science since its beginning. I encourage you to search for videos or articles about this. Bishop Barron has some wonderful ones on his YouTube channel. Also, Father Spitzer has wonderful books and has done fabulous lectures on this topic.
- How to walk with God correctly in your relationship?
    - I hesitate to use the word correctly. Everyone has their own unique relationship with God, just like every child has their own unique relationship with their mom or dad. If you're struggling to find the words you seek in prayer or would like guidance, try out the Hallow Catholic prayer App. It's a wonderful resource and will help you along your faith journey. It definitely can help your relationship lean towards God. It's something the two of you can listen to and do together. We'll get more into what a Christ-centered relationship looks like soon.
- If I don't go to Mass now but start going later, will I still go to hell?
    - I can't answer that. When we come to our judgement day at the end of our lives on earth, only then will we know where we will spend eternity. However, missing Mass is a mortal sin because it breaks the third commandment. Through the Sacrament of Confession and true

contrition, the Church says this sin can and will be forgiven.

- How should you focus on healing after a breakup?
    - *Asking this question is a great start to healing. I learned from my unhealthy, codependent relationship with my then-boyfriend/now-husband that you cannot be whole in a relationship until you are whole on your own. This happens through God's grace. Start healing by working on your own growth and asking Jesus to help and guide you in your healing. He will help you to become whole, meaning the person He willed you to be, and trust me, He has way better plans for you than you have for yourself. Focus on His divine will for your life. The other things will fall into place according to it.*
- How do you know that the relationship should be long-term?
    - *Simply put, do you enjoy each other? Is there mutual attraction and respect? Is there friendship and unconditional love? No relationship between two imperfect humans will be perfect, but it doesn't mean that you compromise your desires for a relationship, especially the desire for it to bring you both closer to God. Remember, you cannot force a relationship to be free, total, faithful, and fruitful. Both people have to be on the same page for longevity to even be on the table.*
- Did you have a good experience with your college community? Please elaborate on the good and bad experiences and how to avoid the bad ones.
    - *I had many great experiences with friend groups in college and a handful of not-so-great, one of which I shared. Looking back, I see the error of not having a Catholic community I could turn to or to be a witness of the faith to me, but thankfully, even so, I had a fun and loving friend group who cared about each other. We even had big Sunday dinners with each other every week for a year or two. It is*

possible to go to college and keep your morals and values. It's a myth that you have to party hard and forget who you are or how you were raised. You may lose some friendships that you expected to last a lifetime, and that is hard, but you may find new friendships that will last a lifetime in their places. You may win the jackpot and not lose any friendships while also gaining new ones! Be mindful of looking at life through the lens of, "Does this bring me close to God or further away from Him?" This question applies to the people in your life just as much as your choices, and it will most definitely help you avoid bad situations. Also, please practice common sense. Don't put yourself in dangerous situations. They are avoidable for the most part.

- I want to know how you found a church that was fit for you and your family when you decided to settle back down in Savannah. You mentioned that you went to Blessed Sacrament, but now you attend St. James for church. I also would like to know how strong of faith you had when you were our age and if that grew from yourself or mainly from your parent's influence.

  - *1. It's a pretty simple answer. St. James the Less is closer to our house. I love the idea of a neighborhood church, and though we're not within walking distance of it, it's nice to be with other families within a few miles of the church. It also makes attending confession and other services or programs in addition to Mass easier. 2. When I was your age, I helped lead retreats. I attended CYO (Church Youth Group) and Mass every week I was in town and not traveling for soccer, and I made sure to say my prayers at night. I was also in a state of sexual mortal sin that I did not confess in confession when I would go, which also led to being in a state of mortal sin for receiving the Eucharist while in a state of mortal sin. I idolized*

*my relationship, my grades, my desired college,
and sports over God. So, I'd say that my faith on
the outside appeared strong, but on the inside, it
was extremely weak and shallow. I did not care to
know or understand God besides what my parents
and school had taught me. I cringe to think of it,
but I am incredibly grateful to God for giving me
the chance to turn to Him and the desire to know
Him. 3. A little bit from my parents' influence and
a lot of bit from my own yearning for more
meaning and fulfillment. At some point, you have
to accept responsibility for your own walk with
God. Your parents cannot do it for you.*

- I would like you to cover more deeply on transitioning from
  a Catholic high school with the faith mentioned every single
  day to a college that is not catholic like UGA. I would also
  like you to talk about how you formed good habits of
  practicing your faith.

    - *It was a tough transition all around. I loved
      attending UGA and how large it was. It's a melting
      pot, and it's so cool to meet people from all over
      and hear their stories, but it was a challenge for
      me to remember my faith and what it means. I
      was always proud to be Catholic, but I eventually
      became a non-practicing Catholic, so there was
      nothing to be proud of (not that we should be
      prideful at all about our faith). I would attend
      Mass every so often and pray at night before bed
      sometimes, but that was really it. Eventually, I
      wanted to be a practicing Catholic. I wanted to
      understand why converts to Catholicism would
      risk everything to become Catholic, why Jesus
      made this one true church, and why martyrs died
      defending it. Forming a habit takes dedication,
      and I became dedicated to learning more, praying
      more, and worshipping more.*

- What to do when your children doubt their faith?

- *Pray unceasingly for them. If you have baptized and raised them in the faith and if you've taught them all that you can about it, entrust their faith to God. Read more about St. Monica and how long and hard she prayed for her son, St. Augustine. All looked lost and hopeless for Augustine, but St. Monica never stopped praying, and she saw the fruits of her prayers in his conversion before her death. We cannot force them. We can only be stewards and teachers of the faith to them and invite them to come along.*
- How do I know when it's time to break up with someone?
  - *What are the fruits of the relationship? Are you able to look at the relationship realistically? It's easy for women to get caught up in how a man makes them feel important or wanted or how handsome and charming he is, both of which can be good, but neither of which will bear good fruits on their own. There has to be development beyond attractions and feelings, development into a self-giving, sacrificial, unconditional love. Our emotions and attractions are ultimately good but are like compasses pointing North to further development if there is potential for this kind of development. This is why dating with marriage in mind and not just to pass the time or solely for fun is so important. It aligns your desires with the ultimate good of finding your spouse and building a relationship on the foundation of God's divine love.*
- Can you recover from mortal sin? If I skipped Mass and started attending, would it prevent me from going to hell?
  - *St. Andre Bessette said, "If you ate only one meal a week, would you survive? It is the same for your soul. Nourish it with the Blessed Sacrament." Confession is a gift. Utilize it, and then nourish your soul.*
- What are some solutions to fight temptations?

- *Strengthen your prayer life. Frequent confession the recommended frequency of at least once a month. Receive the Body of Christ weekly. If you are unsure of how to handle certain temptations on your own, find a good resource (book, channel, or podcast) or ask your priest or a mentor in your church. Arming yourself with knowledge of God and His teachings will help you defend yourself against temptation.*

- I'm interested in how to go about marriage in the eyes of God. I feel like there is a stereotype of Catholic couples living less exciting lives, so what are ways you can have fun but avoid sin?

  - *1. God created marriage to sanctify us. There are many marriages in the Bible, some that were incredible, like Mary and Joseph's marriage, and some that were far less than ideal, like David and Bathsheba's. St. Pope John Paul II had wonderfully helpful things to say about marriage and the family. I recommend diving further into his writings or finding books that help summarize them like "Men, Women, and the Mystery of Love" by Dr. Edward Sri. 2. This question kind of makes me sad. From my experience and witnessing other Catholic relationships, more often than not, they are full of joy! To be clear, I do not mean that they (or we) do not face trials or that they're always in some strange, comatose state of happiness. I mean they're joyful, peaceful people. Even the ones who have experienced immense pain and sadness, such as the loss of a child in a miscarriage, are so filled with the Holy Spirit and love of God that they just radiate hope and peace. We have a lot of fun. We've traveled a lot. We've renovated five houses together. I started my own business. We live on a little farm. The list goes on, and all of it was fun and exciting. We haven't always avoided sin and will, I'm sure, struggle with it in our present and*

*future, but sin does not equal fun. When I've hurt
God with my choices, it's not fun. I'd say it's all
about your perspective. Avoid coming from an
angle of, "I can't do XYZ that are sinful but still
want to." Instead, try approaching sin from the
angle of, "I no longer want to do XYZ, not because
it is sinful, but because ultimately, I love God." It
comes back to understanding attachment to sin.*

- How do I continue to stay in touch with God when I go to
college?

  - *Deliberately. When you have a relationship with
  God, you begin to know him, and when you know
  God, you love Him. You grow in your desire to
  stay in touch with Him. You want to worship Him.
  You want to surrender to His divine will for your
  life. He loves us so much, and He desires for us to
  reciprocate that love. He even tells us how to do so.
  Read the gospels. Try listening to the "Bible in a
  Year" or "Catechism in a Year" podcast or both.
  Daily devotionals are great ways to stay in touch
  with God in our busy lives.*

Class Four

- Did you know your husband was the one?

  - *Not right away. It took me about five to six years
  to figure out that he was the one God had
  answered my prayer with. I used to pray for Him
  to send me a man who loved me for me, and my
  now-husband has truly always loved me for me.
  God provides when we put our trust in Him.*

- What are some examples of mortal and venial sins that
aren't as talked about or common?

  - *In my opinion, venial sins that aren't talked about
  often as sinful are gossiping, selfish pride, abusive
  language, and hatred of neighbor. We typically see
  talking about other people negatively as harmless
  as long as they don't find out or know. We often
  think hating another person doesn't matter in the*

big scheme of things. We can often get heated in the moment and call someone a nasty name. We can often allow our egos to be inflated by the smallest achievements or victories. All of these little things that we might think don't matter much do actually matter and are sinful because they're uncharitable towards others. The main mortal sin that I think many Catholics are unaware of is the skipping of Mass with unjust cause. The other ones, like murder and fornication, tend to be well-known, but the refusal to worship God weekly as He commanded us to is a mortal sin that many of us tend not to think about.

- How to balance church time, sports time, social time, and school time?
    - *Balancing life is and always will be a challenge. By orienting your daily life towards God, your other responsibilities tend to fall into place. Remember to offer your day to Him. Remember to ask, "Does this bring me closer to God or further away from God?" If it's something neutral like playing a sport or going to school, then ask the question within those situations. For example, you could ask, "Does my attitude during school hours or while I'm in strength conditioning bring me closer to God or further away from Him? Am I going about my tasks with a charitable attitude? Am I kind to others while I go about these tasks?" Orienting your daily life towards God will help you learn how to balance your life by also helping you discern what in your life is necessary and unnecessary in terms of bringing you close to or further away from God. Is this friendship helping me grow in holiness, or is it toxic? Does this sport require me to miss Mass on the weekends? Begin looking inward and asking yourself these types of questions.*
- Is there a limitation on confession?

- *Not at all. We can approach the Lord and ask for His forgiveness as often as we'd like. Generally, the suggested frequency of confession is at least once a month. Some people go weekly.*
- What was your turning point in your prayer life that you knew you needed a change?
    - *Entering into marriage made me think about getting closer to God, so I took a few baby steps. Entering into motherhood made me leap to God. When I realized that my husband and I were responsible for teaching the faith and who God is to our children, it wasn't like a game anymore. The desire to know God and our Catholic faith became intensely real and extremely important. Our children need to know God. They need to know He loves them. They need to know why they were created and why they matter. They need to know what Christ teaches us, and they need to know what their purpose here on earth is, just as all of us do. They need that foundation just as we do. The main turning point was when I realized that we have a duty to honor God and lead our children to Him.*
- What are some other examples of times in friendships that you realized it was time to not be friends anymore? How did you try and help your friends to stop sinning before finally realizing you couldn't do anything else to help?
    - *1. Sometimes, friendships just fade. You go separate paths, and you lose touch with one another. Other times, the other person may step away from the friendship, and you may not know why. And still, in other circumstances, you may be the one stepping quietly away. Ask yourself a few questions. Does this relationship bring me closer to God? Is it a healthy, respectful relationship? If the answer to those questions is no, then you may need to evaluate whether or not it is helpful to either of you to stay friends. 2. This is one hard. It was*

really hard to accept that I couldn't force some of my friends to turn away from some of their sins. I talked to them about their choices. I mentioned how we were raised in our faith. I commiserated with some of their sins because I too was making similar choices. At some point, it's important to realize that it's out of your control, give it over to God, and pray for them. Never stop praying for them.

- How did you overcome the challenges and finally be able to grow in your faith?
    - *I wouldn't say that I have overcome the challenges. There will always be challenges. Always. It's being able to approach these challenges with a new perspective because of our faith. When your life is God-centered, the challenges tend to not weigh us down so much. God's love gives us courage and strength that we otherwise would not have. His grace allows us to withstand things we previously thought we couldn't. Check out some of the martyrs' stories. They withstood torture upon torture bravely and stoically with the grace of our Lord. I started growing in my faith when I started participating in the conversation with God. From there, it just keeps growing. His love for us is so spectacular. He calls us to Him through this love. We just have to answer.*
- What happens if you are in a mortal state of sin and you have communion?
    - *One remains in a state of mortal sin. The grace from the Sacrament cannot be received while in a state of irreverence. It is the sin of sacrilege to receive the gift of the Body and Blood of Christ without being in a state of grace. The good news is participating in the Sacrament of Reconciliation and confessing mortal sins with true contrition will once again put you in a state of grace.*
- How do you know that the Catechism is God spoken?

- *Luke Chapter 10 & Matthew Chapter 28. Also, what are its fruits? What is its message? I encourage you to dive deeper and learn more. You may be surprised at what you find.*
- Do people just confess consistently to wash away mortal sins?
  - *They can if they are truly repentant, but ideally, no. They turn away from mortal sin because they are truly sorry for their grave sins and make a choice to stop.*
- What has been the most rewarding part of your Bible study? How to get in the habit of reading the Bible more frequently?
  - *1. Two things I think. One, I enjoy understanding things that I previously did not understand. I thought I understood Mass and some of the Church's teachings. I did not. It was wonderful to learn the sources of many aspects of Catholicism. Secondly, I enjoyed getting to know God. I think I used to treat Him as some being up in the sky who only cared if I was a "good" person. It was revolutionary for me to begin to feel His love for me. 2. I wholeheartedly recommend the 'Bible in a Year' podcast with Father Mike Schmitz. It's 10-20 minutes a day, and his commentary is so helpful during those really tough chapters of the Bible.*
- Where do you go for frequent confession? I can't find anywhere that offers frequent confession at convenient times.
  - *Most parishes have set times for confession that they usually post on their websites. If you're unable to attend their provided times, they also allow you to schedule confession at your convenience. Call or email your parish's office. Priests are usually more than happy to accommodate you for confession.*
- She answered my only questions. *:)*
- I do not have any questions, she went in depth about all of her topics. *:)*

- I don't have many questions, but one would be about how to find the motivation or time for Mass when you are in a dark mind space or are overwhelmed with work?
    - *It's important to remember that we are participants in Mass. We are not spectators. We go to participate, with the priests, all the angels, and saints, in the sacrifice of Christ on the altar. When you are in a dark mind space or feeling overwhelmed, try learning more about the Mass. Find out more about how you can be an active participant. There are videos, podcasts, articles, books, and all sorts of materials that can help you see Mass in a new light, in its truth and beauty. When you realize that you are an integral part of the divine mystery that is the Mass, perhaps the darkness will begin to fade. Mass is not a stage performance. It's an act of communion to glorify and worship our Lord.*
- How would you advise on showing love and support to those who aren't religious, without forcing our beliefs down their throat? How do you support other people even if their views don't align with the church?
    - *Good question. I'd advise turning to the saints. How did they treat others who weren't of the same religion as them? How did they evangelize? Implement some of their habits of kindness, respect, and love. Be Jesus to others. Remember, after receiving the Eucharist, you are a walking tabernacle. Jesus resides in you. How would He treat others whose views don't align with yours?*
- How to show love to those who identify differently? How can we show them love, kindness, and support without forcing our lifestyles onto them?
    - *You can and should treat everyone with love and kindness. You can support others without condoning their actions or behaviors. For example, I love my 4-year-old tremendously, with a love I didn't know was possible until motherhood, but*

when she lies to get her way, I don't support the act of her lying. I support her by not accepting the behavior of the lie. Behaviors have natural consequences, both good and bad, but we can and should still love and respect another's dignity as a person.

- How to introduce your child to your religion without forcing it on them?
  - *By walking in your faith. Children are little sponges. If they see that you have a close relationship with God, see you praying, see you attending Mass, see you helping and loving others, they will imitate you. They will soak it all in, and one day, hopefully, they will turn to God themselves. It's up to us as parents to guide our children to Him.*
- When did community help you most?
  - *I would say when I became a wife and then a mother. I had wonderful friends in college, but we definitely weren't helping each other attain holiness. We were living in a culture and only concerned with having fun, getting good grades, and finding a career path. When I became a wife, I began craving wisdom from women older than me. When I became a mother, I began craving wisdom from my peers who were also mothers. Community gives you the camaraderie of having others around you in the same life chapter as you are now or who have already gotten through the chapter you're currently in. It's a connection with like-minded people who are willing and able to help support one another in a healthy, loving way.*
- What are the main things we should pray for?
  - *Prayer is unique to each person, but generally, if you are looking for ideas for intentions to pray for, pray for your family and friends, all the souls in purgatory, everyone who is sick and their families, for God to help you learn how to love and trust*

Him, for God to reveal Himself to you, for God to help you grow in virtue, for your future husband and your future children. The list of intentions can be endless.

- How do you cope with loss?
    - *I am so sorry if you've experienced loss in your life. Grieving is unique yet universal. Early in my marriage, in one year, my family lost eight loved ones. They were young and old. My mom's brother and sister passed away two weeks apart from each other by way of a heart attack and a brain aneurysm. Loss is never easy. Praying for those who have passed away helps us to give our grief over to God and entrust Him with the souls of those we love. We can also offer up our suffering in grief. Ask God to use it for the intentions of others, and pray for healing. Grief is one of those things you always carry with you, and while healing does not take it away completely, it will help lessen the burden. Give God your grief. "Come unto me, all ye that travail and are heavy laden, and I will refresh you. Take my yoke upon you, and learn of me; for I am meek and lowly in heart: and ye shall find rest unto your souls. For my yoke is easy, and my burden is light" (Matt. 11:28-30).*
- What is the difference in all the types of branches of Christianity?
    - *Jesus sent his apostles out to spread the good news. He designated Peter the rock upon which He would build His Church. The Catholic Church is the fulfillment of Jesus' plans for His Church. All other branches of Christianity broke away from the one, true Church at different points in history, and we pray and hope that all can be rejoined into communion one day. This is why we say, "I believe in one, holy, catholic and apostolic Church" every week in the Nicene Creed during Mass. The differences in the other branches of Christianity*

vary significantly. I encourage you to dive deeper into this through a reputable source.

- How to grow in my faith with peers looking down on me?
  - *I'm sorry if you've experienced peers looking down on you for your faith. Jesus never promised that following Him would be easy, but it's a real struggle when those around us are unkind or cruel about our faith. I encourage you to put yourself out there to find a community of peers who will help lift you up in your faith. Find a youth group or a Bible study. If you can't find one, be brave and start one. Also, read more about the saints. There are so many saints who struggled with this exact same problem. Gain inspiration from their stories and lives. Ask them to pray for you.*
- What are some tips for how to make sure to make time for the Lord, especially when in college and making that transition? How to stay devoted?
  - *How do you make time for other things? Do you schedule them? Do you write them in a planner or set reminders on your phone? Do the same for prayer and Mass. If it's hard to find time for God, make time. Devotion comes through love. Love for God comes through knowing Him. God is love. How do you come to know Him? Through having a relationship with Him and by worshipping Him.*
- What are some personal experiences you've had to recover from sin?
  - *I mentioned before that I went eight years in between confessions one time. When I finally entered the confessional again, I had a quite the list of sins to repent for. I cried. I tried to justify why I sinned as I listed them out. I cried some more. For what felt like the first time in my life, I was truly sorry for the sins I had committed. I don't cry every time I go to confession now. When I walk out of the confessional, it feels like my soul has just had a warm, divine shower. All of the dirt*

and grime from my sins, whether they were small
or large, is lovingly washed away by a Father who
loves me. I watch how my husband gingerly
bathes our baby in the sink sometimes and think
it's a like lot for God when He forgives us of our
sins. He slowly works the ugliness out of our lives.
Sometimes, I sin the same sin again and again,
and I drive myself to the confessional and confess
it again, thanking God for the gift of forgiveness
and praying that He gives me the strength I need
to avoid the sin in the future.

- How do you build stability in a family?
    - *One small moment at a time. Stability or being
    stable relies on many things- our mental health,
    our physical health, our financial situation, our
    home life- but ultimately, it relies on our
    relationship with God. When we model our family
    life after the Holy Family, we bring stability to our
    family. This is not to say that we are perfect or the
    equivalent of the Holy Family, but we have Mary
    and Joseph to turn to to ask for help and guidance
    in our own family lives. We can seek the answers
    to how to be a loving, authoritative parent from
    the Bible. We can look to Jesus as the bridegroom
    and his Church as the bride when we are looking
    for stability in our marriage. God provides us with
    so much guidance. We just have to seek it out. Also,
    we pray as a family. Sometimes, it's complete
    chaos, while other times, it's calm and peaceful.
    Either way, praying together as a family reminds
    us that we have a Creator who loves us and who
    we can turn to in every moment of our lives.*

- What do you do when he is a different religion and you want
him to be your religion? lol
    - *I love the "lol." I think it means that you know you
    can't make him convert. You can pray for his
    conversion, though. You can strengthen your faith
    and hope that through you, he may see what you*

see in your faith. You cannot force him, but you can invite him.

- How do you know if someone is genuine in their faith and not "into" it for another reason?
    - *You don't. I've asked myself this question many times, and the answer is that you don't know for sure if someone is genuine. However, what are the fruits? Do they attend Mass but are hateful and spiteful to others? Are they active in the church but gossip and complain behind others' backs? What are the fruits that you can observe of their faith? How do they treat their family and friends? "You will know them by their fruits."*

Questions & Answers
Chapter Three

Class One

- Do you have any tips on how to make a relationship last through college? How do you manage a Godly relationship in college?
    - *1. From experience, I would say for a relationship to persevere through college, it needs to be built on respect. Arthur and I lacked true, deep respect for one another our freshman year. It's why we had to take a break that summer. We thought we respected each other, but it wasn't until we both really looked inward and at how we treated the other that we saw what we were lacking. Romantic relationships are, of course, built on love, but the success of the day-to-day is strongly dependent upon respect. 2. College will throw you both into a new world with new temptations and opportunities. When you truly love and respect each other, you'll be able to withstand it and come out stronger at the finish line. This also applies to managing a Godly relationship. You can begin by praying for each other and with each other.*
- What has helped you and your husband grow closer to God together?
    - *Our children. Like most parents, we want what is best for them. What is the ultimate best they could ever have? It's their faith. We knew if we were going to pass down a love for our faith to our children that we needed to get closer to God personally and together as husband and wife. Practically, we employed the habit of praying together daily.*
- How to help our future children want to pursue Catholicism?

- *By being a good steward of the faith. They will watch your walk with God. Teach them. Guide them. Provide support. Help them to grow in their faith. Don't let it be a stale religion class for them. Show them the richness and beauty of our faith. We'll get more into the practical side of this later.*
- What made you go back to your now husband after taking a long break?
  - *We came to an understanding. We both, separately, went to counseling before we officially got back together. We worked on ourselves and set up a plan to help us improve in the areas where we were weak. We realized the errors in our relationship, such as codependency and a lack of trust and respect. We agreed that we loved each other so much and that our relationship mattered enough to work through things together. Many people discard relationships when the going gets tough, and I'm not referring to truly unhealthy relationships. There are red flags in relationships that are imperative to take notice of while dating. Praise God that we could look at our relationship for what it was at that time without rose-colored glasses and chose each other. We decided to go the hard route of bettering ourselves and making sacrifices for the other, and I can honestly tell you that I never had doubts again as to whether or not he was the man I should spend my life with.*
- How to trust the Lord's plan for you even though it can be challenging?
  - *This is an age-old question. When I feel myself not trusting the Lord's plan, I look to the saints for examples. It's so challenging to make ourselves vulnerable and fully trust in God, but the many holy saints had their challenges too and still persevered.*
- Would you please come back during religion class?

- *I would love to, but the schedule this semester does not allow it. I do miss the smaller groups and engagement, and I can definitely tell the differences in y'all's responses! I pray that the Holy Spirit is planting some fruitful seeds in the short time we have together.*
- How to prepare to be a Godly wife?
  - *Love this question! It means you're able to look at yourself and realize that you have areas in which you can grow and mature. We don't reach a magical place of perfection. We'll be striving to be good and holy our entire lives, or at least we should be striving to. Look to Proverbs 31:10-31 for a beautiful example of a "woman of worth." Practice and pray for growth in virtue.*

Class Two

- What are some ways to make yourself feel more confident?
  - *This is a tough one. You may remember at the beginning of these talks, I mentioned that I was terrified of public speaking. I would stand in front of a group of people shaking and completely forget what I was there to say. I had zero confidence to speak coherently in front of a large group. Now, after practicing quite a few times with y'all and as a speaker at our parish's Pre-Cana Marriage Prep, I'm much more confident and can thankfully actually remember most of the words I've prepared. Feeling more confident can apply to a multitude of things, such as physical beauty or mental capabilities. I'm not sure if you're talking about one specific area or overall confidence, but I would say practice, if you can, in the area where you lack confidence and pray about it. Always remember your dignity as a child of God.*
- Have you and your husband ever been on the brink of divorce? If so, how were you able to overcome your marital struggles?

- *No. Praise God. We'll touch on this in our intimacy talk when we get to communication, but we have a rule in our marriage about the d-word. We never ever say it, even jokingly. We both come from divorced families, and we committed a long time ago to not repeating that trauma in our own family. If any struggles ever arise, we talk things out in a respectful manner and pray. We're there for each other no matter the hardships that we face. Marriage is not a competition with your spouse. It's a communion between the two of you and God.*
- How to have a stable marriage?
  - *We'll get more into this next time, but for now, build your marriage on God. Remember the table analogy. Turn to the Trinity as the foundation of your marriage. Love selflessly and sacrificially, as God told us. Look to Matthew 7:24-27. Will you build your marriage on sand or rock? We chose rock, and it's made all the difference.*
- How do you manage finances in a relationship?
  - *Great question! This is something many couples fail to discuss before marriage, believe it or not. Talk to your significant other about it. Maybe one of you is more adept in the finance area, or maybe you'd like to tackle it together. Personally, my husband handles our finances. Though I'm not bad at math, budgeting our family's finances is way more stressful for me than it is for him, so we decided early on that he would technically be in charge of it for us. It's worked beautifully.*
- When do you know you're ready for the one?
  - *It's easy to get caught up in fear when committing yourself entirely to another person for the rest of your life. Look at yourself. Look at the fruits of your relationship. You may not be exactly where you'd like to be, but if you're both walking with Christ and think you can honestly vow to love each*

*other freely, totally, faithfully, and fruitfully, then
you're ready.*

- How do you know how to be a mother when it's time?
  - *God is amazing, and He made women amazing.
    Many nurturing instincts arise when you have a
    baby. Some women are more natural at
    motherhood than others, but there are so many
    resources to help us as mothers take care of our
    children's bodies and souls. Read. Join local mom
    groups. Turn to women older than you for support
    or advice. Technology isn't all bad. There are some
    really great blogs out there written by real women
    with real babies. Sometimes, it's nice not to feel
    alone in the early stages of motherhood, and
    reading or hearing about other women's
    experiences helps that.*

Class Three

- How do you pray with your husband?
  - *We go to Mass and confession together, pray
    nightly with our children, and then just the two of
    us before bed. Sometimes, talking to God in front
    of each other is awkward. Sometimes, the words
    gracefully flow. Either way, we make sure to say
    the Act of Contrition and St. Michael prayer and
    then give thanks for our many blessings.*
- How do we balance fun and morals?
  - *What do you define as fun? Living in a state of
    grace doesn't prevent us from having fun. In fact,
    I'd argue that it makes our lives much more fun.*
- How do I know if I am following the church?
  - *It can seem daunting, but thankfully, with
    podcasts like 'Bible in a Year' and 'Catechism in a
    Year' and countless other resources, it is easier
    than ever to learn more about what the Church
    teaches and how it applies to our lives. You could
    always ask someone you know who is
    knowledgeable in the matter.*

- Can you come back on a more personal note, like in our religion class?
  - *I do wish I could. I'm sorry.*
- What is the process of helping your husband to heaven?
  - *We'll get more into this next time, but for now, it's the same as getting yourself to heaven. Love and to listen to God. Let Him lead your lives together, and love others as Christ did.*

Class Four

- I am an Atheist. My father is an Atheist, and my mother is Catholic. My boyfriend of 3 years comes from a devout Catholic family, but he is on the fence. He is older than me and waiting for me to graduate to start a life. The topic of what religion we will raise our kids has come up multiple times from all four parents. I feel pressured, and I want to stay true to myself without pressuring him one way or the other. I need help.
  - *I agree. It all sounds stressful. I'd recommend finding a good counselor. It is respectful of you not to pressure your boyfriend to abandon his faith.*
- Why is raising a child with two different religions in the household frowned upon?
  - *It's challenging and has its hardships because, in a Christian marriage, your faith is your foundation. If you are Catholic and your spouse is of another denomination or religion, there will be division in the very foundation of your marriage. Some people compromise and work through these challenges. Some cannot overcome their differences in beliefs, and these hardships are often pushed onto their children. Parents need to be unified for their children. Children need stability, and the unification of their parents provides that for them.*

- What questions do you ask yourself when you think you are in a wrong relationship?
  - *Are the fruits of the relationship good or bad? I know it seems too simple to be helpful, but it's true. Does the relationship bring you closer or further away from God? Is it a healthy, respectful relationship? Look at it for what it really is. Don't sugarcoat it, and ask yourself these questions and more to help you discern. Also, pray about it.*
- How do you handle peer pressure?
  - *I struggled with this as we matured in our marriage and our love of God. Psalm 1 was helpful.*
- What if some people aren't called to marriage?
  - *Not everyone is. It means they have another vocation God is calling them to.*

Questions & Answers
Chapter Four

Class One

- Do you read the Bible with your husband? If so, has it helped y'all having that time to relax and read and discuss the Lord with each other? Also, how often do y'all read it together, if you do?

    - *1. No, we currently do not. Reading the Bible with your husband is a beautiful habit to do together, and though I'd love to implement this habit one day in our future, it's not one we practice now. 2. We absolutely discuss the Lord and His will for us daily. When we started offering our day to the Lord and seeing the magnificent fruits of that offering, we couldn't help but talk about it all the time. We tend to think God is hard to hear, and don't get me wrong, He can be at times, but truthfully, when you're open to His love and make time to be still with Him, it's sometimes shocking how loud the Holy Spirit can be. My husband and I are amazed daily at the opportunities He gives to us to show His love to others. Things we could have never imagined, such as an old, wayward friend suddenly reaching out right when we're creating the invitation list for Farm to Jesus or a chance to help a stranger with the heavy door at the store. There are moments where, in the past, we would have clung to our pride or bitterness, but now, in the light of Christ, we see the opportunities He presents to us to help us grow in holiness and humility and shed our resentment. God touches our every moment if we allow Him in, and His work in our lives never gets old, so we can't help but discuss it! 3. My husband doesn't process learning well through reading. I went through the*

'Bible in the Year' podcast in 2021, and he's slowly working through it now. It's allowed us to have conversations we haven't had previously about scripture, but I've tried to give him the space to go through the Bible at his own pace. If I ever read something profound or impactful that I'd like him to hear, in the Bible or otherwise, I'll read it out loud to him for us to think on and talk about, but I think it's important to also honor how God reaches his heart. It looks different than how He reaches mine, but the end goal is the same.

- What if you're a widow, do you still have to live a life of chastity? Our school slogan is "Women who lead." But you tell us to let the man lead. Why does everything have to be about lifting your husband up?
  - *1. Yes, we, as baptized Catholics, are all called to live a chaste life, married or otherwise. Chastity is a virtue. The Catechism of the Catholic Church tells us, "All the baptized are called to chastity. The Christian has "put on Christ," the model for all chastity. All Christ's faithful are called to lead a chaste life in keeping with their particular states of life. At the moment of his Baptism, the Christian is pledged to lead his affective life in chastity." (CCC, #2348). The line, "in keeping with their particular state of life," is an important one to keep in mind here. Your practice of chastity, assuming you are currently unmarried, looks different than my practice in chastity as a married woman. Your current state calls for you to abstain from the sexual embrace. Mine does not. However, in both situations, chastity places a call on our lives to live in total cooperation with God's grace and authorship without resentment. An unmarried widow's state in life would call for abstinence. 2. Yes, I shared that message today and didn't get to fully talk through it as I had planned due to time. Christ died for both men and women. Men and*

women have many differences, but God loves them equally. Both have inherent dignity, and submitting to our husbands does not change that fact. In their very nature, men are more adept at guarding and protecting, while women are proficient at nurturing and being caregivers. This does not mean that these attributes are exclusive to either sex or that every single man or woman possesses these qualities. Still, overall, a woman's physical body and mental inclinations are to provide nurture and care, while a man's is to guard and provide. Remember that God gave Adam the job of guarding and cultivating the garden and everything in it. Again, these natural inclinations are not absolute, though there are specific distinct, unchangeable differences between men and women, such as the ability to birth children. In a marriage where, for whatever reason (alcoholism, narcissism, etc.), the man or woman is unable to fulfill their responsibilities to these natural inclinations, then it is the responsibility of the other spouse to step into the other's role to the best of their abilities. Now, that being said, scripture tells us as wives that we are under the authority of our husbands. "But I want you to understand that the head of every man is Christ, the head of a woman is her husband, and the head of Christ is God." (1 Cor. 11:3). Scripture says that a husband is to be the spiritual leader of his family just as Christ is to the Church. Some husbands cannot fully fulfill this call, and therefore, it falls to the wife to do so for herself and her family. However, in a Catholic marriage, with the Trinity's love set as its foundation, the natural and spiritual roles of husband and wife should be ordered as God-authored. This does NOT diminish our worth as wives or as women. It enhances it and allows us the space and freedom to grow in virtue and lead in the ways we are called to. In Fulton Sheen's 1950s show, 'Life is Worth Living', he once said that, "an honest and noble man seeks to be deserving of the love of a virtuous and noble woman and that the cultural barometer of moral exceptionalism resides solely in the heroic disposition and attitude of virtuous womanhood." Sheen argues that a culture's morals rest **solely** in the hands of women. I'd say that we, as women of God, have a definite call to lead. 3. For the same reason, I said I don't want to win a conflict that may arise and for my husband to lose because it would mean that we both lost. Our marriage is built on God, not ourselves. I do not lose my dignity or worth as a person or fail to have God's love by building my husband up and vice versa. We share the common goal to love God and to help get each other and our children to heaven. This allows us to build **each other** up in a healthy, non-codependent, loving way. There are times when I need more support than he does and times when he needs more than I do, and that's okay and normal in a self-giving, loving relationship. Marriages are not 50/50. They are 100/100. We give all of ourselves to each other and to God. St. Paul tells us in Galatians Chapter 5, "Serve one another, rather, in works of love, since the whole of the Law is summarized in a single command: Love your neighbor as yourself. If you go snapping at each other and tearing each other to pieces, you had better watch, or you will destroy the whole community."

Questions & Answers
Chapter Seven

Class One

- Questions about motherhood!! I love the topic of becoming a mother, and I can't wait till my time comes to become one. I would love to hear what you have to say about it! Thank you so much for coming and talking with us, I feel like I can ask you questions and gain knowledge on topics without any judgement, as I am a Christian and want to live my life for Christ, and raise my kid in Christ.
  - *Motherhood is hard but so fun! I'm excited to talk about it, too, with y'all. And, you're so welcome. Thank you for making this a two-way conversation with your responses! Your desire for more understanding and knowledge about our faith and our Lord is beautiful!*
- What is our purpose, and what are we called to do in life?
  - *This is the question of all mankind, isn't it? Our purpose is to glorify God by loving Him and serving Him. Saying "yes" to His divine will for our lives and surrendering to Him is what we are called to do.*
- How do we wait for physical intimacy?
  - *With lots of self-control and self-denial. Ask God to help give you the strength you need to resist temptations. And, enjoy the fun of the physical intimacy that isn't sinful before marriage such as holding hands, hugging, and kissing.*
- What is the importance of physical intimacy after marriage and having kids?
  - *Sex is a form of physical intimacy that brings you closer to your spouse than anyone else in the world. It's a powerful act of divine love and the ultimate physical giving of one another to each other. Even when a husband and a wife are past*

338

childbearing age, the unification of the sexual
embrace is still there. Physical intimacy, whether
in the sexual embrace or in another form such as
kissing, is important because it is the outward
show of a couple's love. It brings them closer to one
another and connects them.

Class Two
- What traits should a good husband have?
  - *Remember the scripture we talked about from*
    Corinthians. He should be a man of integrity and
    virtue, one who will selflessly love, guard, and
    protect, and one who loves the Lord.
- How to start preparing for marriage while already in a
  serious relationship?
  - *Numerous opportunities arise daily that will help*
    you prepare for marriage, but start with showing
    each other respect and kindness. From there, build
    up to communicating effectively and serving one
    another lovingly. Shed your ego and practice
    humility. These and more will help you set the
    groundwork for your future marriage. It's as
    simple as being Christ to one another.

Class Three
- How to listen to God?
  - *How often do you sit in silence? Like true silence*
    with no outside noise or distractions. It can be
    hard to hear God, especially when we surround
    ourselves with noise, but God is in the words of
    someone close to you. God is in the prayers you
    pray, the scripture you read, the saint quote you
    come across. God's voice is not just a commanding
    presence. It's the quiet whisper in your heart that
    directs you along your path and leads to Him.

- If you do have sex before marriage, how can you come back from that sin as a couple to build back up your relationship with God?
    - *If you are both Catholic, you can go receive healing in the Sacrament of Confession, and from there I'd say, talk through your relationship. What do you enjoy about each other? In what ways can you love each other without using one other? How can your relationship bring you closer to God?*
- How to start preparing for marriage while already in a serious relationship?
    - *If you both think that you may want to marry each other one day, today is the perfect day to start preparing yourself for marriage in your relationship. Look at your relationship. What areas can you work on growth in self-giving love? In what ways can you be Christ's love to one another within your romantic love? Your commitment to each other is beautiful. When that commitment helps you both turn to God, it's magnificent. Your love will mature, but you can start practicing and growing in virtue now.*

Questions & Answers
Chapter Eight

All Classes

* What if childbirth is not part of God's plan for me?
    * *It might not be. If you and your spouse still desire a child, then open your heart to the option of adoption. What an incredible gift you could be to a child.*
* Why does God not bless some women with children?
    * *I don't know. Often, when things don't go as we plan or how we want, we get angry with God, but in reality, He has a reason for everything. We just might not understand it. We might never understand His reason until we hopefully get to heaven one day. God knows what is best for us. We just have to trust Him.*
* Is it ok to not want kids?
    * *I think it depends on why you don't want them. If it's purely out of selfishness, then no, it's probably not okay. If it's for just reasons, then yes.*
* How do I make sure I raise my kid right?
    * *You can't, but you can try very hard to raise them with the love of God. Instill that in their hearts, and they'll be "right."*
* Do you think it's worth it to put a pause on your work to be with your child the first few years, then go back once they get into pre-k? I plan my life, and with everything, I usually have a plan and an answer, but this always stumps me. I would love nothing more than to put a pause on work and be with my child for the first few years, but I do not want to struggle and only have one income. Do you think it's worth it to not work?
    * *1. Oh, I see a lot of me in you with this question. The first answer is to pray. Give Him your anxieties. Give Him your fears. Give Him your*

*plans. 2. I think it's absolutely worth it to be with
your child as much as you can starting from birth.
3. Discern His will for you. I understand the fear of
relying on one income, but many people do it
beautifully. It can be done and done well. When the
time comes, talk and pray with your husband
about it. God will show you the way. You just have
to open your heart to hear Him.*

- How to ensure your marriage stays strong and you
remember to prioritize each other when you have your
children?
    - *Love this question! This was one of the things my
    husband and I wrote down before we had children.
    When you order your life how it's supposed to be,
    1. God, 2. Husband 3. Children, you prioritize your
    husband. Some people advise to never stop dating
    each other. Some people say to set aside at least
    ten minutes a day to catch up. The point is to do
    what works for you to stay connected emotionally,
    mentally, physically, and spiritually.*
- How to be patient with your child?
    - *There are times when this is tough. It takes self-
    control, sometimes self-denial, deep breaths, and a
    lot of prayer.*

Acknowledgments

Thank you to...

+ Our Lady, for your comfort and guidance. + The Holy Spirit, for giving me the words. + Our Lord, for giving me the way. + God, our Creator, for love. + St. Ambrose, for interceding for my rhetoric. + St. Gianna Molla, for being a champion for devoted wives and adoring, self-sacrificing mothers. + My husband for often being the voice of reason I need when I lose my way and for being the rock for our family. You amaze me every single day with your dedication and love for me and our family. + My two beautiful girls who practiced patience during this book-writing and talk-giving process. Coming home to you when I felt as if I had given everything I had for the day away rejuvenated my soul. + Father Barnabas O'Reilly for swooping in to help without question and for the impact you're making through your vocation. + All of the women who read this book as it was flowering. Thank you for your feedback, your criticism, your proofreading skills, and your friendship. Thank you, especially to the one who would only respond with, "Just keep writing," when I would get discouraged. + My parents, for the sacrifices they made to put me through Catholic schools. Thank you for raising me in the one, true faith. + Mel, for pushing my limits of understanding and showing me the way. Thank you for your faith in me that I could reach a deeper level of faith and for living out your life in a way that blesses others through your suffering. + Ysabel, this all began with you. Thank you for your questions and our conversations. Summer afternoons spent with you discussing life have been such a gift. + The students who sat through these talks, thank you for your patience as I got over my fear of public speaking and for participating in the conversation. I don't know all of your names, but I know your faces. Thank you, especially to the ones who wrote thoughtful responses and asked raw questions and to the ones who provided glimmers of hope when all seemed lost. I appreciate your kindness. + The president, principal, and vice principal, for your trust in me and the message and for dealing with me storming into your office for five minutes here and there whenever I needed to talk. I don't know how y'all do this every day. You're amazing. + The teachers, especially the religion teacher who let me take over her classroom. + St. Vincent's Academy, for providing young women the space and room to grow in love of the Lord. + The parents of all of these young women, for bravely trying to raise your child Catholic in a culture that's turned its back on God. + Father Mike Schmitz, for touching my heart with your homilies in 2020, for educating me on the Bible in 2021, for gently walking me through the Catechism in 2023, and for inviting me to join you in your love for God. + You, dear reader, for yearning for more understanding of our faith and desiring to know our great God. Remember, you are in this world but not of this world.

Great Catholic Resources

- www.morningoffering.com
- Hallow Prayer App
- Ascension App
- *Men, Women, & The Mystery of Love* by Edward Sri- (*This should be required reading for every couple before they get married.*)
- *Spousal Prayer* by Deacon James Keating
- *Theology of the Body For Beginners* by Christopher West
- *The Discernment of Spirits: An Ignatian Guide for Everyday Living* by Fr. Timothy M. Gallagher
- *The Hidden Art of Homemaking* by Edith Schaeffer (*not Catholic but still a wonderful resource for women*)
- *Small Steps for Catholic Moms* by Danielle Bean & Elizabeth Foss
- Abiding Together Podcast
- Bishop Robert Barron's YouTube & wordonfire.org
- Bible in a Year Podcast
- Catechism in a Year Podcast
- Ascension Presents & Sundays with Ascension YouTube
- Theology of the Body Institute YouTube
- Pints with Aquinas Podcast
- The Catholic Talk Show Podcast
- FOCUS Catholic YouTube
- GabiAfterHours YouTube
- Godsplaining Podcast
- Coffee & Catholics Podcast
- Aly Aleigha music
- Brother Isaiah music
- Sensus Fidelium YouTube

Sources

- Catechism in a Year Podcast- https://ascensionpress.com/pages/catechisminayear
- Father Ripperger Lecture (basic prayer)-https://www.youtube.com/watch?v=TiGjeKoIufo
- Father Ripperger Lecture (defects in virtue)- https://www.youtube.com/watch?v=nnYopNgQloo&t=3026s

- St. Maximilian Kolbe video/prayer- https://www.youtube.com/watch?v=Y9SwMO36u_0&t=13s & www.militiaoftheimmacultata.com
- Father Mike Schmitz Talk on Marriage (love vs respect)- https://youtu.be/xoXTTXg--4M?si=hvyYQ494XkEb-NpZ
- Bishop Barron Homily (worshipping God)- https://youtu.be/s4uuPF-NpAo?si=9Dq4YmMHTG4lfjqD
- Bishop Barron Homily (God is love)- https://youtu.be/IQ6TkhS0M-s?si=FdpCoStEfWMoHMv1
- Story of Elisabeth Leseur- https://www.catholiccompany.com/getfed/whats-the-incredible-story-of-elisabeth-and-felix-leseur/
- Albom, M. (2017). Tuesdays With Morrie. Sphere.
- Wojtyla, K. (1993). Love and Responsibility. William Collins Sons & Co. Ltd.
- Wojtyla, K. (1997). The Theology of the Body Human Love in the Divine Plan. Pauline Books & Media
- Mother Teresa story- https://aleteia.org/2021/11/19/the-time-mother-teresa-was-late-for-an-appointment-with-john-paul-ii/
- Corrie Ten Boom Story- https://www.youtube.com/watch?v=x8z2R7DaKMM
- Augustine of Hippo. Confessions. Translated by Henry Chadwick, Oxford University Press, 1991
- St. Ignatius of Loyola. "Prayer for Generosity." Spiritual Exercises of St. Ignatius of Loyola. Translated by Luis Gonzalez, Institute of Jesuit Sources, 2007.
- Keating, James. Spousal Prayer: A Way to Marital Happiness. Our Sunday Visitor, 2013.
- Sheen, Fulton J. Three to Get Married. Scepter Publishers, 2003.
- Gaudium et Spes: Pastoral Constitution on the Church in the Modern World." The Holy See, 1965, www.vatican.va/archive/hist_councils/ii_vatican_council/documents/vat-ii_const_19651207_gaudium-et-spes_en.html.

About the Author

Kira lives with her husband and children on a 4-acre homestead in Savannah, Georgia. After graduating from the University of Georgia with a bachelor's degree in Journalism, she envisioned herself climbing the ranks in the big career world, but God had other plans for her. In the wake of marrying her middle-school sweetheart and running her own social media marketing company, she began to hunger for more. More love. More purpose. More order. Thankfully, God provided the more. When she began to walk in her faith and started saying "yes" to the Lord, the fruits were overly abundant and sweet to taste. She shares these fruits now with whoever will take the time to slow down to have a real, meaningful conversation.

Oh, I almost forgot! Thank you to everyone who continued sending me their questions and responses even when it was no longer homework. They were incredibly insightful and helpful. I couldn't in good conscience pick just one class that had the best questions/responses, so everyone got the trophy. Parma and Cora had a great time coming to see you. :)